IEE PROFESSIONAL APPLICATIONS OF COMPUTING SERIES 3
Series Editors: Professor P. Thomas
Dr. R. Macredie

D1413103

Troubled
IT Projects

prevention and turnaround

Other volumes in this series:

Troubled IT Projects

prevention and turnaround

John M. Smith

The Institution of Electrical Engineers

Published by: The Institution of Electrical Engineers, London,
United Kingdom

© 2001: The Institution of Electrical Engineers

The Institution of Electrical Engineers,
Michael Faraday House,
Six Hills Way, Stevenage,
Herts. SG1 2AY, United Kingdom

British Library Cataloguing in Publication Data

Smith, John
Troubled IT projects: prevention and turnaround
(IEE professional applications of computing series; no. 3)
1. Industrial project management 2. Information technology
I. Title II. Institution of Electrical Engineers
658.4' 04

ISBN 0 85296 104 9

Typeset by HWA Text and Data Management, Tunbridge Wells, Kent
Printed in England by MPG Books Ltd, Bodmin, Cornwall

DEDICATION

This book is dedicated to my children – Jason, Justin, Kate, Spike and Georgie – and to my wife, Lizzie. Thank you all for your encouragement, support and understanding during the last two years.

I am also indebted to my colleagues at IBM – Deborah Young, Steve Ingham and Simon Barber – for their valuable suggestions while reviewing the manuscript.

Grateful thanks also to the many great professionals and characters with whom I have worked and who have taught me so much in the process, including: Graham Strickland, Des King, Arthur le Boutillier, Larry Allen, Q. Wallace, Mike Stevens, John Longley, Gordon Chase, David Dundas, Peter McKee, J. Alan Thomas, Bill Barrow, Rick Greengrass, Ian Reid, John Farley, Jim Philip, Steve Feldman, Mike Griffiths, Clive Wootton, Tony Lowe, Huw Evans, Paul Clarke, Ian Keith, Bob Lowe, Alice Smith, Derek Alway, Colin Brooks, Arthur Davies, Jim Stuart, Mike Johnson, Jim Moncrief, Graham Nixon, Lynne Brindley, Steve King, Patrick Whale, Neale Whyatt, Simon Fellows, Deborah Hanson, Roger Blake, Phil Taylor, Ray Weaver, Pieter Lindeque, Peter Counter, John Pridmore, Dave Farquharson, Gill Gray and Christian Noll.

The views expressed in this book are mine, based on 30 years in the IT services industry. They do not necessarily represent IBM policy, nor do they reflect an endorsement of any commercial products.

CONTENTS

FOREWORD

Having worked with John some years ago, I was intrigued when he called to ask me to write a foreword to his book. I had known John as a deeply thoughtful senior consultant, able to grasp the essence of the most complex system requirements and to evolve creative solutions. I wondered what new insights a book from John would offer to executives engaged in the challenging world of large and complex systems projects.

Upon delving into the book I was delighted, and it is a great pleasure for me to warmly recommend the book to all engaged in information systems projects. The subject is timely. The increasing sophistication of telecommunications and information technology offers huge scope for business benefit. However, as IT becomes ever more pivotal to an organisation, project failure can be more than just expensive, it can bring down the business. Bigger potential rewards imply bigger risks.

It is sad to note that projects today fall prey to the same basic problems that were apparent 20 years ago. Questions have to be asked about whether organisations are learning. Questions must also be asked about the quality of training given to our project managers and developers. Are academic courses failing to prepare IT graduates for the issues they will face when they work on projects in the 'real world'? Must IT professionals make these mistakes for themselves before they can learn to avoid them?

John is well placed to write this book. His experience of IT projects is wide-ranging. He has developed real-time software for air traffic control radars, managed commercial software development projects and programmes, spent time as a sales executive and managed a branch of a systems business. In recent years, his focus has been on strategic and technical consulting and on the investigation and turnaround of troubled projects.

What impresses me about this book is that it is based on John's personal experience. He is open about how he has learned from his mistakes. He is not afraid to admit his failures. We can all learn from this experience.

This is a practical book, with examples of how to translate its recommendations into improvements in our own processes. As chief executive of a major electronics systems business, I know the challenges faced in large system developments. This book goes deeply into root causes and clearly demonstrates solutions for us all. At the same time it is eminently readable, full of interesting examples and clear summaries.

This is essential reading for all in the IT services industry engaged in selling and delivering application development and systems integration projects. It is a valuable handbook for anyone engaged in information systems development. I commend it to you.

Peter McKee
Managing Director
Raytheon Systems Limited

PREFACE

I once visited a leading systems Vendor in a specialised market sector. A Buyer had contracted with this Vendor and the project was slipping. The project was to modify the Vendor's standard product to meet the specific requirements of the Buyer's business and technology environment. I was asked to provide an independent view on whether the Vendor could deliver the project – to a revised plan – or whether the Buyer should 'pull the plug'. I found that:

- the Vendor's product had no documented architecture;
- when a small customisation was undertaken, it was normal to proceed without any design specifications or program specifications;
- there were no design, coding or testing standards;
- there was no Quality Assurance function;
- no formal unit testing was undertaken;
- a small number of standard product tests were defined, but not all of these would be exercised before a new product was released into the field;
- no project planning was undertaken (e.g. a time-line plan) and there was no means of assessing how much effort had been spent on a particular project.

In short, the company had almost none of the basic management systems, development processes, standards and disciplines needed to succeed in the IT industry. Yet it *had* succeeded. The informal development approach was clearly a part of the culture of the company which the management valued and did not wish to change.

Their challenge was that projects were getting larger – too large to reside in the heads of one or two developers, however capable they might be. They had 'hit a wall' and only a painful culture change and the introduction of an appropriate degree of formality to their processes would enable them to move the company forward.

A varied and always challenging career in the IT services industry has taught me that IT projects often get into difficulty. If the problems are acute, the project will fail and both Buyer and Vendor may suffer substantial loss. More likely, it will become 'troubled', usually implying that costs greatly exceed those budgeted and the project requires a substantially longer timescale than planned.

Sometimes, the problems can be laid at the door of technology. More frequently, as in the example above, the problems are to do with the people and processes being used to deliver the project. I have seen a recurring pattern in these problems and noticed the same mistakes being made time and time again. I have reached the conclusion that there is little mystery about why IT projects become troubled. Part 1 of this book sets out an analysis of the 40 most common troubled project root causes, based on available studies and personal observation.

The problems besetting many of the projects that I have reviewed can be traced back to avoidable mistakes made at the planning or bid stage. Part 2 of this book takes you through the activities required to scope, solution, plan and bid for a project opportunity and shows how, by being vigilant, you can avoid many troubled project root causes. It requires work. It requires you to ruthlessly reject inherently risky opportunities. It requires substantial investment in the opportunities for which you decide to bid. It requires thorough definition of the project in terms of the architecture, the deliverables and the approach that you are going to take to deliver them. It requires full engagement with your potential Buyer. It requires a skilled team and mature software development processes. However, it is not rocket science.

Before they will award contracts, clients need to gain confidence that you understand their requirements and are capable of delivering to your plans. A well-specified and low-risk solution is also a winning solution. I believe that Part 2 of this book will help Vendors contract more business and deliver both more consistent business performance and higher customer satisfaction. I hope that Part 2 will also help Buyers to ensure that Vendors jump through all the necessary hoops to generate a high-quality, implementable solution.

Of course there will always be some problems to be solved during delivery. Part 3 of this book sets out an approach to reviewing projects, which I have proved does uncover the important issues. The approach can be used for regular project healthcheck reviews. It can also be used when attempting to turn around projects in real trouble. Part 4 of this book covers how to prepare an implementable 'Turn-around Plan' for such a project.

This is not a book of IT horror stories to shock and entertain. There are several of these available already. They are valuable as they tell us *what* went wrong and sometimes *why*, but they don't always provide much guidance on how to avoid problems on our own projects. I hope that this book will, and that you will find it a practical handbook, whether you are deciding whether or not to bid for an opportunity, brainstorming possible solutions, writing a proposal in the early hours of the morning, or reviewing a project which is foundering.

If you are a purchaser of IT services, this book is also for you, because not all the root causes of troubled projects are the responsibility of the services Vendor. Many are down to the Buyer and often it is *your* money which is at risk.

I've been strongly motivated to write this book as I believe that the simple concepts expressed here can help Buyers and IT services Vendors become smarter at project definition, contracting and project delivery. We might not be able to eliminate troubled IT projects, but we can reduce their incidence.

At the end of some of the chapters there are suggested exercises. This sounds terribly patronising and reminiscent of school homework. However, I've included them simply to encourage you to note down your own experience of the topic under discussion, and to take some actions in your organisation which might make a positive difference.

John M Smith
Summer 2001

Part 1
WHY PROJECTS FAIL

Part 1

WHY PROJECTS FAIL

Chapter 1

WHAT *IS* A TROUBLED PROJECT?

Project failure

In this book I am going to distinguish between projects which are *troubled* and projects which *fail*. A definition of a failed project is quite easy – it is a project which does not make the journey from conception through to successful implementation. I'll give you an example.

> I was once given two weeks to prepare a set of 'scripts' for use at a dozen or more locations around the world. By following the scripts, unskilled staff would be able to migrate all user data from a variety of desktops and servers – many with different architectures and operating systems – to the 'strategic' replacement desktops and servers, which would have a common architecture. Users would be able to access all their data files on their new PCs and servers using the latest versions of applications. A salesman had observed that the Buyer's incumbent Vendor was approaching data migration in different ways at different locations and that skilled staff were being used. He made an assumption that our company could undertake the work more cheaply using unskilled staff and standard scripts. He sent the Buyer three presentation foils which represented an offer to migrate all their global data at a very low, fixed price per desktop. I looked into the assumptions which underpinned our proposal to the Buyer and found them to be flawed. Data migration could not be approached in this way. The project was basically not feasible and, if the offer was accepted, the project would represent a huge risk to our company. The proposal was withdrawn.

This is an example of a project which failed virtually at conception. Others might fail during design or development. Others can fail during implementation, like the recent Mars Polar Lander spacecraft, which traversed the vastness of space and entered the Martian atmosphere before contact with the spacecraft was lost. Some projects travel right through their life cycle to operational use; it then becomes clear that the system delivered by the project does not, and never can, meet the business needs and it is quickly withdrawn from service.

The focus of this book is troubled projects and I shan't be saying anything more about failed projects, other than to point out that all failed projects were once troubled projects. It is our goal to detect and correct the causes of a project's troubles before it fails.

Let's start by discussing and categorising terms used by the leading authors in the field of troubled projects. John Boddie, in his book *Crunch Mode*,[1] describes projects which have very challenging schedules. They are achievable, just, but only through the use of very skilled people, using an approach which breaks some of the traditional 'rules' of system development.

Ed Yourdon, in his book *Death March*,[2] considers projects in rather worse shape than this. Of the four categories he defines, only the 'Mission Impossible' category holds out any hope of a glorious result, against all the odds. The implication is that most 'death march' projects end in failure.

'Runaway Project' is a term coined by KPMG Management Consulting in the UK. KPMG defines a runaway as a project which has significantly failed to meet its objectives and/or is more than 30 per cent over budget. The implication is that some 'runaways' will eventually be successful.

Robert Glass uses the same term in his book *Software Runaways*,[3] although Glass uses a slightly different definition. He believes – and I agree with him – that a project is a true 'runaway' only if it is over budget by at least 100 per cent. But all Robert Glass's 'runaway' case studies ended in failure and I don't believe that this is always the case. If we were to consider a continuum of 'predicted cost to complete' divided by 'original budgeted cost' it might look a little like Figure 1.1.

The meaning I extract from the Figure 1.1 is that:

- most projects get into crunch mode at some stage when the chips are down, but most projects with the potential to succeed eventually do complete;
- 'death march' and 'runaway' projects are hard to separate, but most 'death march' projects fail (the word 'death' gives it away);
- troubled projects include some 'crunch mode' projects and all 'death march' and 'runaway' projects. I know one project very well which is five times over budget. I believe that it will complete successfully. It is certainly a 'runaway' and it has certainly been a 'death march' for the team, many of whom have been on the project for five years.

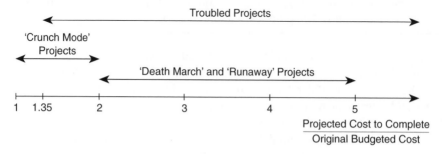

Figure 1.1   *A Taxonomy of Problem Projects*

The project life cycle

Every project passes through a number of stages. Vendors tend to concentrate on those for which they are responsible – typically design, development and implementation. But the seeds of project problems can be sown well before a contract is placed with a Vendor, and projects which appear to be implemented successfully can become troubled in operation. Therefore, we need to look at the full project life cycle. This is shown in Figure 1.2.

The diagram shows that most projects move through six stages. These stages often overlap to some extent. For example, moving from project initiation/mobilisation to system design in cases where an external Vendor will undertake the design, implies the placing of a contract. A contract cannot be placed until the Vendor has learned enough about the requirements to estimate the price of the design phase. This means that the Vendor must undertake some of the design work up front, prior to contract. Also, the input from one or more Vendors will invariably modify the Buyer's perspective on the scope and scale of the project, which will modify their plans and budgets, the firming up of which is part of the project initiation/mobilisation stage.

As we will be considering the root causes of troubled projects and where in the life cycle they might become visible, we need to sketch out the likely activities within each phase. As I do not want to prescribe a set of business processes, I will do this by listing some typical inputs and outputs of each stage. These are shown in Table 1.1.

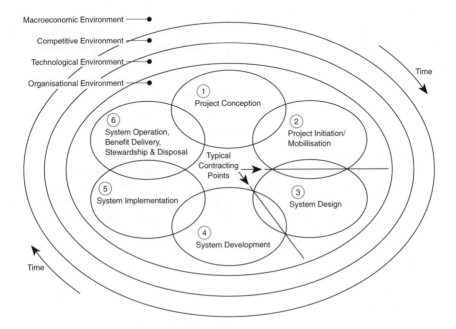

Figure 1.2   *The Project Life Cycle*

Table 1.1 *Typical Inputs and Outputs of Each Life Cycle Stage*

Project Conception	
Typical Inputs/Stimuli • Drive for revenue/profit growth • Board directives/vision • Recognition of a business need/opportunity • Competitive pressure • Technology advance • New management/strategy	Typical Outputs • High-level IS/IT strategy or road map • Investment appraisal/business case • Allocated budget • Board-level sponsorship • Identified projects • High-level requirements and plans
Project Initiation/Mobilisation	

Typical Inputs/Stimuli
• High-level IS/IT strategy or road map
• High-level requirements and plans
• Investment appraisal/business case
• Business process map
• Procurement strategy:
  • Outsource/In-house decision
  • Prime integrator or multiple Vendors
  • Bespoke or packaged solution
• Bidders list
• Proposals and tenders
	Typical Outputs
	• Programme/Project (P/P) organisation
	• P/P infrastructure and tools
	• Project and contract management processes
	• Lower-level requirements
	• Request for Information/Proposals (RFI, RFP)
	• Invitation to Tender (ITT) and evaluation criteria
	• Risk log
	• Selected Vendor and contract
	• Acceptance strategy and benefit measures
	• Firm budget and plans
	• Defined in-house supporting projects

System Design	
Typical Inputs/Stimuli • RFI, RFP, ITT • Discussions with Buyer's Project Manager (PM) and team • Discussions with end-users • Market and Buyer intelligence • Knowledge of budget, competition and evaluation criteria • Existing solutions and candidate technologies • Estimates based on function point counts etc	Typical Outputs • Requirements clarification • High-level solution/architecture • Outline project and resource plans • Development and implementation approach • Detailed estimates for design • Proposal/tender • Low-level design • Detailed development plans and estimates • Quality plan

(*continued*)

Table 1.1 *Typical Inputs and Outputs of Each Life Cycle Stage (continued)*

System Development	
Typical Inputs/Stimuli • Resource and time-line plans • Project budget • Agreed requirements baseline • Agreed design baseline • Documented approach • Schedule of work products • Project infrastructure and tools	Typical Outputs • Programs and documentation • Test plans and scripts • Change requests/contract changes • Progress reports • Project work products and deliverables • One or more drops of software • Factory acceptance tested system
System Implementation	
Typical Inputs/Stimuli • Live data and data migration strategy • Users to be trained • Platforms and infrastructure • Software/systems for site/user acceptance • Site acceptance test plans and scripts	Typical Outputs • Operational platforms and infrastructure • Site/user accepted system with live data • Trained users • Initial user feedback • Schedule of faults and enhancements
System Operation, Benefit Extraction, Stewardship and Disposal	
Typical Inputs/Stimuli • Live system supporting business processes • Benefit measures • Consolidated user feedback	Typical Outputs • Analysis of business benefit • Proposals for process/software change • Schedule for ongoing review of the system

Definition of a troubled project

We need to define a troubled project in more than simply qualitative terms. The problem with quantitative measures is that they don't always scale. For example, if a three-month project takes six months, it may not be a total disaster for either the Vendor or the Buyer – provided that no major time imperative has been breached and the system is successful in operation. If a four-year project takes eight years to complete, this implies expenditure of a totally different magnitude. Also, the business need that the project is endeavouring to meet will almost certainly have changed by the time the project completes.

Here is my best shot at a definition.

> A troubled project has one or more of the following characteristics:
>
> 1. It exceeds the planned timescale by more than 50 per cent, excluding the timescale impact of agreed changes in scope.
> 2. It exceeds the build cost by more than 35 per cent, excluding the cost of agreed changes in scope.
> 3. It is the cause of major Buyer dissatisfaction to the extent that the future of the project is called into question.
> 4. The Buyer lacks the commitment to make the project succeed.
> 5. It substantially fails to support the intended business processes.
> 6. It substantially fails to deliver the anticipated benefits.
> 7. The outcome for Buyer–Vendor is not win–win.

Note that the above are characteristics of *how* a project is troubled. In the next chapter we will set out the typical reasons *why* a project becomes troubled.

By 'planned timescale', I mean the timescale embodied in the contract between the parties. You may regard a 50 per cent overrun of planned timescale as excessive. My experience is that the average timescale overrun is 30 per cent, only some 5 per cent of projects come in to time (mostly very small ones), and about half of all projects overrun by more than 30 per cent of planned timescale. As organisations achieve higher levels of software maturity, average timescale overrun improves dramatically.

An overrun in build cost may predominantly hurt one of the contracting parties, depending on the contractual environment (fixed price or time and materials). The average planned gross profit on fixed-price deals is around 25 per cent. It takes a cost overrun of 33.3 per cent for the Vendor to reach break-even. I've chosen a cost overrun of 35 per cent as this represents the point where the Vendor is typically running into loss.

The 'impact of agreed changes' is excluded from the calculation of timescale or cost overrun. I have often heard it said that Vendors bid low and make their money on the changes. I'm sure that this is sometimes the case, but my experience has been that the value of changes is typically less than 20 per cent of the original contract value. At this level, even if you make a very large gross profit (GP) on the changes, you are not going to restore a loss-making project to its planned level of GP.

All projects provide the potential for dispute between Buyer and Vendor, whether they be contracted at fixed price or on Time & Materials (T&M) terms. There will be peaks and troughs of Buyer satisfaction. This is to be expected. By 'major Buyer dissatisfaction' I imply that the Buyer is discussing withholding payment or terminating the contract.

By 'Buyer lack of commitment' I mean that the Buyer organisation does not do all in its power to make the project a success, tending to blame the Vendor for all problems which occur through the life cycle of the project. Examples of lack of commitment on the part of the Buyer include failure to champion the project within the organisation and failure to take culture change and user training challenges seriously.

By 'substantially failing to support the intended business processes' I mean that the delivered IS/IT project is basically unusable, even after the inevitable post-implementation bug-fixes and enhancements. It might comply with the requirements specification, it might have passed acceptance tests, but it does not support the business.

By 'substantially failing to deliver the anticipated benefits' I mean that the IS/IT system is usable, but the anticipating cost savings, efficiency improvements, or other measures specified in the business case are not delivered.

The 'outcome for Buyer and Vendor' should be win–win. If either or both parties feel exploited by the other, the project is troubled and the prospect of a mutually rewarding business relationship in the future is slim.

Some troubled project examples

I once managed a project to design and develop a criminal information system for a UK police force. We had underestimated the amount of main memory required in the server. The Buyer did not see why they should pay for additional memory – after all, this was a fixed-price project. To save money, I took a decision to code the application in assembler rather than a high-level language so that the code would fit the available memory. This saved me money in the short term, but both timescale and budget were greatly exceeded as a result of this decision. Also, the eventual system, although it performed superbly and was very robust, required very specialised skills to maintain. This project exemplifies troubled project characteristics 1, 2 and 7.

Another project with which I have been associated in an advisory capacity was badly underestimated. A subcontractor providing subject matter expertise which was crucial to the success of the project went into liquidation. The project was scheduled to complete in two years but took four. This project exemplifies troubled project characteristics 1, 2, 3 and 7.

In talking to the two Buyers above, it was clear that there was little sympathy for the financial pain of the Vendor (these were both fixed-price projects). The Buyers were feeling the pain of not having the systems to support their businesses and therefore losing the business benefit the systems would bring. In the case of the police system, lives might even have been at risk. Sometimes it pays to take a 'second position' standpoint and view a project from the Buyer's perspective.

I once acted as an expert witness in the High Court on behalf of a services Vendor who was being sued by a manufacturing company for failing to deliver a system which was usable, or could be made usable, within a reasonable timescale. My report demonstrated that the functional specification had been signed off by the Buyer, that this functionality was demonstrable, that the Vendor's team had produced good quality code and documentation, and that they had achieved high productivity (this was demonstrated using function point analysis). My conclusion with hindsight is that the Buyer may have lost interest in the system, baulked at the investment of time required to implement the system and train users, and wanted their money back. This project exemplifies troubled project characteristic 4.

I was once employed to undertake a performance study of a turnkey system supplied to Her Majesty's Stationery Office. It was a stock control and ordering system. The system had been accepted and the Vendor had been paid, but performance was rather worse than poor. A transaction to fulfil an order with some half a dozen items required several minutes to complete, during which time the user could do nothing other than watch the screen. The Vendor was uninterested in supplying additional hardware (which would have gone some way to improving performance). In their view, the contract had not specified a performance level, their contractual obligation had been met and that was that. I was able to achieve an improvement of 300 per cent with very minor software changes and file repositioning, but this was hardly enough! This project exemplifies troubled project characteristics 3, 5, 6 and 7.

Summary

Projects can fail at the very start of their journey to implementation, right at the end, or anywhere in between. Not all troubled projects fail, but all failed projects were troubled projects. Troubled projects include some 'crunch mode' projects and all 'death march' and 'runaway projects' – to use terms prominent in the literature.

A project life cycle of six stages has been defined:

1. project conception;
2. project initiation/mobilisation;
3. system design;
4. system development;
5. system implementation;
6. system operation, benefit delivery, stewardship & disposal.

Typical inputs/stimuli and outputs have been summarised for each stage.
Finally, a definition of a troubled project has been given in terms of the characteristics which might be evident (*how* the project is troubled).

Exercises

1. Make a list of the troubled projects with which you have been associated.
2. Which characteristics of troubled projects were evident in each case?

References

1. John Boddie, *Crunch Mode*, Yourdon Press, 1987.
2. Ed Yourdon, *Death March*, Prentice Hall, 1997.
3. Robert Glass, *Software Runaways – lessons learned from massive software project failures*, Prentice Hall, 1998.

Chapter 2

ROOT CAUSES OF TROUBLED PROJECTS

Sources of information

There are a number of sources of information on the root causes of troubled projects. These include some notable books, surveys of troubled or 'runaway' projects conducted by management consultants, reports prepared by government accounting watchdogs such as the US General Accounting Office and the UK Committee of Public Accounts, and internal studies conducted by IT services companies. And then, of course, we all have our own experience.

Books

There are a number of excellent texts in the field of software risk management which enumerate problems and issues likely to be encountered during software projects. These include:

- *Software Risk Management*, Barry W Boehm, IEEE Computer Society Press, 1989.
- *Software Engineering Risk Analysis and Measurement*, Robert N Charette, McGraw-Hill, 1989.
- *Assessment and Control of Software Risks*, Capers Jones, Yourdon Press, 1994.

Surveys

Two surveys on 'runaway projects' were conducted by KPMG Management Consulting in 1989 and 1994. The results of the 1994 survey were reported in *Software World* [1] in 1995 and are summarised with permission from A P Publications Limited. The surveys were conducted by an independent research organisation over the telephone, presumably using a pro forma approach. This is important, as such studies do tend to 'lead the witness' to some extent by providing multiple choice questions.

About 250 organisations participated in the 1989 survey and some 120 in the 1994 survey. Several market sectors were represented including the manufacturing, distribution, retail, energy and finance sectors and public sector organisations.

Respondents to the 1994 survey voted the following as the top six root causes of runaways:

- project objectives not fully specified – mentioned by 51 per cent of respondents;
- bad planning and estimating – mentioned by 49 per cent of respondents;
- technology new to the organisation – mentioned by 45 per cent of respondents;
- inadequate/no project management methodology – mentioned by 42 per cent of respondents;
- insufficient senior staff on the team – mentioned by 42 per cent of respondents; and
- poor performance by hardware/software suppliers – mentioned by 42 per cent of respondents.

Around 30 per cent of respondents also identified the following as root causes of runaways:

- inadequate communication;
- lack of senior management involvement;
- inappropriate project staffing;
- insufficient user training.

KPMG also found that 55 per cent of runaway projects had not been subjected to any form of risk assessment or ongoing risk management.

KPMG concluded that:

- 'runaways' occur with equal frequency across all market sectors;
- 47 per cent of runaways involved a mixture of packaged and bespoke/custom application software, 22 per cent involved the implementation of packaged software, and 24 per cent were bespoke software development projects – so packaged software did not provide a safe haven;
- a quarter of projects had become problematic during the initial planning stage (project initiation/mobilisation in our terminology);
- the use of new technology was becoming an increasing contributor to runaways.

Government enquiries

A very interesting and informative report, *Improving the Delivery of Government IT Projects*,[2] was issued by the UK House of Commons Committee of Public Accounts on 24 November 1999. This report is available from the UK Stationery Office and can be viewed on the Internet at www.parliament.the-stationery-office.co.uk/pa/cm/cmpubacc.htm

While it is true to say that government IT projects are procured and managed rather differently from private sector projects, this report has much valuable advice to offer. It has two main strengths. First, it is presented unashamedly from the taxpayer's perspective and concentrates on extracting key lessons from troubled projects for the benefit of UK Government Buyers. Second, as a cross-party committee, the Committee of Public Accounts does not shrink from plain speaking and Government Buyer criticism. A number of 'war story projects' are exposed. The key conclusions and recommendations of the report are shown below and the report's 'key lessons' are included in the Appendix. Look at the website for the war stories! Parliamentary copyright is reproduced with the permission of the Controller of Her Majesty's Stationery Office on behalf of Parliament.

'Decisions about IT are crucial to the development and success of the business of public bodies, and cannot be treated in isolation from other aspects of their work. Failure to deliver an IT system can have a profound effect on an organisation's ability to provide services to its customers. Key decisions on IT systems are, therefore, business decisions, not technical ones, and should involve senior management. And the commitment of senior management can be a critical factor in securing a successful outcome.

Projects are conceived and grow from identified business needs. However, what seems a clear objective at the beginning can easily become blurred and confused as events progress. The end-users must be identified before the project commences so that their needs are taken into account fully during design and development.

The scale and complexity of projects is a major influence on whether they succeed or fail. Departments should consider carefully whether projects are too ambitious to undertake in one go. This consideration is particularly important if a project connects with the business operations of other parties, or depends on the development of IT undertaken by other parties.

The management and oversight of IT projects by skilled project managers is essential for ensuring that projects are delivered to time and budget. But the successful implementation of IT systems calls for imagination and well-conceived risk management, as well as sound project management methodologies.

The increasing use of complex external contracts for the delivery of major public sector IT projects and the supply of strategic IT services has highlighted the need for a high degree of professionalism in the definition, negotiation and management of IT contracts. It is essential that public sector bodies get the right contracts in place. With large sums of public money at stake, any lack of clarity, or debatable interpretation in a contract, can lead to expensive misunderstandings that might have to be resolved in the courts.

The implementation of an IT system is not an end in itself. It is important that sufficient attention is paid to ensuring that staff know how to make full and proper use of it. Without this it is unlikely that the anticipated business benefits will be realised. Training of staff can take up considerable resources, often a significant proportion of the overall cost of the project. Training must address the needs of users, and of those operating and maintaining the system.

As well as wasting enormous sums of public money, failures in IT can have disabling impacts on public services and on citizens. These have included the failure to pay social security benefits to vulnerable people and major delays in issuing people their passports. In addition to planning and managing projects positively, departments should therefore have contingency plans in place to maintain adequate levels of service in the event of project failures.

It is essential that organisations learn lessons from the projects undertaken. A post-implementation review is designed to establish the extent to which they have secured the business benefits anticipated. The review may encompass whether the project has met its business objectives, user expectations and technical requirements.'

Summarising this down to bullet points, the report finds the following root causes of troubled projects in the UK public sector:

- lack of senior management involvement and commitment;
- failure to focus on key business and end-user needs;
- failure to break complex projects into manageable, separately contracted 'chunks';
- poor and unimaginative project management;
- poor risk management and contingency planning;
- unclear contracts and poor contract management;
- insufficient focus on user training needs and the design of training interventions.

IT services companies

All successful IS/IT professional services Vendors spend time considering what has gone wrong with their projects in order that they can identify and learn lessons which will improve their competitiveness, delivery and financial performance. Many companies set out a list of the most common root causes of project problems. The lists I have seen concentrate on the system design and system development stages of the project life cycle, as these are the most tangible stages where the Vendors are active. The degree of overlap with published surveys and public inquiries is substantial.

My analysis

It is clear that there is a measure of agreement between the various sources of information on troubled project root causes. For example, KPMG and the UK Public Accounts Committee are in agreement about the following root causes:

- poor specification of objectives/failure to focus on key business needs;

- inadequate project management;
- lack of senior management involvement;
- poor user training;
- poor risk management.

It is also clear that both KPMG and the Public Accounts Committee have individually valuable suggestions for root causes, such as:

- bad planning/estimating (from KPMG);
- insufficient senior staff (from KPMG);
- failure to break complex projects into manageable 'chunks' (from the Public Accounts Committee).

In my conversations with IT professionals from a variety of IT services companies, I also find a strong measure of agreement on the root causes of IT project problems.

In his book *The Thirty-six Dramatic Situations*,[3] Georges Polti sets out to prove that there are only this number of basic plots in the world's treasury of literature and drama. Some of the situations could even have some relevance to troubled projects – disaster, falling prey to cruelty or misfortune, daring enterprise, fatal imprudence, rivalry of superior and inferior, erroneous judgement – for example.

It is an interesting fact that, after analysing the above sources of information and my own experience, I was unable to find more than 40 generic root causes of troubled projects. My list is shown in Table 2.1. Root causes which are the responsibility of the Buyer or the Vendor are clearly shown. Root causes which do not refer to the Buyer or the Vendor can bedevil both parties. Note that these are generic root causes of troubled projects. I am not advocating that you should not capture and manage project-specific risks, but you may well find that many of your project-specific risks are actually specific manifestations of some of the 40 generic root causes.

Projects can become troubled at any life cycle stage

As we saw in Chapter 1, problems can arise in any stage of the project life cycle. Thus, Table 2.1 positions each root cause within the project stage where its effect is likely to become apparent.

Detection and correction of troubled project root causes

A services provider's first contact with the Buyer is usually within the Project Initiation/ Mobilisation stage. At this stage, the Vendor must be on the lookout for root causes RC07 through RC17. However, Vendor staff often have opportunities

Table 2.1   *Root Causes of Troubled Projects*

Project Conception

RC01 Project based on an unsound premise or an unrealistic business case

RC02 Buyer failure to define clear project objectives, anticipated benefits and success criteria

RC03 Project based on state-of-the-art and immature technology

RC04 Lack of Buyer Board-level ownership/commitment or competence

RC05 Buyer's funding and/or timescale expectations unrealistically low

RC06 Buyer failure to break a complex project into phases or smaller projects

Project Initiation/Mobilisation

RC07 Vendor setting unrealistic expectations on cost, timescale or Vendor capability

RC08 Buyer failure to define and document requirements (functional and non-functional)

RC09 Failure to achieve an open, robust and equitable Buyer-Vendor relationship

RC10 Vendor failure to invest enough resources to scope the project prior to contract

RC11 Buyer lack of sufficient involvement of eventual end-users

RC12 Vendor underestimation of resources (predominantly person-effort) required

RC13 Vendor failure to define project tasks, deliverables and acceptance processes

RC14 Failure to actively manage risks and maintain robust contingency plans

RC15 Poor project planning, management and execution

RC16 Failure to clearly define roles and responsibilities in the contract/sub-contracts

RC17 Full-scope, fixed-price contracting (requirements, design and development)

System Design

RC18 Failure to 'freeze' the requirements baseline and apply change control

RC19 Poor choice of technical platform and/or architecture

RC20 Vendor starting a phase prior to completing a previous phase

RC21 Poor choice of design/development method

RC22 Failure to undertake effective project reviews and take decisive action

RC23 Vendor lack/loss of skilled resources

RC24 Poor Vendor standards deployment (design, coding, testing, configuration management etc)

RC25 Poor Vendor requirements traceability (requirements > design > code > test)

(continued)

Table 2.1   *Root Causes of Troubled Projects (continued)*

RC26 Buyer retains design authority with right to approve/reject low-level designs
System Development
RC27 Delays cause the project to be overtaken by advances in technology
RC28 Vendor failure to 'freeze' the design (& technical platform) and apply change control
RC29 Inadequate Vendor training and supervision of junior staff
RC30 Inadequate Vendor review of designs/code/documentation
RC31 Poor Vendor management of subcontractors
RC32 Lack of a formal, 'engineering' approach to integration and testing by Vendor
RC33 Insufficient attention paid by Vendor to non-functional requirements
System Implementation
RC34 Buyer failure to manage the change implicit in the project (people, processes, technology)
RC35 Inadequate user/systems training
RC36 Catastrophic failure of the system, with no effective contingency arrangement
RC37 Missing a crucial 'go live' date
System Operation, Benefit Delivery, Stewardship and Disposal
RC38 Buyer failure to measure actual delivered benefit and take corrective action
RC39 Buyer failure to maintain/enhance system post-implementation
RC40 Changes in the competitive or macroeconomic environment

to meet members of the Buyer's project team who have been involved with the project from its conception. This gives them an opportunity to also probe for evidence of root causes RC01 through RC06. Part 2 of this book covers this stage of the project life cycle and gives guidance on detecting and correcting (or possibly walking away from!) root causes RC01 through RC17 (and several more).

Root causes which can affect a project during the design and development phases (RC18 through RC33) can be detected during the process of regular delivery reviews. This process is covered in Part 3 of this book. Root causes which can affect a project in later stages (RC34 through RC40) are detectable if the process of project review is continued through the system implementation and system operation stages. The need for such reviews is strongly recommended in the UK Government Public Accounts Committee report.

Which root causes are the 'big hitters'?

Any of the root causes in Table 2.1 can have a profound impact on the outcome of a project, and the problem is that they hunt in packs. Many troubled projects are beset by, perhaps, half a dozen of these root causes. This is confirmed by the KPMG surveys.

Not all root causes are equal. For example, a project which is based on an unsound premise (RC01) is, arguably, more likely to fail than a project in which the Vendor fails to provide sufficient training and supervision for junior staff (RC29), but both root causes are potentially fatal. Similarly, a project which should have been broken up into a set of smaller projects in order to make it more manageable (RC06) is, arguably, more likely to become troubled than one in which the Vendor fails to 'freeze' the design and apply change control (RC28). Precisely because these are difficult arguments to win in a convincing manner leads me to conclude that it is unwise to try to rank the root causes into 'big hitters' and 'the rest'. However, such ranking is definitely of value for an individual project as it will inform the prioritisation of 'Turnaround' actions.

Summary

There are a number of sources of information on the root causes of troubled projects. These include some notable books on the subject of software risk management, surveys of troubled or 'runaway' projects conducted by management consultants, reports prepared by government accounting watchdogs and internal studies conducted by IT services companies. And, of course, we all have our own experience to call upon. The information is out there. There is no mystery.

There is a good measure of agreement between the various sources, but some root causes are mentioned by only one or two sources. It seems sensible to combine the information from these sources into a table. This is what I have done, eliminating repetition and extracting specificity to provide a list of 40 generic root causes of troubled projects. I have highlighted where in the project life cycle these problems might be detectable and correctable.

Root causes which can affect a project during the Project Conception and Project Initiation/Mobilisation stages can be detected during the planning or bid stage of a project. Guidance on how to achieve this is given in Part 2 of this book. If Vendor and Buyer fail to agree that one or more of these root causes is threatening the success of the project and that something needs to be done about it, the Vendor can always walk away from the business. Sometimes this brave step does need to be taken.

Root causes which can affect a project during the System Design and System Development stages can be detected during project delivery reviews, enabling corrective action to be planned and executed. Guidance on how to achieve this is given in Part 3 of this book.

Root causes which can affect a project during the System Implementation and System Operation, Benefit Delivery, Stewardship and Disposal stages can be detected if ongoing project reviews are undertaken throughout the life of the project/system.

Exercises

1. Choose a troubled IS/IT project which you have worked on and, on a large piece of paper, draw six circles to represent the six stages of the project life cycle (as in Figure 1.2). Review the list of root causes in Table 2.1 and note down on the diagram each root cause of the project's troubles. Write each root cause in the life cycle stage at which it first became apparent (or, with hindsight, when it should have become apparent).
2. Make a note of any important generic root causes which are not in Table 2.1 and e-mail them to me at john@thelearningworks.co.uk. as I am always interested to hear of new root causes of troubled projects!
3. Think about and note down any interventions that might have been made to address the issues during the life of the project.

References

1. Andy Cole (KPMG), *Runaway Projects – Cause and Effects*, Software World Vol. 26, No. 3, 1995.
2. House of Commons, Session 1999–2000, Committee of Public Accounts, First Report – *Improving the Delivery of Government IT Projects*, The UK Stationery Office.
3. Georges Polti, *The Thirty-six Dramatic Situations*, 1921, ISBN 0-871161095.

Exercises

1. Choose a troubled IS/IT project which you have worked on and, on a large piece of paper, draw six circles to represent the six stages of the project life cycle (as in Figure [illegible]). Review the [illegible] root causes in Table [illegible] and write down on that diagram each root cause of the project's troubles. Write each root cause in the life cycle stage where it first became apparent (or, with hindsight, when it should have become apparent).
2. Make a note of any important alternative root causes which are not in Table [illegible] and send them to me at [illegible] [illegible] of new root causes of troubled projects.
3. Think back and note down the interventions that might have been made to address the causes during the life of the project.

References

1. [illegible] Group (CHAOS), [illegible] Software World, Vol. [illegible], No. [illegible], 1995.
2. House of Commons, Session [illegible] Committee of Public Accounts, [illegible] Report [illegible] Management of Projects, The Stationery Office.
3. [illegible] 197[illegible] ISBN [illegible]

Chapter 3

A TROUBLED PROJECT CASE STUDY – THE *SS GREAT EASTERN*

Introduction

There are several high-profile IT projects in recent history which would be excellent candidates for analysis in this chapter. These would include the UK Passport Agency system replacement project, the Denver International Airport baggage-handling system, and the Taurus project for the UK Stock Exchange. However, it would be hard to present an account and analysis of one of these projects without causing potential dissent and strong emotions in the community of the project participants, many of whom are still active in the industry. Taking a project example from another industry – such as the Channel Tunnel or the Millennium Dome – would not solve this issue. For this reason, I have chosen a historic project from a time well before the invention of the computer (with apologies to Charles Babbage who conceived his Analytic Engine in 1834 but did not live to see it realised). This example clearly illustrates that the same generic root causes which beset IT projects are equally troubling to other types of project.

Isambard Kingdom Brunel

I have long been interested in the life and work of Isambard Kingdom Brunel, having been born and raised in Maidenhead on the route of the Great Western Railway (GWR). It is only comparatively recently that I have come to realise that, despite his very obvious engineering genius, he sometimes made rather fundamental professional errors.

One example is the rail section he designed for the GWR. Its resistance to bending in the vertical plane was low (which made for a very bouncy ride), while its resistance to bending in the horizontal plane was very high (which made it extremely difficult to bend the rails to accommodate the required curves on the line). This was a very basic mistake for one so familiar with the theory of the bending of beams.

However, much greater weaknesses were apparent in his business acumen and interpersonal skills. The adoption of the broad gauge for the GWR in the face of the universal use of the standard gauge by other railway companies was clearly unwise. It made it impossible for traffic to be transferred conveniently between the GWR and other railway networks and it was inevitable that the gauge would subsequently have to be converted – at substantial expense to the company. Clearly Brunel was unprepared to compromise his view that the broad gauge was inherently superior from a technical point of view, and unable to concede that business considerations could be more important than technical ones. Another example is apparent in his estimating for the construction of the GWR from London to Bristol. Brunel's original indicative price following a funded, high-level design study was £2.805 million. After detailed design, Brunel reduced his estimate to £2.5 million. The directors state in a prospectus of September 1834:

> 'The sum required for the construction of the entire line of 118 miles, including depots, locomotive engines etc., will be £2,500,000. The difference between this and the original estimate of £2,805,330 arises from the Engineer having now sufficient data to calculate the cost with accuracy; in the absence of which data on the former occasion, the Directors preferred stating a sum which should exceed rather than fall short of the greatest probable cost.'

The actual cost – including £90,000 of unplanned legal fees – was £6.282 million. It would seem that, for all his engineering genius, Brunel lacked commercial nous. He should not have reduced his original estimate. It is better to under-promise and over-perform, than to over-promise and under-perform. In addition, the directors also showed a good deal of naïveté – a very early example of how not to run a railway. Incidentally, the original timescale estimate for completing the line to Bristol was 29 months; the actual timescale was 73 months.

The GWR clearly meets the definition of a troubled project as presented in Chapter 1. However, it is also an outstanding example of the fact that a troubled project can go on to be a resounding commercial success.

The *Great Eastern*

The project I have chosen to use as a case study is one in which Brunel played a major part – the design, construction and operation of the steamship *Great Eastern*. I am indebted to an excellent book by George S Emmerson, *SS Great Eastern – The Greatest Iron Ship*,[1] which has provided much of the information. If you are not interested in ships, join me at the end of this chapter for a summary of the root causes of this troubled project.

Project conception

In 1851, gold was discovered in Australia, leading to an increase in emigration from the UK. The Australian Royal Mail Steamship Company employed Brunel as a consultant to assist them in specifying and placing contracts for two steamships, the *SS Adelaide* and the *SS Victoria*. Brunel had a track record in steamships. When constructed, his 236ft long *SS Great Western* was the largest paddle-driven steamship in the world, making 74 round trips across the Atlantic. His 322ft long *SS Great Britain* was the largest ship in the world when constructed and the first to be driven by a screw propeller. It made 32 voyages to Australia and saw service in the Crimean War and the Indian Mutiny.

Brunel then mused about the possibility of a steamship so large that it could make the round trip to Australia without refuelling. It would need to be faster than sailing ships, which took between 100 and 120 days to make the journey. Brunel calculated that an average speed of 14–15 knots would be required to make the ship an attractive proposition. Sketches for such a ship can be seen in a surviving notebook of Brunel's, alongside drawings for Paddington Station.

Brunel approached the Eastern Steam Navigation Company, a company formed to compete for two Royal Mail contracts to carry the mails to India and Australia. Despite the Commons recommending two competing services, the company had lost both contracts to P&O and was somewhat at a loose end, having no actual ships and no real business to run. They found the concept of a ship able to steam at 18 miles per hour and reaching Australia in 30–35 days extremely interesting. The ship would be about 600ft long with a displacement of some 18,000 tons, making it six times larger in terms of displacement than any other ship in the world. It would be designed to carry 800 1st class, 2000 2nd class and 1200 3rd class passengers, plus a ship's company of 400 officers and men.

Project initiation/mobilisation

The company set about the task of raising capital; a high return on investment was predicted. Brunel set about the task of specifying the requirements for the vessel and producing what was, in essence, a high-level design. He decided that the ship would be powered by a pair of paddles and a singe screw propeller. The two independent power plants would provide a degree of redundancy and make for a very manoeuvrable ship.

Brunel estimated that it would cost about £500,000 to build the ship. His estimate of timescale was 18 months from project start to launch of the hull, plus about six months for fitting out and working up into service.

Tenders were invited from shipbuilders for the hull, complete with paddle engines. Only one bid was received, for £332,295, from John Scott Russell. Russell was an established naval architect with his own shipbuilding yard at Millwall on the Isle of Dogs. He had contributed much to the advancement of steamship design, particularly with regard to the design of 'wave-line' hulls to provide minimal resistance to movement through the water at the designed cruising speed. Russell's bid was a little more expensive than Brunel had estimated, but it was accepted and the contract signed in May 1854. Russell agreed to accept one quarter of the contract price in shares to ease the company's cash flow and provide an element of risk/reward.

System design

Detailed design was the responsibility of the Vendor. Many novel ideas were considered by Russell and discarded. Some survived, including the use of a telegraph to transmit steering signals from the bridge to the helmsman at the stern – essentially a fly-by-wire system. Others would be added later, after the ship had been in service for several years. One such was power-assisted steering, which was fitted in 1867. Design features included:

- a wave-line hull to minimise energy loss;
- a system of longitudinal girders running the whole length of the hull, rather than conventional framing (this longitudinal framing system was much favoured by Russell);
- longitudinal bulkheads running the whole length of the engine and boiler rooms to help support the vast weight of the machinery and to provide convenient storage for fuel between these bulkheads and the hull;
- transverse bulkheads dividing the ship into 11 watertight compartments. These, in conjunction with the longitudinal bulkheads, the longitudinal framing and the double-skinned upper iron deck, provided great strength and rigidity;
- a double-skinned hull, one skin on each side of the longitudinal framing;
- standardisation of materials to just two Commercial Off The Shelf (COTS) sizes of iron angle sections and three thicknesses of plate.

During this stage of the project, the method of launching the ship had to be determined. The construction of a dry dock was considered, but the cost was thought to be prohibitive. Engines and boilers had to be fitted prior to the launch due to the lack of dockyard facilities for fitting them subsequently. In a lengthwise launch, the substantial unsupported weight of this plant might have overstressed the hull. There was also the problem that the river is only 1000ft wide at Millwall. The plan was formed to launch the ship broadside into the Thames.

During the design of the ship, Brunel insisted on approving all detailed designs and drawings. This was very time-consuming and caused much delay and re-work. The relationship between Russell and Brunel deteriorated. Construction began in May 1854. In April 1855, Brunel was concerned that the designs had not been completed. It would seem that for the first year design and construction proceeded in parallel.

System development

During the construction of the ship, Brunel displayed an irresistible desire to alter the design and specification as work proceeded. This gave rise to a large number of changes.

Six months into the build, the largest financial backer of the project died, forcing the company to seek additional funding. The rate at which funding could be made available began to determine the rate at which progress on the construction of the ship could be made.

The Crimean War (September 1854–February 1856) created a large national demand for skilled labour and materials, causing prices and wages to rise and putting Russell's margin under threat. There was a recession in shipbuilding and several Thames shipyards were closed. Russell advised Brunel that an additional £40,000 would be required to fund the changes. Brunel resisted this, perhaps because he was reluctant to admit to the ESN directors that he had cost the company this level of additional expenditure.

After the war, there was a fall in trade and reduced demand for shipping, putting the whole enterprise at risk. The ship became the focus of much press interest and speculation.

Russell had much of his capital locked up in ESN shares which had reduced in value and were virtually impossible to convert into cash. He came close to bankruptcy and the relationship between Brunel and Russell worsened as Brunel refused to accept all of Russell's arguments for more money. Russell repudiated the contract and went into voluntary liquidation. A price was agreed between the company and the liquidators for the completion of the hull and engines.

Brunel, who was falling ill with the kidney complaint which would eventually kill him, was still insisting on approving every detail and requesting further changes. Matters came to a head and the liquidator imposed a budgetary limit of £20 on any change.

System implementation

The launch of the ship was a hugely troubled and expensive process. The slope of the launch-way had been designed to enable a controlled rather than a free launch to take place. The dead weight of the ship on the launch-way proved too much for the hydraulic rams to move and a huge amount of additional ram capacity had to be installed, moved and re-installed as the vessel was inched down the 250ft launch-way to the low water mark. It took 12 weeks to float the ship, in the full glare of publicity from the national press. The cost estimate for the launch was £14,000; the actual cost was £170,000.

When the ship was finally afloat, on 30 January 1858, it had cost £640,000, almost double the tender value. A further £140,000 was needed to complete the fitting-out and the Eastern Steam Navigation Company was £90,000 overdrawn at the bank. It had taken 45 months to build and launch the hull, two and a half times the timescale originally planned.

Little was accomplished in 1858. The Far East trade had been affected by the Indian Mutiny and the bank rate was rising. There was little demand for shipping and the company found it hard to attract new investors. Efforts to gain government funding were unsuccessful, as the government did not wish to encourage irresponsible and speculative projects.

In November 1858, the ship was sold for £160,000 to a new company set up by some of the existing directors plus external backers. The Great Ship Company raised the capital required to complete the ship, now known as the *SS Great Eastern*. In the prospectus for the new company, the plan to use the ship for the American trade was apparent. Eight round trips to the US each year were planned and a 15 per cent dividend was forecast.

In January 1859, Scott Russell submitted a tender for £125,000 to complete the ship. A maiden voyage to the US was planned for the summer. This would be preceded by a trial sailing out into the Atlantic in order to prove the completed vessel.

On 6 September 1859, the ship moved down the Thames under her own steam, en route for Weymouth, surprisingly carrying over 150 1st class passengers. The design of the ship featured heat exchangers, fitted around the paddle boiler flues, to pre-heat boiler feed water. These took the form of water jackets around the flues. A supplementary purpose of the water jackets was to insulate the main saloon, through which the flues passed, from the heat of the exhaust gases. This feature had been specified by Brunel, despite objections from Russell. A flaw of the design meant that water could be introduced into the water jackets while the inner surface was almost red hot, causing steam to form instantaneously at high pressure. This occurred on the trip to Weymouth, causing the forward water jacket to explode. Fortunately, no passengers were in the main saloon when this happened, but several stokers were badly burned and five later died from their injuries.

Repairs took three weeks and cost £5000. The company pressed to have the work completed at Russell's expense, despite the feature having been mandated by Brunel. The planned trip to the US was cancelled and the ship wintered at Southampton.

The new company accused Russell of not fulfilling the contract satisfactorily and withheld the final milestone payment of £6000. Russell took the dispute to arbitration and was awarded £18,000. Shareholders became impatient at the lack of dividends and the share price fell to one-fifth of face value. There was a tempestuous meeting of directors and shareholders in January 1860 at which the directors reported that the ship had been mortgaged for £40,000. They then resigned. A new Board was appointed, no member of which had any previous experience of running a steamship line.

£20,000 of work was commissioned to enable Board of Trade requirements to be met and the ship was readied for service.

System operation, benefit delivery, stewardship and disposal

The public had become afraid of the *Great Eastern* and only 38 fee-paying passengers embarked on the ship's maiden voyage on 16 June 1860. The ship reached New York in 10 days and 19 hours and performed faultlessly; there was no vibration, little noise and only modest rolling in the Atlantic swell. Tours of the ship were offered at the exceedingly high price of $1, and several short excursion cruises were run. These were badly managed and did no credit to the directors of the company. The ship travelled home uneventfully.

In 1861, the ship sailed for the US again and on her return she was chartered by the Admiralty to carry 2500 troops and 200 artillery horses to Quebec.

On her next trip from Liverpool with 400 passengers, the ship encountered a heavy storm. In an incident during which the ship was reversed with the rudder hard over (the equivalent of 'pilot error'), the rudder head fractured and steerage was lost. The ship rolled terribly and heavy objects broke free, including a roll of lead in the engine room. The paddle engines had to be stopped to avoid the danger that the roll of lead might foul the oscillating cylinders. When this was done, the paddles were badly damaged by the heavy seas. The screw engines had to be stopped as the damaged rudder was fouling the propeller. The ship was without power or steering in a storm of frightful proportions. A temporary rig was set up to steer the ship, devised by an American engineer on board who later successfully claimed $15,000 salvage from the company.

In 1862, there were three return trips to the US. Arriving off New York on the third trip, the ship hit an uncharted reef which damaged the outer skin of the hull. This incident would have sunk a lesser ship.

1863 was the *Great Eastern*'s most successful season, during which she made three return trips to the US, carrying 3650 passengers. Despite comparative success, costs exceeded revenue by £20,000 – exactly the amount by which fares had had to be cut to compete with the Cunard and Inman Lines which were engaged in a fierce price war. The company found itself in the red to the tune of £142,350 and a liquidator was appointed.

The ship was put up for auction in January 1864. There were no bids but behind the scenes plans were being laid to acquire the ship for a new purpose. Some of the directors had been approached by Cyrus Field, the prime mover behind the Atlantic Cable Company, which had sponsored two failed attempts to lay a cable across the Atlantic. These directors bought out as many bond-holders as were necessary to give them control over the disposal of the ship. They then put it up for auction, having formed a new company – the Great Eastern Steamship Company. The ship went under the hammer for £25,000, just one quarter of the scrap value and 2.5 per cent of the build cost. They had themselves a bargain.

The ship was immediately chartered to the Telegraph Construction Company, the forerunner of Cable & Wireless, in return for a share of the cable revenue. At last, here was a mission for which the ship was ideal. Her huge bulk meant that she could carry the 21,000 tons of cable required and provide a steady platform from which it could be laid.

The first attempt in July 1865 was nearly successful. Twelve hundred miles of cable were laid, leaving 600 miles to go, when the cable parted. Three attempts were made to retrieve the cable from the ocean floor, 2.5 miles below, using grapnels. On each occasion the cable was located and lifted about a mile off the sea bed before the stress overcame the lifting gear and the cable fell back. The ship returned home with plans for another attempt, it having been proved beyond reasonable doubt that the enterprise was feasible.

The *Great Eastern* set off for Newfoundland on her second attempt in July 1866, carrying an improved cable. The cable was laid successfully without any breakages and the ship arrived in Hearts Content Bay, Newfoundland, 14 days later. In a further success, the cable lost the previous year was located and retrieved from the sea bed. It is hard to imagine the skill which made this possible in the days before Global Positioning System (GPS) technology and unmanned underwater exploration vehicles. The cable was spliced to 600 miles of cable on board which had been ferried across from the UK. The ship then paid out the cable back to Newfoundland. Two submarine cables were now in place. The ship returned home to a hero's welcome. Knighthoods were bestowed and shareholders received a dividend of 70 per cent.

The ship was then chartered to a French company to ply between New York and Brest in conjunction with the Paris Exhibition of 1867, carrying Jules Verne on the one trip made.

In July 1869, the *Great Eastern* laid her third cable across the Atlantic, this time from Brest to Newfoundland on behalf of the Societé du Cable Transatlantique Français, whose principal was P J Reuter of news agency fame. Also in 1869, the Suez Canal opened, providing a final nail in the coffin of the ship's original mission to be the premier vessel to ply the Far East trade; her draught was too large for her to use the canal safely.

In 1870, the ship laid a cable across the Indian Ocean. In 1873, she laid her fifth cable, from Ireland to Newfoundland. In 1874, she laid her final cable, this time from Newfoundland to Ireland.

Business was good, with shareholders receiving a dividend of 10–15 per cent per annum, but the future of the great ship was now less certain. While her hull was in good condition, her power plant was obsolete. Modern steamships had no paddles. Instead, they had multiple screws and triple expansion engines. The cost of converting her to a modern luxury liner was prohibitive. After nearly 10 years of idleness, she was sold for £26,200 in October 1885 and the company wound up. After a few years of ignominious use as a floating amusement arcade – fulfilling a prophetic cartoon drawn in 1857 – she was sold for scrap. She made her last journey under her own power in January 1889 and was broken up. It would be another 10 years before a ship was built which exceeded her length of 680ft and 17 years before the ill-fated *Lusitania* exceeded her displacement.

The root causes of the project's troubles

Project conception

The *Great Eastern* was a state-of-the-art high-technology project. The ship would be six times larger than any built previously anywhere in the world. It was an inherently risky and speculative enterprise.

The company commissioning the project was a start-up company with little capital of its own and, equally importantly, no experience of running a steamship line. This must raise questions as to whether the business case was realistic.

Project initiation/mobilisation

The Buyer underestimated both the cost and timescale required to build the ship. So did the Vendor. This was not surprising as they could not call upon previous experience of constructing a ship of this size.

System design

Timescale pressure led the project to adopt an approach whereby design and construction could proceed in parallel. This is always problematical, causing much unnecessary rework.

The Buyer insisted on reviewing and changing the detailed design. This caused a great deal of rework and delay, adding to the Vendor's cost.

System development

The Buyer insisted on making changes to the requirements and the design. These were not managed well by the Vendor and the contract value was not increased commensurate with the changes. Russell should have insisted on a contract variation for each change, agreed up front, rather than issuing a retrospective claim.

The relationship between Buyer and Vendor was poor, both regarding the other party with extreme suspicion. There was little evidence of reasonable behaviour on the part of the Buyer.

Macroeconomic factors conspired to increase the Vendor's costs and to reduce the likelihood of the Buyer making a good return on their investment.

System implementation

Implementation costs escalated dramatically due to the difficulties faced in launching the ship.

Macroeconomic factors continued to bite, with Far East trade volumes falling and rising interest rates putting exports under further threat.

The new owners of the ship abandoned the original mission for the ship (the Australia route) and pressed her into service on the US route for which her design was sub-optimal.

The catastrophic failure which led to five deaths on her first short voyage further marred the ship's already poor reputation in the eyes of the public.

There was further evidence of a poor working relationship between the Buyer and the Vendor.

System operation, benefit delivery, stewardship and disposal

The Buyer failed to deploy the ship for the purpose for which she was designed and built.

End-users (the public) were fearful of the ship and she never achieved a passenger volume which would have provided a good return on investment.

Margins were also under pressure as a result of a price war between steamship lines.

She reached the end of her useful life when the cost of re-fitting her as a luxury liner exceeded the most optimistic profit forecast.

Analysis of the root causes of the *Great Eastern's* troubles

Table 3.1 shows which of the 40 generic root causes of troubled projects are apparent in this case study. Also shown is a personal view of the relative importance of the root causes, where '1' is the most important. Note that there are always going to be some problems which do not appear in the standard list but which are nevertheless important. One example in the case of the *Great Eastern* is the poor esteem in which the ship was held by the public, probably as a result of damning press publicity. We have a recent example of this in the UK in the Millennium Dome.

There is always going to be a degree of subjectivity when assessing the relative importance of the problems on a project. My advice is to write the root causes/problem statements on 'Post-its®' and sort them manually until you are happy with your ranking. The really important thing is to separate the 'big hitters' from the rest. Too many reports have one long list of 100 or more findings; this detracts from the importance of the *key* findings, blunts the impact of the report and makes it easier for those responsible for corrective action to focus on the easy actions rather than the high-priority ones.

In the case of the *Great Eastern*, the 'big hitters' were the lack of competence on the Boards of the companies which commissioned and ran the ship, the challenge of scale and new technology, and the unforeseen changes in the competitive and macroeconomic environment. Interestingly enough, none of these fall inside the system design and system development stages of the project life cycle, which are the normal high-focus areas when considering troubled projects and the causes of their failure.

The most telling analysis of the project's troubles came from her builder, John Scott Russell, who states:

> 'she fell into the management of amateur directors, among them men who had commanded ships, but not steamships; among them men who had made money by ships, but not steamships; among them men who

had built engines, but not marine engines … The *Great Eastern*, the largest of all Brunel's conceptions, has read us all a lesson.'

(This quotation is reproduced by permission of David & Charles.)

Postscript

In April 2000, P&O's latest cruise liner, *Aurora*, was named by the Princess Royal at Southampton. A magnum of champagne failed to break when struck against the ship's bows. At 886ft, *Aurora* is nearly 200ft longer than the *Great Eastern*.

Table 3.1   *Prioritised Root Causes of the* **Great Eastern's Troubles**

	Relative Importance of Root Cause
	Project Conception
2 RC01	Project based on an unsound premise or an unrealistic business case
3 RC03	Project based on state-of-the-art and immature technology
1 RC04	Lack of Buyer Board-level ownership/commitment or competence
5 RC05	Buyer's funding and/or timescale expectations unrealistically low
	Project Initiation/Mobilisation
7 RC07	Vendor setting unrealistic expectations on cost, timescale or Vendor capability
9 RC09	Failure to achieve an open, robust and equitable Buyer–Vendor relationship
6 RC12	Vendor underestimate of resources (predominantly person-effort) required
	System Design
12 RC20	Vendor starting a phase prior to completing a previous phase
10 RC26	Buyer retains design authority with right to approve/reject low-level designs
	System Development
11 RC28	Vendor failure to 'freeze' the design (& technical platform) and apply change control
13 RC32	Lack of a formal, 'engineering' approach to integration and testing by Vendor
	System Implementation
8 RC36	Catastrophic failure of the system, with no effective contingency arrangement
	System Operation, Benefit Delivery, Stewardship and Disposal
14 RC38	Buyer Failure to measure actual delivered benefit and take corrective action
4 RC40	Changes in the competitive or macroeconomic environment

Her 76,000 tons is more than three times the gross tonnage of the *Great Eastern*. On Monday 1 May, the ship left Southampton on her maiden voyage – a 14-night Mediterranean cruise – carrying some 2000 passengers. A few hours later, she was limping home at reduced speed with a propeller shaft bearing having been damaged by overheating. P&O and their insurers faced a £6 million bill for lost revenue and compensation. 140 years on from the maiden voyage of the *Great Eastern*, and despite huge strides in technology, this incident reminds us that any ambitious project can suffer from unexpected problems.

References

1. George S Emmerson, *SS Great Eastern – The Greatest Iron Ship*, David & Charles, ISBN 0 7153 80540.

Part 2

PREVENTING TROUBLED PROJECTS AT THE PLANNING STAGE

Chapter 4

A PROFESSIONAL SERVICES SALES PRIMER

Introduction to Part 2

Table 4.1 shows the root causes of troubled projects which are detectable and preventable at the planning or bid stage.

An effective Quality Assurance (QA) function can detect many but not all of the potential root causes. But leaving QA to detect the issues and risks of a bid is an indictment of the professionalism of your business. It is everyone's responsibility to de-risk a project.

The Vendor should discuss Buyer-induced root causes with the potential Buyer and suggest ways of de-risking the project. Strategies might include:

- for a 'full scope' development, breaking the project into a number of phases, starting with a requirements definition phase;
- phasing delivery of a complex project to provide a number of software 'drops'. This provides usable functionality early and early proof of project viability;
- the concept of a 'pilot' or 'proof of concept demonstrator' to enable requirements to be honed or infrastructure to be proved before more substantial investment is made.

The problem is that procurements have a momentum all of their own. Buyers have planned their procurement strategy and have formed a picture of how the project will be structured and implemented. They are reluctant to change the approach they are taking on the advice of a potential Vendor – it makes them look ill prepared and requires them to change the procurement approach and timetable in flight. Buyers are also understandably wary of contracting with a single Vendor for a requirements definition phase as they feel they would have burned their boats and would be 'over a barrel' with regard to the price of subsequent phases. Placing a requirements definition study with two potential Vendors is unattractive to Buyers as it implies additional expense and a substantial time commitment from end-users and the Buyer's project team. The approach of placing parallel, funded design studies with two potential Vendors has somewhat fallen out of favour. This is a great pity as this approach does allow the potential Vendors to thoroughly shape the development project for the benefit of both parties to the contract. In addition, the funding goes some way to meeting the Vendors' costs for the design work and development planning.

Table 4.1   *Troubled Project Root Causes Preventable during the Planning Stage*

Chapter	Preventable Troubled Project Root Causes	
5 Opportunity Qualification	RC03	Project based on state-of-the-art and immature technology
	RC05	Buyer's funding and/or timescale expectations unrealistically low
	RC06	Buyer failure to break a complex project into phases or smaller projects
	RC08	Buyer failure to define and document requirements (functional and non-functional)
	RC17	Full-scope, fixed-price contracting (requirements, design and development)
6 Engaging the Potential Buyer	RC01	Project based on an unsound premise or an unrealistic business case
	RC02	Buyer failure to define clear project objectives, anticipated benefits and success criteria
	RC04	Lack of Buyer Board-level ownership/commitment or competence
	RC09	Failure to achieve an open, robust and equitable Buyer-Vendor relationship
	RC11	Buyer lack of sufficient involvement of eventual end-users
7 Shaping the Solution	RC03	Project based on state-of-the-art and immature technology
	RC19	Poor choice of technical platform and/or architecture
	RC21	Poor choice of design/development method
8 Defining the Solution	RC13	Vendor failure to define project tasks, deliverables and acceptance processes
	RC26	Buyer retains design authority with right to approve/reject low-level designs
9 Project Estimating and Planning	RC12	Vendor underestimation of resources (predominantly person-effort) required
	RC15	Poor project planning, management and execution
	RC16	Failure to clearly define roles and responsibilities in the contract/subcontracts
10 Quality Assurance and Risk Management	RC01	Project based on an unsound premise or an unrealistic business case
	RC03	Project based on state-of-the-art and immature technology
	RC05	Buyer's funding and/or timescale expectations unrealistically low
	RC06	Buyer failure to break a complex project into phases or smaller projects

(continued)

Table 4.1 *Troubled Project Root Causes Preventable during the Planning Stage (continued)*

10 Quality Assurance and Risk Management	RC07	Vendor setting unrealistic expectations on cost, timescale or Vendor capability
	RC08	Buyer failure to define and document requirements (functional and non-functional)
	RC10	Vendor failure to invest enough resources to scope the project prior to contract
	RC12	Vendor underestimation of resources (predominantly person-effort) required
	RC13	Vendor failure to define project tasks, deliverables and acceptance processes
	RC14	Failure to actively manage risks and maintain robust contingency plans
	RC15	Poor project planning, management and execution
	RC16	Failure to clearly define roles and responsibilities in the contract/subcontracts
	RC17	Full-scope, fixed-price contracting (requirements, design and development)
	RC19	Poor choice of technical platform and/or architecture
	RC21	Poor choice of design/development method
	RC23	Vendor lack/loss of skilled resources
	RC24	Poor Vendor standards deployment (design, coding, testing, configuration management etc)
	RC26	Buyer retains design authority with right to approve/reject low-level designs
	RC32	Lack of a formal 'engineering' approach to integration and testing by Vendor
	RC33	Insufficient attention paid by Vendor to non-functional requirements
11 Writing the Proposal	–	

If the project bears the hallmarks of a troubled project due to Buyer-induced root causes and the Buyer is unprepared to de-risk the project, the Vendor must be prepared to walk away from the opportunity.

In Part 2 of this book we consider the bid stage of a project from the perspective of risk reduction and troubled project root cause prevention. Part 2 is written primarily for Vendors. However, I very much hope that it will be of value to Buyers also, as it highlights the activities and deliverables of a well-thought through solution. If you are a Buyer, you should expect to see evidence of these activities and deliverables from each of your prospective Vendors.

A well-scoped and thoroughly worked-through solution is not only a low-risk solution, but is also a winning one. Buyers want to see evidence that you understand their business drivers and the system requirements they have documented.

They want to see a full description of what they will get if they contract with you. They want a route map of the project, showing what the deliverables are and when they will be provided. They want to know who your project manager will be and have confidence that they can forge an effective working relationship with your team. They want to know how you will manage the project and ensure that deliverables are of high quality. If you can deliver this package during the bid stage, you have the potential to win. The chapters in Part 2 should help you to win more business, while achieving more consistent business performance and delivering higher levels of customer satisfaction.

Introduction to this sales primer

This is not a book on selling. However, whatever role we play in a professional services business we need a basic understanding of the sales process. If you have not had much contact with the sales side of the business, this 'sales primer' will give you enough to get by.

Well-known facts about selling

- Sales are the lifeblood of a company
- It is easier to sell to an existing Buyer than to a 'Prospect'
- You should not have all your eggs in one basket
- Without a continuous flow of new business a company will shrink
- You must know your product and your marketplace

Lesser-known facts about selling

- Sales is an honourable profession; to succeed you must be proud of what you do
- Sales is more of a science than an art
- You don't have to be an extrovert to succeed in sales
- Every Vendor staff member who interacts with a potential Buyer is selling
- Sales is a game of percentages – not a game of chance
- You maximise your sales by concentrating your efforts on what you can win

Orders, sales and backlog

Orders

Let's be precise. When you bid for an opportunity and win you may have 'closed a sale' but you have actually won an order. The total value of orders received by your business, division or branch in a given accounting period (month, quarter or year) is your Gross Orders Received (GOR) figure. A sales professional's earnings are usually geared to the value of orders won rather than to the profitability of the business. This is unfortunate as they can be responsible for winning business which is troubled and loss-making.

Sales

Your sales (or revenue) in a given accounting period is the total of all invoices raised less credit notes issued (exclusive of VAT/sales tax) in that period. I will use the words Sales and Revenue interchangeably. Sales revenue comes from new business and follow-on (or repeat) business.

Unless the project is contracted on a Time & Materials (T&M) basis, it is normal for the Buyer to pay a defined proportion of the contract value on the achievement of each of several payment milestones. The Buyer and Vendor will typically negotiate what these milestones will be and how much value should be attributed to each one. Examples of milestones would be 'delivery of a detailed design specification', 'completion of Factory Acceptance Testing', and 'delivery of Software Drop 2'. The Vendor will normally endeavour to maximise the value of early milestones in order to achieve a positive cash flow and to take some profit from the contract early.

When a milestone is achieved, it is normal to 'write off' the cost of 'Work in Progress' associated with that milestone against the value of the milestone. This gives a Gross Profit (GP) figure for the milestone. Total project GP to date is then:

$$\frac{\text{(Total Sales to Date (total of all invoices raised)} - \text{Total cost written off)}}{\text{Total Sales to Date}} \times 100\%$$

If the project is performing to its planned budget, its percentage GP to date will be similar to its target percentage GP for the whole project.

Early milestones are often achieved relatively painlessly, even on projects which will become troubled at a later stage. Later milestones might be delayed due to the project getting into difficulty. When they are achieved, options available include:

- booking the total milestone revenue and writing off all Work in Progress against the milestone;
- booking the total milestone revenue and writing off all Work in Progress plus a provision for future costs against the milestone;

- booking a proportion of the milestone revenue and writing off all Work in Progress against the milestone, accruing a proportion of the milestone revenue to be taken later, when the financial status of the project is clearer.

Backlog

Your Backlog is your potential future sales from contracted business. In simple terms, it is the difference between your GOR and your Sales to Date. The larger the Backlog as a proportion of annual sales, the more of a cushion your business has against a short-term downturn in business. Many professional services businesses have a frighteningly small Backlog of between three and six months. A small Backlog means a great deal of pressure on salespeople to win orders.

Some businesses use the word Pipeline instead of Backlog. I've no problem with that except that I think it is a word best applied to the flow of Leads, Opportunities and Bids which results in orders won.

The sales pipeline

The Sales Pipeline is shown in Figure 4.1. Let's start at the top of the diagram. A 'LEAD' is a 'SUSPECT' with a potential business opportunity. 'Leads' need to be generated by getting out there and talking to 'Suspects' in your chosen market sectors about the products and services you want to sell. This is the 'LEAD GENERATION' stage. It goes without saying that your salespeople will only uncover a tiny fraction of all potential Leads for your products and services; many Leads will be missed by your company and pursued and developed by your competitors.

Leads need to be converted into 'OPPORTUNITIES'. An 'Opportunity' is a 'Prospect' with a business requirement and a budget who wants to place a contract. The process of converting your Leads into Opportunities is called 'OPPORTUNITY GENERATION'. Ideally, you are looking to gain the Prospect's agreement to the submission by your company of a proposal for services on a single-tender basis. Of course, not all Leads will resolve down into single-tender Opportunities. Often, Buyers will be engaged with several potential Vendors and you will have to compete for the business. But generally, Opportunities that you have developed:

- have fewer competitors and therefore offer you a better win chance;
- give you a far better insight into the Buyer's requirements than you can achieve purely by reading an invitation to tender (ITT) or request for proposals (RFP);
- provide the opportunity to develop a RELATIONSHIP of respect and trust with the decision-makers and decision-influencers in the Buyer organisation which is to the mutual advantage of Buyer and Vendor.

If you have also influenced the requirement, discussed your potential solution, demonstrated how it will meet the Buyer's requirement and obtained positive

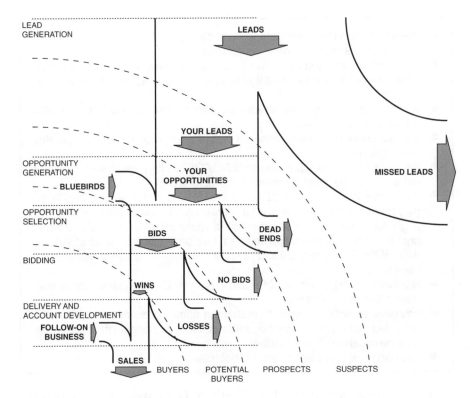

Figure 4.1   *The Sales Pipeline*

feedback on the attractiveness of your solution, you have an 'INSIDE TRACK'. It is often the case that a Buyer will not agree to visit Vendor companies or reference sites once the ITT has been issued, so if you have not held such sessions before the ITT arrives through your letterbox, it is too late. Not all Leads turn into Opportunities; some become 'Dead Ends'.

Once your Lead has become an Opportunity, you have a real chance of winning some business. The Suspect is now a Prospect. You can now show the opportunity on your 'DISCOUNTED SALES FORECAST' as a potential source of future revenue.

A Discounted Sales Forecast shows each Opportunity, its likely contract value, a conservative estimate of your win probability and the discounted value of the business (contract value multiplied by win probability). The sum of the discounted values gives you at least a crude indication of future sales.

Enter 'BLUEBIRD', stage left. A 'Bluebird' is an Opportunity which arrives unexpectedly. It is a real Prospect with a real business requirement, a budget and a desire to place a contract. However, it is highly likely that it is an Opportunity which one or more or your competitors have been developing.

Bluebirds are intrinsically attractive, but:

- there are often many Vendors to compete against;
- other Vendors probably have inside tracks;
- you don't understand the Buyer's business drivers and system requirements as well as the Vendors that have been tracking and developing the Opportunity;
- another Vendor may have shaped the Opportunity to match a particular off-the-shelf solution;
- another Vendor may have prepared the ITT and the proposal/tender evaluation criteria;
- the Buyer may not allow you to 'ENGAGE' to fully understand the requirements and present your candidate solution;
- the competition may be a 'BEAUTY PARADE'. In other words, the Buyer may have a strong preference for a particular Vendor's solution and you might have been invited to bid either to 'make up the numbers' and demonstrate that procurement procedures have been followed, or as a 'STALKING HORSE' to pressure the favoured Vendor to quote a particularly keen price;
- Bluebirds divert valuable bid resources from Opportunities where you have a better win chance;
- you have an uphill struggle to match the quality of some other Vendors' solutions and proposals as they will have been working on them for some time before the ITT was issued;
- You can't build a business from Bluebirds.

You are now at the 'OPPORTUNITY SELECTION' stage, where you have to decide whether or not to bid. This is the process of Qualification, which is covered in Chapter 5. Good qualification is key to winning profitable business and avoiding troubled projects. Opportunities you decide to bid become 'BIDS'; those you don't become 'NO BIDS'.

When you are at the bid stage you are engaged with a 'POTENTIAL BUYER' and the outcome is either a 'WIN' or a 'LOSS'. There are no second prizes or awards for the fastest loser! The ratio of your Wins to your Bids is your 'CONVERSION RATE'. The rest of the chapters in Part 2 of this book cover aspects of the bidding process and show how to eliminate the risk of a troubled project throughout this process.

What should your conversion rate be?

1 in 1	Pinch yourself, you're dreaming!
1 in 2	Superb. You must have a hot product and a world-class team.
1 in 3	Very Good. This is top-class qualification, solutioning and bidding.
1 in 4	Good. Room for some improvement though.
1 in 5	Average. Bidding is costing you too much.
1 in 6–10	Poor. You're not going to grow your business in this way.

If you reach the bottom of the Sales Pipeline, you have a 'WIN' and a real 'BUYER' at last. There is nothing quite so satisfying in business as an order – particularly if it's a large one where you have developed the Lead and Opportunity, crafted the solution and the proposal, and know exactly how to deliver the project.

The even better news is that every new Win brings with it the prospect of 'FOLLOW-ON BUSINESS' which no other Vendor can compete for. We are not just talking about a few changes to the requirements. You will have opportunities to assist the Buyer in their planning for system implementation. There may be change management consultancy to deliver. There may be a large-scale end-user training programme to design and deliver. Major enhancements and further system developments may lie ahead. You are in the 'DELIVERY AND ACCOUNT DEVELOPMENT' stage. This is where services Vendors obtain most of their business. However, there is a balancing act. You have to keep converting new business opportunities if you want to grow the business.

I noted earlier that Selling is a game of percentages, not a game of chance. You will have seen that the Sales Pipeline is a leaky one. The science of sales is to reduce the leakage as much as possible. This means:

- maximising the Leads you generate;
- maximising the Opportunities you develop from Leads;
- maximising your conversion rate by bidding only those opportunities which you have a strong chance of winning.

Summary

Twenty four out of the 40 root causes of troubled projects can be detected and prevented at the bid stage, given a professional approach by all in the business. A strong and independent QA function can detect most but not all of these.

The Sales Pipeline is a leaky one. Your salespeople need to work hard at Lead Generation and Opportunity Generation to provide sufficient new business opportunities for your business to grow. You can't afford to rely solely on follow-on business.

Good qualification of the potential Opportunities increases your conversion rate and filters out many potentially troubled projects.

Exercises

1. If you don't have a process for monitoring the conversion rate of your business, design and implement one.
2. Monitor your follow-on business conversion rate as well as that for new business.
3. Make a list of 'Bluebirds' you have bid for in the last six months. What was your conversion rate on these?

4. Covering every deal lost in the last 6–12 months, construct a histogram showing the reasons why you lost (from de-briefs with the potential Buyers). What are the three main reasons why you lost? What could you do to improve your conversion rate? What *will* you do?

Chapter 5

OPPORTUNITY QUALIFICATION AND SELECTION

Introduction

On my first day at a professional services company, I was asked to help on a bid for a Criminal Information System. An Operational Requirement (OR) had dropped through the letter box unexpectedly. It was a very good OR with clear functional and non-functional requirements. We had no relationship with the Force and had never developed a police information system before. We had no information on the size of the budget or how many Vendors had been invited to propose. Conventional wisdom said 'No bid'. What we did have in our favour was a charismatic principal, a technical architect who was very able and convincing, and me – a software engineer in his first commercial IT job – who was keen to make an impression. We decided to bid. I designed the database, using a file management system with B-tree indexes. My previous experience was in real-time systems; I had never worked on a system with a disc drive before, let alone a database. We worked hard. We worked nights and weekends. We wrote a detailed and persuasive proposal. I nearly fell asleep at the wheel driving the proposal to Norwich after working all night typing, copying and binding. We won the business.

Years later, I was working for another services company when another police ITT arrived unannounced. We had no relationship with the client and little recent experience in this sector – which is perceived as a disadvantage by Buyers in this marketplace. The requirements were expressed at a very high level, amounting to full-scope, fixed-price development (RC17). The client's timescale aspiration was very ambitious. We did not know the size of the budget or who the competition was. We were not allowed to engage with, or even meet, the Prospect. We decided to bid, but were not successful.

The two examples above introduce the topic of Opportunity Qualification and Selection. They illustrate that this is not an exact science. We should have 'No Bid' the first opportunity, but we bid it and won. We should have 'No Bid' the second opportunity, but we bid it and lost.

Troubled project root causes to avoid at the opportunity qualification stage
Be on the look out for:
RC03 Project based on state-of-the-art and immature technology

> **RC05** Buyer's funding and/or timescale expectations unrealistically low
> **RC06** Buyer failure to break a complex project into phases or smaller projects
> **RC08** Buyer failure to define and document requirements (functional and non-functional)
> **RC17** Full-scope, fixed-price contracting (requirements, design and development)

Qualification is important because:

- it enables you to filter out Opportunities which have the clear potential to become troubled and loss-making projects;
- good qualification increases your conversion rate, which maximises the business generated by your bid resources;
- a lost bid costs exactly the same as a winning bid and prevents you from bidding another Opportunity which you have a better chance of winning;
- qualification is a means of achieving your business strategy in your chosen vertical markets;
- a target rifle is more accurate than a scatter gun.

Qualification worksheet

A Qualification Worksheet is shown in Figure 5.1. The purpose of the worksheet is to help you to target the Opportunities that you can win. Work through this for every Opportunity (especially 'Bluebirds') you are considering bidding. The worksheet prompts you to consider 11 factors and 'mark' them qualitatively on a scale of 'Low' to 'High'. These are the factors:

> *T*angible requirements?
>
> Does the Request for Proposal (RFP)/Invitation to Tender (ITT) contain the clear and crisp functional and non-functional requirements needed to form a sound foundation for a design and development project?

If requirements are expressed at a high level only and the Prospect is requesting a fixed price for requirements clarification, design, development and implementation, then you have a potential full-scope, fixed-price project on your hands. This is not necessarily a reason to 'No Bid', but if your company does not have a great track record of delivering profitable full-scope, fixed-price projects then you should certainly consider 'No Bidding'. You have to be very good to succeed at these. You need to provide in your proposal a full set of the assumptions on which your price is based. These must be sufficiently solid to provide a mechanism for gearing the price if the system turns out to be more feature-rich or complex than you assumed.

Opportunity Qualification Worksheet

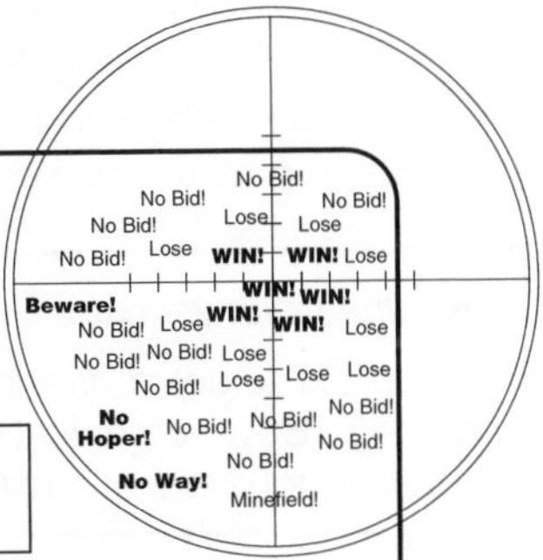

Opportunity:

No Bid! No Bid! No Bid!
No Bid! Lose Lose
No Bid! Lose WIN! WIN! Lose
WIN! WIN!
Beware!
No Bid! Lose WIN! WIN! Lose
No Bid! No Bid! Lose
No Bid! Lose Lose Lose
No Bid! No Bid!
No Hoper! No Bid! No Bid! No Bid!
No Bid!
No Way!
Minefield!

We will WIN because…

If we lose, it will be because…

The Top 3 risks are:

1.

2.

3.

Tangible requirements?   LOW ☐ ☐ ☐ ☐ ☐ ☐ HIGH

Aligned with your strategy?   ☐ ☐ ☐ ☐ ☐ ☐

Relationship with this prospect?   ☐ ☐ ☐ ☐ ☐ ☐

Good solution?   ☐ ☐ ☐ ☐ ☐ ☐

Effort available to bid and execute?   ☐ ☐ ☐ ☐ ☐ ☐

Time available to prepare a winning bid?   ☐ ☐ ☐ ☐ ☐ ☐

Size of budget known/adequate?   ☐ ☐ ☐ ☐ ☐ ☐

Competition known + strengths/weaknesses?   ☐ ☐ ☐ ☐ ☐ ☐

Only me! Do you have uniques?   ☐ ☐ ☐ ☐ ☐ ☐

Price that will win?   ☐ ☐ ☐ ☐ ☐ ☐

Engagement with prospect possible?   ☐ ☐ ☐ ☐ ☐ ☐

Beware Troubled Project Root Causes:
RC03 Project based on state-of-the-art and immature technology
RC05 Buyer's funding and/or timescale expectations unrealistically low
RC06 Buyer failure to break a complex project into phases or smaller projects
RC08 Buyer failure to define and document requirements (functional and non-functional)
RC17 Full-scope, fixed-price contracting (requirements, design and development)

Figure 5.1   *Qualification Worksheet*

Full-scope, fixed-price bids require more resources than other types of bid due to the need to specify this comprehensive framework of assumptions. If the project is full-scope, fixed-price *and* large, then consider very carefully whether you want to play this game; these projects usually become troubled.

Aligned with your strategy?

If you bid and win, is the project going to strengthen your presence in a strategic Buyer organisation or market sector, or will it blur your focus and be a distraction? Is it a 'Must Win' Opportunity?

This is a particularly important factor to consider for 'Bluebirds'. They might be large and attractive Opportunities, but if they take you into a sector in which you have decided not to compete, then don't bid them. This presupposes that you are clear about which products and services you wish to promote to which key Buyers and in which vertical markets.

I once made a very good living as a generalist IT consultant. I undertook system performance tuning studies, IS/IT strategy studies, LAN/WAN strategy studies, cellular telephone system studies, dbms selection studies and project trouble-shooting studies. If I did not have the knowledge of a particular technology, I could read up on it and be pretty credible within a couple of days. Those days are over! Technology has exploded and it's simply not possible to be an expert in more than a couple of areas of IT. The same is true for systems integration and application development project work. Buyers want to contract with Vendors who understand their business sector and who have off-the-shelf solutions which can be quickly and cost-effectively implemented. You have to specialise to survive.

Relationship with this prospect?

Do you have either an existing/previous business relationship with this Prospect or, preferably, have you had ongoing contact with this Prospect while the Opportunity was maturing?

The ideal situation is that you have an 'Inside Track' and have helped the Prospect to articulate their business requirements. No relationship at all is a big disadvantage. Without a contact in the Buyer organisation with whom you have rapport, you will find it hard to discover the size of the budget for the project or the Prospect's 'Hot Buttons' (the features, technologies or project parameters which really count in the Vendor selection process). You will also lack a sounding board with which to test the attractiveness of your solution as it develops. Beware Bluebirds!

> ### *G*ood solution?
>
> Do you have the building blocks with which to construct a solution which meets all the essential requirements and most of the desirable ones, is low risk, can be delivered quickly, fits within the Prospect's budget and is sufficiently tangible that it can be demonstrated, at least in part, at your facility or at a reference site?

A good solution increasingly means one based predominantly on Commercial Off-The-Shelf (COTS) products which can be integrated to meet the Prospect's requirements very quickly and with a minimum of bespoke development. Also attractive to Prospects are solutions based on packaged applications which can be implemented without requiring them to fundamentally change their business processes. Totally bespoke projects are time-consuming, costly and risky. The Prospect's project team will be motivated by success and demotivated by risk. When considering your solution, brainstorm what your competitors might be offering. If you don't have high-quality building blocks for a good and price-competitive solution, you should 'No Bid'. Also beware Prospects with particular brand loyalty; you can usually detect this in the RFP/ITT. If you are bidding one of the competing brands, you might be on a hiding to nothing. Again, you need a Relationship with the Prospect to test whether your preferred solution will receive serious consideration on its merits and price.

> ### *E*ffort available to bid and execute?
>
> Do you have sufficient skilled resources to prepare a winning solution and proposal, including an experienced project manager, a technical architect, a development manager, and a business analyst or subject matter expert with understanding of the Prospect's business? (Some individuals may be able to cover more than one speciality.)

If your bid resources are busy and it is not possible to obtain the skills you need to define a winning, low-risk solution and write a high-quality proposal, you should 'No Bid'. This qualification factor also relates to your ability to resource the project if you win. It's motherhood, I know, but you require really good people to run successful projects. You do your company a disservice when you staff up a project with inexperienced and unproven resources.

> ### *T*ime available to prepare a winning bid?
>
> Do you have sufficient elapsed time to deploy your bid team, discuss requirements with the Prospect, develop a systems architecture, define project deliverables, prepare estimates and plans, document the solution, check it with the Prospect, and write the proposal (which may require a paragraph-by-paragraph response to RFP/ITT requirements)?

Buyers sometimes provide a very short period of time for an RFP or ITT response. If, in your view, insufficient time is available to do justice to the RFP/ ITT, manage your risk and provide the best added value for the Buyer, then ask for an extension. It is not in the Buyer's interest to have a set of ill-considered solutions and proposals to evaluate, and it is not a sign of weakness on your company's part to ask for more time. If you don't have sufficient time to manage your risk and produce a response worthy of your company, and the Buyer will not grant an extension, then 'No Bid'.

Size of budget known/adequate?

Bids cost a great deal of money. The potential revenue from a project has to be above a certain threshold for the Vendor to be prepared to invest bid effort. Bids for low-value projects can cost as much as bids for high-value projects, particularly if a very detailed response is mandated. The key question here though is 'Do you know the Buyer's budget and is it sufficient?'

This is a key qualification factor as it is a waste of your time and money to prepare a bid which will be dismissed with no more than a cursory glance because your price is above the Buyer's budget. I have never understood why Buyers are so often unwilling to disclose the budget for a project. Do they suspect that all potential Vendors will automatically bid right up to the budget ceiling? Who knows?! It is definitely in the interests of both Buyer and potential Vendors to have a figure to work with. It provides the Buyer with instant feedback from Vendors on the adequacy of their budget. It gives the potential Vendors the opportunity to suggest possible scope reductions, the resultant savings from which might be of great interest to the Buyer. Always ask the Prospect what the budget is. If they won't tell you, take care!

Competition known + strengths/weaknesses

Do you know how many potential Vendors have been invited to respond? Do you know who they are, what they are likely to bid and whether there is a Vendor with an inside track?

Once again, Buyers are often unwilling to disclose who they have invited to bid. Knowing who your competitors are is important as:

- If you are competing against 8, 10 or even 20 companies, your win chance – purely on a mathematical basis – is too low for the Opportunity to be worthwhile unless you have a compelling Inside Track or are certain that you will reach the shortlist. Also, it only takes one credible Vendor to underbid for you to lose the business and for the Buyer to potentially catch a serious cold. This could be a waste of your bid budget.

- Knowing your competitors and the strengths and weaknesses of their likely solutions helps you to hone your own solution. This can make you more competitive and it provides the Buyer with a better set of candidate solutions to evaluate.

---

*O*nly me! Do you have uniques?

Do you have a means of differentiating yourself from the pack by being able to offer features attractive to the Buyer which no other Vendor can match?

If all potential Vendors offer to meet the Buyer's business requirements to more or less the same extent, then it is going to come down to two key factors in the Buyer's mind – Price and Risk. The perceived risk in the Buyer's mind of selecting your company will be driven by their experience of using your services in the past, your reputation in the marketplace and the quality of your relationship with the Buyer. Price is generally subservient to Risk. Any Unique Sales Propositions (USPs) that you can offer will set you apart from other 'Me Too' Vendors and will help you to win even if Price and Risk are not in your favour.

---

*P*rice that will win?

By virtue of your excellent solution and, potentially, by innovative approaches to pricing the project, do you have a price that is within the Buyer's budget and lower than most of your competitors?

This factor is tightly linked to the 'Good Solution' factor. We all know that the lowest price does not always win. The quality of your solution and your people, your company's reputation and your USPs can allow you to win even when more expensive than several of your competitors. However, you are in a much stronger position if you offer a really keen price.

---

*E*ngagement with prospect possible?

Will the Buyer allow your bid team and potential project manager to meet the Buyer's team so that you can:

- discuss the requirements in detail?
- understand the Buyer's priorities?
- understand their business, budget and timescale imperatives?
- 'test sell' your solution in order to hone it to best match the Buyer's requirements?
- discover how the Buyer will evaluate the responses?

This is an absolutely key factor to consider in qualification. If a Buyer refuses to hold two short meetings – one at the start of the bid and one towards the end – then simply 'No Bid' the Opportunity as you would be wasting your bid budget and time. A Buyer who refuses to meet potential Vendors to enable them to maximise the fit of their solutions to the business needs and the budget is throwing away a valuable opportunity to de-risk the project.

Also consider how well the cultures and value systems of Vendor and Buyer organisations match. If there are fundamental differences here, building a relationship will be difficult.

Making the bid/no bid decision

When you have considered all factors and 'marked' them using the tick boxes on the qualification worksheet, determine the centre of gravity of your 'marks'. The really key factors – the 'big hitters' – are:

- the quality of your RELATIONSHIP with the Prospect;
- the quality of your SOLUTION;
- your UNIQUES;
- whether you have a WINNING PRICE;
- whether you can ENGAGE with the Buyer.

Before making your Bid/No Bid decision, consider which of the troubled project root causes shown on the qualification worksheet are potentially present. Finally, answer the three questions shown on the worksheet:

1. We will win because …
2. If we lose, it will be because …
3. The top three risks are …

What can you do to make the reason why you will win even more compelling? What can you do to eliminate the reason why you might lose? What can you do to eliminate or mitigate the 'big hitter' risks?

You are now ready to decide whether to Bid or No Bid.

Qualification hints and tips

- Qualification is the responsibility of the business, not of the salesperson, principal or partner who 'owns' the Opportunity. Sales, your 'bid factory', resourcing, operations, finance, production, QA and contracts functions all have a legitimate voice in the qualification decision. Ask your QA professional to undertake an independent risk assessment of the opportunity ahead of the qualification meeting.
- Qualification should be a formal and documented business process.
- Be honest and have the courage of your convictions. However attractive a win would be, if the Opportunity has TROUBLED PROJECT written through it like a stick of rock, 'No Bid' it.

- Once you have made your decision, stick to it unless you fail to develop a winning solution – in which case, withdraw at that stage.
- Don't allow your bid resources to be over-stretched. If you have a dedicated 'bid factory', the team can't work late every night and at weekends.
- Play to win the Opportunities you select. Give them 150 per cent effort.
- A good guide for the bid budget for a large fixed-price software development project is 5 per cent to 7 per cent of the contract value – and shouldn't T&M clients expect the same level of solutioning and budgeting accuracy?

Summary

Qualification is not an exact science. It is a crucial process for filtering out potential troubled projects and increasing your conversion rate. Qualification is a formal business process in which all functions of your business must participate. Be honest with yourself when qualifying an Opportunity as a lost bid costs the same as a winning one. Play to win the Opportunities you select.

Exercises

1. Think of troubled projects you have known. Use the qualification worksheet and 20:20 hindsight to determine which projects you would have been able to qualify out if you had used the worksheet.
2. How clear are your people about your company's products, services and marketplace strategy? They need to know this for good qualification.
3. Use the TARGET SCOPE qualification worksheet, really focus on the deals you are best placed to win, and monitor your conversion rate. It will improve!

Chapter 6

ENGAGING THE POTENTIAL BUYER AND BID PLANNING

Introduction

I once responded to a Request for Proposals (RFP) for a software strategy study. The potential Buyer provided a national, mainframe-based service. The RFP was clear about what was required; the potential Buyer was seeking advice on the best dbms and software development environment (SDE) on which to base the redevelopment of the applications providing the service. I sketched out the shape of a study, starting with a phase to capture and prioritise the demands of the applications and then evaluating available dbms/SDE products against these criteria. I proposed to use 'Smith's Triangle of Needs', a device I had used successfully before, modelled on Maslow's Triangle of Needs for the human condition. In this case, the triangle would show the dbms/SDE 'needs' imposed by the applications of the new system – with the most fundamental at the bottom and the 'nice to have' needs at the top. As the existing hardware platform would need replacing and this was a government procurement, it would be important for the dbms/SDE to be an open software platform to allow competition for the hardware sale. I discussed my outline approach with a senior colleague who was planning to lead the study. He had also sketched out an approach to the work, which involved investigating the memory utilisation, CPU loading and disc channel capacity of the existing mainframe and making recommendations for a hardware upgrade. He felt that if the current applications could be made to run better, the Buyer could postpone the system redevelopment and would be delighted. I was bemused by this strategy and I met with the senior civil servant responsible for the service to discuss their outcomes for the study. He told me that his objective was to replace the existing system as quickly as possible. He also made it clear that what he wanted was a report which recommended a dbms/SDE which was open. It would be unfortunate if the selected software could not be run on the current mainframe supplier's hardware platforms, but we should not regard this as a 'show-stopper'. I received the distinct impression that the relationship between the Buyer and the incumbent hardware supplier was rather strained.

If we had not had an opportunity to engage with the potential Buyer, we would never have understood their real objective. The story also illustrates how easy it is for readers of an RFP to have completely different views on the best solution to offer.

Engaging the potential Buyer is important because:

- You need to satisfy yourself that none of the root causes listed in this chapter are present. If they are, you will want to revisit your decision to bid. If you do decide to proceed with your bid, you will want to share your concerns with the potential Buyer and ensure that effective containment plans are put in place by both parties to address these risks.
- You need to test your understanding of the business needs and the expressed system requirements. Do they match? If you delivered the system as specified, would it support the business?
- You need to understand the relative importance of the system requirements – which are essential, which are 'nice to have' and which are really not very important at all. This information gives you the means of extracting from the base proposal any 'nice to have' requirements which are particularly expensive to provide. These can be offered as separately priced options.
- You need to work with the potential Buyer to 'polish' your solution so that you can achieve the best possible match between your solution and the Buyer's requirements. This includes gaining the Buyer's agreement to any structuring of your proposal into a base offer and separately priced options.
- People buy people first – you need to put the project manager who will run the project in front of the potential Buyer and ensure that there is the basis of a strong working relationship between them.
- You need to know how proposals/tenders will be evaluated and the real 'hot buttons' which will sway the decision one way or the other.

When discussing engagement with the potential Buyer, we need to consider the two categories of 'decision maker' and 'decision-influencer'. The choice of Vendor may be made by a selection panel whose members have essentially the same degree of authority. In other cases, the choice might be made by one or two key decision-makers, based largely on the advice of several other decision influencers. You need to understand the dynamics of decision making in the Buyer organisation. If at all possible during the bid phase, you need to engage with both decision-makers and decision influencers. This is not manipulative provided that you do not attempt to play one person off against another; your objective is to understand the 'hot buttons' of as many decision-influencers and decision-makers as possible in order to craft a solution which is attractive to all.

> When I was working as a sales executive and branch manager in a services company, I made a habit of always asking for a de-brief after winning or losing a bid. I was often surprised to hear that we had won, not because we had offered the lowest price or the best technical solution, but because we were the only supplier to give the decision-maker/selection panel the opportunity to meet the person who would manage their project.

Remember that the output of the sales process is not a proposal. It is a potential Buyer who wants to buy your solution and your people.

Risk management

You have been through the qualification process and filtered out, or decided to manage, the root causes relating to the opportunity qualification and selection stage:

RC03 Project based on state-of-the-art and immature technology
RC05 Buyer's funding and/or timescale expectations unrealistically low
RC06 Buyer failure to break a complex project into phases or smaller projects
RC08 Buyer failure to define and document requirements (functional and non-functional)
RC17 Full-scope, fixed-price contracting (requirements, design and development)

If you are going ahead with the bid knowing that RC03, RC06 and/or RC17 are present, then you have accepted that this is a high-risk project. This implies additional bid resources (including the intensive participation of contracts/legal and QA professionals) to reduce the impact of these root causes as much as possible through tight project definition, contractual protection and adequate contingency on your estimates.

If root causes RC05 and/or RC08 are present, you have an opportunity to share your concerns with the potential Buyer. To address RC05, you can establish whether any additional funding or time can be made available and start to discuss whether some areas of functionality can be de-scoped or phased to give the Buyer an affordable first tranche of functionality within an acceptable time period. To address RC08, you can promote the concept of a funded requirements capture phase or set out your approach to handling the risk of scope creep – which would typically be to set out a comprehensive set of assumptions bounding your current understanding of the scope and scale of the requirements.

You also have the opportunity to establish, in your meetings with the potential Buyer, whether any of the following additional troubled project root causes are apparent:

Troubled project root causes to avoid when engaging the potential Buyer
Be on the lookout for:
RC01 Project based on an unsound premise or an unrealistic business case
RC02 Buyer failure to define clear project objectives, anticipated benefits and success criteria

RC04	Lack of Buyer Board-level ownership/commitment or competence
RC09	Failure to achieve an open, robust and equitable Buyer-Vendor relationship
RC11	Buyer lack of sufficient involvement of eventual end-users

If you sense that RC01 is present, you have an opportunity to help the potential Buyer to change the focus of the project or re-scope it so that the potential business benefits can be matched to the investment being made. If you sense that RC02 or RC11 is present, you can advise the Buyer of the benefits of clear objectives and anticipated benefits in order that project success can be measured. You can also assess whether there has been sufficient end-user involvement and remind the Buyer of the pivotal importance of this, perhaps using the Public Accounts Committee report, discussed in Chapter 2 of this book, as a reference. If you sense that RC04 or RC09 is present, you will have an opportunity during project delivery (the system design, system development and system implementation stages of the project life cycle) to address these issues with the Buyer. On the other hand, you may decide after the initial meeting to withdraw from the bid.

Opportunity ownership

The first important task is to decide who in your business is going to 'own' the opportunity. Opportunity ownership is not about who receives the commission on the sale or which business owns the revenue. It is about who has the energy, passion and commitment to live and breathe the opportunity right through the bid stage and convert it into a win. The opportunity owner must immerse themselves in the deal so that they understand the requirements and issues inside out, and take the lead in nurturing the relationship with the Buyer. This is traditionally a sales executive, principal or partner role, but it clearly also makes good sense for this role to be taken by the project manager who will manage the project if you win. If this role is taken by a bid manager who will take no further part in the project during delivery, then no matter how effective they are:

- the investment made by the Buyer to forge a relationship with the bid manager is wasted; they will have to do it all over again with the actual project manager;
- there is a discontinuity at the very start of the project delivery phase which can be very disruptive, especially if the project manager disagrees with the estimates, the approach or the plan.

The bid process

Figure 6.1 presents an overview of the bid process. Part 2 of this book is devoted to the different stages of this process, with particular reference to how the potential root causes of troubled projects can be detected and managed. Note that the bid process is largely sequential, with the exception of quality assurance and risk management, which is ongoing and continuous.

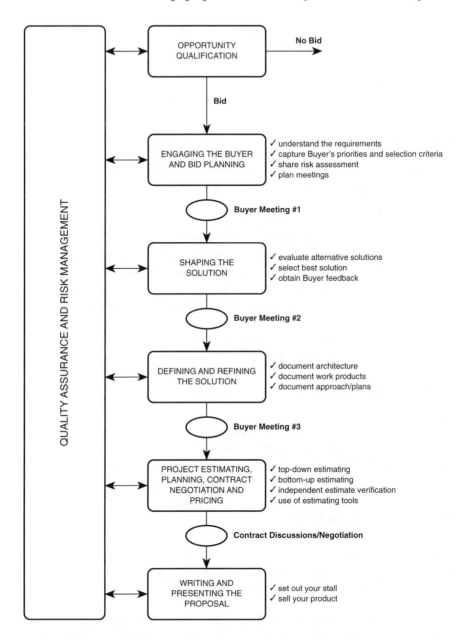

Figure 6.1   *The Bid Process*

We saw in Chapter 5 that the ability to engage with the potential Buyer is one of the key qualification criteria. To have got this far, the potential Buyer must have indicated a willingness to take at least one meeting. Right at the start of the bid, before the first face-to-face meeting, you need to establish how many opportunities you will have to meet with the potential Buyer, so call them to explain the purpose of the meetings. You don't need to mention the items in italics; these are parts of *your* agenda. Ideally, you want three meetings prior to the formal presentation of your proposal. The purpose of these meetings is as follows:

Buyer meeting #1 is to:

- test your understanding of the business drivers and the Buyer's objectives and success criteria for the project;
- understand, *and assess the viability of*, the Buyer's business case;
- understand how the project will be managed by the Buyer's team, *the quality of the Buyer's team*, the level of commitment which is apparent from Buyer senior management and the extent of end-user participation in the project so far;
- clarify any system requirements which are unclear, contradictory or apparently not addressed by the RFI/RFP/ITT/Statement of Work (SOW);
- discuss your initial Risk Management Plan with particular focus on any budget and timescale challenges and any lack of detail in the documented requirements. Determine what can be done, by both parties, to address these issues;
- capture the Buyer's priorities, motivators and Vendor selection criteria – their 'hot buttons';
- seek agreement to further, pre-submission meetings to help you to give the Buyer the best possible solution.

Buyer meeting #2 is to:

- discuss your outline solution;
- check that it meets the Buyer's selection criteria;
- capture changes suggested by the Buyer;
- discuss the Risk Management Plan, particularly the containment actions;
- introduce your project manager, if you have not already done so.

Buyer meeting #3 is to:

- take the Buyer through the detailed solution;
- obtain feedback;
- discuss any areas of potential non-compliance;
- discuss possible cost-saving options.

Note, and stress to the potential Buyer, that these are working meetings, the purpose of which is to achieve the best possible match between your solution and the Buyer's requirements. They are for the benefit of both parties. They are meetings where you will primarily *listen* to the Buyer rather than *sell* to them. If the Buyer is only prepared to meet with you twice, then go for meetings 1 and 2. If you only have one meeting opportunity, combine the agendas of meetings 1 and 2 and delay the meeting until you have shaped your solution.

Unless they can be combined with the working meetings outlined above, don't waste meeting opportunities on:

- visits to laboratories, executive briefing centres or other Vendor facilities;
- meetings with executives from your organisation who cannot be expected to understand the opportunity in depth, cannot personally contribute to the bid process, can only promise that the project will receive the highest priority, and whom the Buyer will probably never meet again;
- general sales presentations of Vendor capability;
- reference site visits; there will be time for these when you are on the shortlist;
- expensive lunches or golf days with the prospective Buyer; there will be time for these when you have won the business.

Preparing the bid plan

Based on the number of meetings the Buyer will take, prepare a plan showing, with target dates:

- all steps in the bid stage (covered in Chapters 6 through 11);
- all meetings with the Buyer;
- all review points internal to the bid team;
- external solution, risk and proposal reviews;
- key deliverables, with assigned owners;
- if possible (at this early stage) the proposal structure, with section owners;
- the logistics of proposal production and delivery.

Remember that the bid plan is not solely about producing a proposal; it is primarily about working with your potential Buyer to develop an attractive, high-quality, affordable, low-risk and winning solution.

Strategies for resourcing the bid

There are two main strategies:

- maintain a 'bid factory' – a team dedicated to evaluating RFI/RFP/ITT/SOW documents, solutioning, estimating, planning and proposal writing;
- form an ad hoc team for each opportunity from staff who are either 'on the bench' (currently unassigned to a project) or who have particular domain skills and are currently assigned to a project but can be made available for a short time.

The relative merits of these approaches are as follows:

Dedicated Bid Factory	
Advantages	**Disadvantages**
✓ Easier to resource,	✗ Staff are unlikely to have relevant domain expertise,
✓ Staff are familiar with the bid process and the 'house' proposal style,	✗ Bid factories tend to be 'back office' functions which do not engage the Buyer,

✓ Staff have access to potentially relevant material from previous bids/proposals.	✗ Any relationships built up with the potential Buyer are transitory, ✗ Staff in this function can become jaded, ✗ This function is, but is not seen to be, at the sharp end of the business, ✗ There is a risk that material from previous Proposals will be pressed into service when it is not really relevant.

Ad Hoc Bid Team	
Advantages	**Disadvantages**
✓ Can use specialist domain experts, ✓ The candidate project manager can establish credibility and the basis of a good working relationship with the Buyer, ✓ The team can be highly motivated – if they win, they have an interesting new project to work on.	✗ Harder to resource – it is especially difficult to obtain staff from an existing project, ✗ Staff will be less familiar with the bid process and the 'house' proposal style.

I have a personal preference for the ad hoc approach as, in my experience, these teams are more highly charged and better able to forge a close and lasting relationship with the potential Buyer.

> I have often heard Vendors criticised for bidding using an 'A team' and then switching in a 'B team' once the deal has been won. Personally, I think this approach does make sense. The 'A team' will do a thorough job of developing a solution that the Vendor can deliver and the Buyer wants to buy. This then makes it possible for a 'B team' to deliver the project successfully. If you use a 'B team' to bid, you probably won't win. If you do, you will need the 'A team' to deliver and, as all Vendors have more 'B teams' than 'A teams', the 'A team' is probably already busy.

Summary

A summary of the required activities of this stage is shown in Figure 6.2.

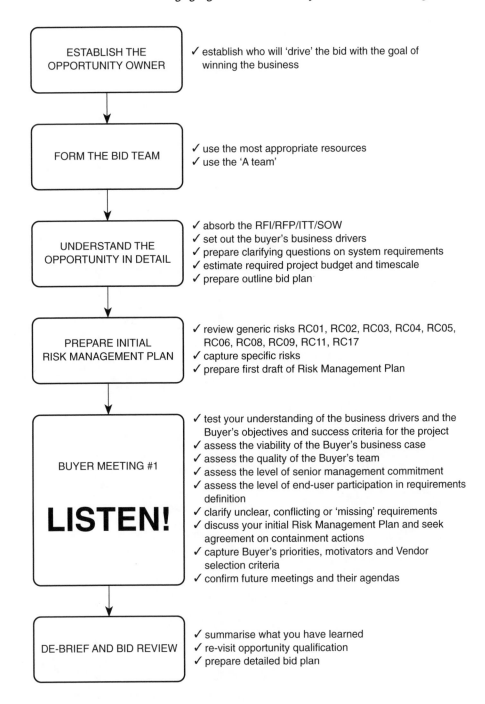

Figure 6.2   *Engaging the Potential Buyer – Summary of the Process*

Chapter 7

SHAPING THE SOLUTION

Introduction

I once led a study to define a strategic LAN architecture for a whole government department. The Invitation to Tender (ITT) was clear about what was required. Divisions within the department were purchasing a variety of LANs from different suppliers and the IT Division felt that a strategy was needed to prevent the proliferation of LAN products from getting out of hand. The LAN architecture had to be compliant with UK Government Open Systems Interconnection Policy (GOSIP), which was attempting to promote open, rather than proprietary, protocols. This was in the days when TCP/IP was labelled 'proprietary' and was to be avoided at all costs by the purists. We found out which LANs were currently in use in the Department and what they were used for. We found that it was possible to define a range of typical LAN configurations for different types of workgroups. We then evaluated products to establish the degree of compliance with GOSIP requirements. This narrowed the field down substantially – basically to one product, and a new one at that. Following the brief, we prepared a recommendation, submitted the report and waited for the accolades to roll in. They didn't arrive. The customer was unhappy with the recommendation. One large division, which had invested heavily in Novell networks, was very unhappy about the prospect of moving to a new 'strategic' network which did not offer many of the features of their existing network. It turned out that users were not prepared to sacrifice usability and functionality on the altar of Open Systems Interconnection (OSI) purity. Whose fault was this? It was mine! The fact that there was a basic disconnect between the demands of the GOSIP policy and the real day-to-day needs of users was a problem that I should have realised and discussed with my client. This was not my natural style. I did all the thinking and the client followed my recommendations. This was the way it was done and it had always worked. It was not until I joined a management consulting firm later in my career that I learned the value of the 'workshop' approach in securing the buy-in of the client every single step of the way.

The approach to solutioning outlined in Part 2 of this book is based on close engagement with the potential Buyer. The Buyer can help you to shape and refine your solution to best match their requirements.

What *is* a 'solution' anyway?

A solution for an application development or systems integration project covers *what* you are going to build, *how* you are going to build it and *who* is going to undertake the work. It covers:

- what – the architecture of the system [technology];
- how – the approach and plan for the project [process];
- who – the project organisation[people].

Take the analogy of building a house. The architecture is the blueprint prepared by the architect, the project organisation is the builder who is going to build the house for you (and their team), and the process is the sequence of tasks that they will follow. Most of us have commissioned a builder to undertake works on our homes. Generally, we have plans prepared. We select the builder with care, taking up references and forming an opinion as to their trustworthiness and professionalism. However, the process by which they intend to undertake the construction is usually a complete mystery to us. How nice it would be for the builder to show us a plan of the work, with milestones and dates, but this is rare. Now think of a Buyer of an IT project. They have similar needs. They want to understand in detail what you are going to build for them. They want to feel that they have selected a skilled team that they can trust to produce high-quality work. In addition, they want to see a detailed plan which demonstrates that you have thought carefully about the tasks to be undertaken, their sequence and how long each task will take to complete.

A well-defined solution is not only an essential foundation for estimating your costs, it is also a powerful sales aid.

Troubled project root causes to avoid when shaping the solution
Be on the lookout for:
RC03 Project based on state-of-the-art and immature technology
RC19 Poor choice of technical platform and/or architecture
RC21 Poor choice of design/development method

It is always a temptation to use the latest versions of operating systems, software development tool-sets and software building blocks such as content management software. If you do decide to use state-of-the-art or immature technology (RC03), ensure that you adopt an approach that recognises the risks you are taking. For example, build a technology demonstrator or prototype into your plan. This will provide a test bed for the technologies and the design and development processes. It will also provide a means of proving that the technologies will scale to meet the challenges of the real system. Share the Risk Management Plan with the Buyer and make it clear that there may be hard decisions to take in the event that the new technologies or processes fail to provide a sound foundation for the project.

To avoid RC19 and RC21, always ask yourself whether you are using a hardware or software platform, architecture or method in a very different way from that intended by its designers. If you are, consider whether there is a more appropriate choice.

Specify solution requirements

Start by reviewing the Buyer's business drivers. What is most important to them? Is it getting a new service available to their customers as quickly as possible to steal a march on their competitors? If so, timescale is probably more important than delivering all the eventually required functionality with the initial release. Is it upgrading an existing system? If so, the timescale for the upgrade is probably less important than achieving continuity of service and the most effective support for existing users. Is it the Buyer's first foray into a new technology, like data mining or digital document management? If so, the Buyer's key driver might be to invest just enough to prove the viability of the technology and assess the level of business benefit which can be achieved. This might point to a 'quick and dirty' Commercial Off-The-Shelf (COTS) implementation as the ideal approach.

Next, review the system requirements, both functional and non-functional, the Buyer's stated budgetary constraints and their timescale aspirations. Even if you have not yet had an opportunity to meet with the potential Buyer, the RFI/RFP/ITT/SOW will normally indicate whether the Buyer is anticipating a custom or packaged/COTS solution. Finally, review the Buyer's stated Vendor selection criteria. You are now ready to search for candidate solutions.

Research intellectual capital

You may not have an intellectual capital repository, complete with a browser front end and advanced search capabilities, but all Vendors need access to basic information on previous corporate experience. You need to:

- Look for similar types of projects and similar systems, not necessarily within the same market sector. Is there a proven architecture which you can reuse for this opportunity? What lessons were learned the last time you attempted a project like this? What 'know-how' and documentation do you have which you can leverage on this opportunity?
- Find out who within your organisation worked on these projects. They might be available to work on the bid and they should be able to advise you on your solution.
- Research what market sector experience you have. Which customers had similar requirements? What reference sites do you have? Which existing customers could help you to understand the dynamics of their marketplace and the comparative strengths of your competitors in that marketplace?

- Determine whether you have any existing building blocks – such as code modules, data models, front-ends, middleware, device drivers, interfaces, test tools etc – which you could reuse to reduce the development effort on this project.
- Research what COTS products and packaged applications are available in the market which you (and your competitors) could use to construct a solution.

Brainstorm potential solutions

First, consider what solutions your competitors might offer using their own intellectual capital, application products or offerings, and their preferred hardware and software platforms. Visit competitors' websites. It is amazing just how much useful information you can find. You will often find a complete architecture of the product they will bid, together with 'white papers' and case studies. Sometimes you will find that the match between the capabilities of a competitor's product and the RFI/RFP/ITT/SOW is so uncannily close that it will give you second thoughts about bidding. This is good. You won't waste your bid budget and spoil your conversion rate. On one recent occasion, I visited one of the competing Vendor's websites and found a case study relating to the same potential Buyer. The case study reported that the system was so successful that the Buyer was rolling it out throughout their business. This left us with the distinct impression that we were in a beauty parade.

Brainstorm alternative approaches to meeting the Buyer's requirements. The first of these should always be the cheapest, quickest and dirtiest solution possible. It might lack elegance, it might be rather inconvenient to use, it *will* be based on COTS or packaged application software or software you have previously developed for another customer, but if it will more or less meet the requirements, it could be just what the Buyer is looking for.

Include the solution you would design and build if time and money were of no consequence – in other words, the best system you can think of.

Consider whether it is possible to build and deliver the application incrementally, starting with an 'entry-level' system with a subset of the required functionality and building remaining features and facilities into later releases.

Consider whether it is possible to install the hardware platform incrementally, starting small and adding processors, memory, disc subsystems or additional servers as demands on the hardware increase.

If system availability demands are onerous, consider your preferred high-availability hardware architecture, but also determine how close you could get to the availability target without the expensive high-availability solution. The potential Buyer might value the opportunity to trade off availability and cost.

Evaluate and select your preferred solution

From your knowledge of the Buyer's business drivers, budget and timescale targets and Vendor selection criteria, compare 2–3 of your most promising candidate solutions. For each candidate solution, list the:

Benefits	Remember to take the Buyer's perspective. You need to identify the best solution for the Buyer, as this is likely to be the solution which you are most likely to be able to sell. List any unique selling propositions.
Weaknesses	As perceived by the Buyer, relative to your other candidate solutions and probable competitors' solutions.
Risks	Consider risk from both Buyer and Vendor perspectives. Consider:

- commercial risks – risks leading to financial exposure;
- technical risks – risks that the solution technology will not provide appropriate functionality, availability, reliability or performance;
- delivery risks – risks threatening the successful design, development, integration and testing of the solution;
- implementation risks – risks to the Buyer's business during user training, data take-on and early live running;
- operational risks – risks to the Buyer's business during subsequent enhancement and maintenance of the solution.

Describe your preferred solution

Select your preferred solution and document it at a high level, ideally as a set of presentation foils which can be used in a later meeting with the Buyer. Cover the architecture, the approach and the people – the *what*, the *how* and the *who*. If you haven't already done so, now is the time to nominate the project manager and get them on board the bid team.

Qualities required in a project manager

A project manager has a demanding role. They are the prime interface with the Buyer. They are the prime interface between the project and Vendor management. And, of course, they are the prime interface to the project team.

To deal with the Buyer, they need:

- self belief;
- presence and strength of character;
- people skills – influencing skills, selling skills, negotiating skills, presentation skills, and the ability to build rapport;
- business acumen and good judgement;
- decision-making ability.

To deal with Vendor management, they need:

- to be seen as having a 'safe pair of hands';

- load-bearing ability;
- financial management skills;
- familiarity with Vendor business processes and financial systems;
- the ability to fight the project's corner assertively.

To run the project and manage the team, they need:

- leadership – the ability to inspire and motivate the team;
- energy – to be seen to be leading from the front;
- good listening skills;
- good project management skills;
- the ability to delegate;
- broad technical knowledge, to prevent the wool from being pulled over their eyes;
- the ability to 'chunk-up' to see the big picture;
- the ability to 'chunk-down' to examine and manage a particular issue.

Less is more – think 'outside the box'

If you think about it, there is a basic conflict of interest between Vendor and Buyer. The Vendor wants to develop good solutions for their clients, but large and highly profitable contracts are particularly attractive. The Buyer wants a good solution too, but he wants it quickly and cheaply. He wants you to stay in business and be able to feed your children, but he does not want you to make excessive profits.

Always review your candidate solutions to find creative ways of improving them. For example:

- How could you deliver the project in (say) 30 per cent less time? For example, is it possible to split a substantial development project into sub-projects and to run these in parallel?
- How could you shave (say) 20 per cent off the price to fit within the Buyer's budget?
  - Example #1. What price reduction can be achieved by cutting out everything that is not absolutely central to the Buyer's business requirements, including even highly desirable requirements? These features can be priced separately, as options. This makes your 'entry-level' price more competitive and you give the Buyer more choices. Your prices will be lower and you will win more business.
  - Example #2. Buyers often calculate the full-life cost of a project by adding the initial upfront costs to the recurring costs over a number of years. This makes it absolutely crucial for you to minimise the recurring costs. If you are quoting for application maintenance, for example, don't quote for a team of 3–4 people (who may be required if the Buyer requires substantial

enhancements); just quote for the half a person needed to fix faults. This is fair and reasonable. You don't know what level of enhancement will be required, so don't spoil your win chance by assuming that the Buyer will want extensive changes. Less is More.

- How could the key risks be eliminated or their impact reduced? Update your Risk Management Plan.
- Are there innovative ways of financing the project? For example, can you offer a leasing arrangement for hardware platforms and software, or a reduced services price in return for a share of future revenues or cost savings?

Buyer meeting #2

Plan for your nominated project manager to take a leading role in the meeting.

Take the potential Buyer through the thought processes you went through when evaluating candidate solutions. Describe your chosen solution. Capture feedback and 'steers' from the Buyer. If the Buyer prefers one of the solutions you have discarded, find out why. Establish whether either you have misunderstood the Buyer's Vendor selection criteria or the criteria have changed.

Discuss any options you have identified to pull back the timescale, phase the delivery of functionality, or de-scope functionality. Identify which of these options are of interest to the Buyer and how you should present them in the proposal – for example, as additional/reduced cost options to an otherwise compliant response, or as a separate, non-compliant response. Determine whether a 'compliant' response is needed at all; if it isn't you can concentrate on an agreed, non-compliant solution and save a substantial amount of time on the proposal. On this topic, you need to ensure that your Buyer contact has the authority to speak on behalf of the Buyer's contracts and procurement functions.

Discuss your Risk Management Plan, with particular reference to the containment actions you have identified for both parties.

Confirm the date and agenda of any future meetings prior to proposal submission.

Summary

A summary of the required activities of this stage is shown in Figure 7.1.

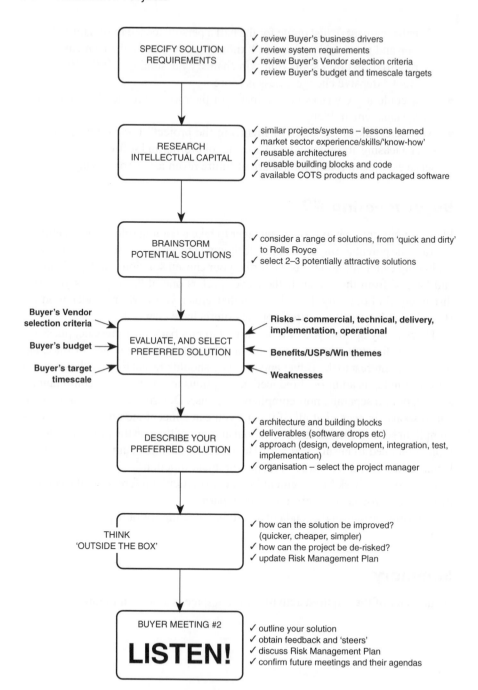

Figure 7.1   *Shaping the Solution – Summary of the Process*

Chapter 8

DEFINING AND REFINING
THE SOLUTION

Introduction

> **Troubled project root causes to avoid when defining and refining the solution**
> *Be on the lookout for:*
> **RC13** Vendor failure to define project tasks, deliverables and acceptance processes
> **RC26** Buyer retains design authority with right to approve/reject low-level designs

RC13 is what this chapter is all about. Regardless of whether a project is contracted on a fixed price or a T&M basis, handling the task of project scoping and planning by means of workshops with the client *after* the contract has been signed is commercial hara-kiri. If you've ever been the project manager running those workshops and experiencing the icy finger of dread as the realisation dawns that the Buyer's expectation of scope is vastly greater than yours, you will know how attractive the 'falling-on-one's-sword' option is.

RC26 doesn't appear too often. When it does, it pays to build a strong relationship between Vendor and Buyer technical architects and to assume in the estimating and planning that 25 per cent additional design work will be needed for each design deliverable.

What can be avoided with a well-defined solution?

- Acute Vendor embarrassment when a budgetary estimate, which has been used by the potential Buyer to secure funding, turns out to be unrealistic. The result of this is usually extreme pressure on the Vendor to deliver at or near the original indicative price.
- Underestimation of effort and timescale, with serious financial consequences for the Vendor or Buyer – depending on whether the contract is on a fixed-price or a T&M basis.
- High stress levels within the project team on Day 1 as they get to grips with what has been sold and how they are going to deliver it.

- Scope expansion and slippage very early in the project, which is damaging to the Buyer–Vendor relationship.

Define solution outputs and level of detail

The outputs of the detailed solutioning process and, more importantly, the level of detail which is appropriate depends on:

1 The nature of the response

- A firm price tender or T&M proposal needs to be defined sufficiently to ensure that you can deliver the work for which you have quoted a price open for acceptance within about 10 per cent of your estimated cost and timescale. You are doing very well if you can routinely estimate more accurately than this. T&M projects need precisely the same care in project definition as fixed-price projects if the Buyer–Vendor relationship is to be preserved.
- An RFP (Request for Proposal) response with an estimated price not open for acceptance, which will be followed a few weeks later by a tender response, can leave some detailed solutioning work to be done later. However, this exposes you to the risk that your tender price will be higher than your estimated price, which will look very sloppy.
- An RFI (Request for Information) asking for an indicative or budgetary price requires sufficient solutioning work to develop a price which is within about 25 per cent of a later tender price. Buyers cannot expect more accuracy than this, and you need to ensure that you advise the Buyer to add an appropriate amount of contingency if the indicative price is to be used to secure funding for the project.
- An RFI asking for a rough order or magnitude (ROM) price requires sufficient solutioning to develop a price which is in the same ball-park as any eventual tender price. I suggest that this means within +/– 50 per cent of the eventual tender price. You need to advise the potential Buyer that the ROM price should be used for consideration of strategic options rather than for budgetary purposes.

2 The size of the deal

- The bigger the deal, the more the Vendor stands to lose if the solution is defined in insufficient detail to enable reasonably accurate estimates to be prepared.
- Small deals inevitably feature a high cost of sale and can often be justified only in terms of later account development potential. On larger deals, a bid budget of between 5 per cent and 7 per cent of total services value is likely to be required.

3 The scope of the development

- Full-scope, fixed-price deals – where the Vendor works with the Buyer to define the requirements, then prepares the design, writes the code, tests the code and commissions the system – are terrifying. You *must* put industrial-strength stakes in the ground to bound the scope of requirements, set out a robust high-level design and estimate the scale of the development in quantitative terms which can be linked to a price escalation mechanism. An assumed number of function points or use cases can be agreed upon. Any increase in function points or use cases can be directly linked to a variation of price (VOP) formula.

- Design & Build projects are just scary. Regardless of the method of contracting, you *must* undertake a high-level design before the contract is signed to satisfy yourself that the project is feasible. You also have to prepare some kind of functional decomposition or application architecture to define the number, size and complexity of programs to be written. Grouping these into high, medium and low complexity will provide a starting point for estimating the effort required.

- Projects which are partitioned into separately contracted design and development phases are 'business as usual'. You still need to do enough solutioning work to derive estimates which are within 10 per cent of reality for the next phase of work.

- If you are offering a product-based solution or a reusable architecture, you will have less work to do on high-level design and more solution material available.

4 How much you want to win

- The more solution detail you put into the proposal, the more credibility and Buyer confidence you will build.

5 How much time and resource is available for the bid

- If you have very little time, you had better be offering a product-based solution!

The process of solution definition is shown in Figure 8.1.

Figure 8.1 also indicates the range of solution outputs that you might need to produce. You must decide which of these outputs is required. The high-level design outputs would typically be grouped together in a high-level design document. The outputs relating to the project approach, work products (deliverables and non-deliverable work products), estimating and planning can form a project initiation document (PID). The typical contents of a PID are shown in Table 8.1. It is primarily the level of detail which will vary; even on the smallest deal the Vendor needs to consider all the PID headings and write a sentence or two on every topic. The Quality Plan and Risk Management Plan are often prepared as separate documents, referenced from the PID.

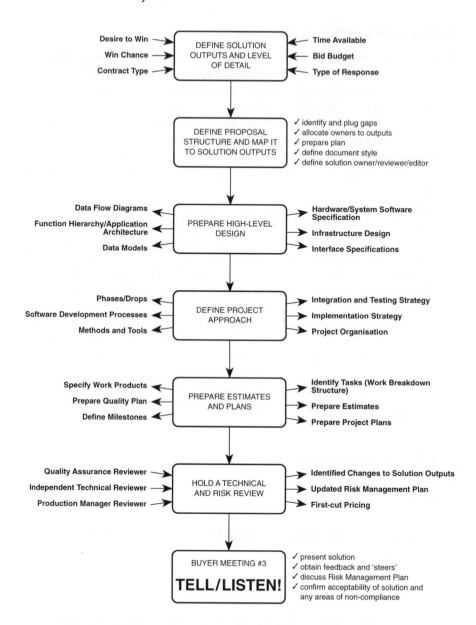

Figure 8.1   *Defining and Refining the Solution – Summary of the Process*

Table 8.1 *Project Definition Document Format*

Introduction Purpose of this Document Maintenance of this Document **Project Mission, Goals and Objectives** Background Project Mission Business Goals Project Objectives **Scope** Project Context and Boundaries Architecture Overview The Scope of the <PROJECTNAME> Project Specific Exclusions **Approach** Introduction Project Stages Design and Development Methods Tools to be Deployed Integration and Testing Strategy Acceptance Strategy Implementation Strategy Support Strategy **Project Work Products** Introduction Project Definition Work Products Project Management/Control Work Products Documentation Work Products Verification and Validation Work Products Code Work Products Hardware/Software Work Products Logistics and Commissioning Work Products Training Work Products Maintenance and Support Work Products **Project Organisation** Organisation Chart Roles and Responsibilities	**Project Plan** Introduction High-level Plan Plan Commentary Low-level Plans (where appropriate) **Project Management, Control and Reporting** Method to be Deployed Progress Monitoring and Project Control Progress Reporting Contract Management Issue Management and Escalation **Quality Plan** Introduction Quality Management Quality Requirements Quality Attainment Plan Quality Control Plan Quality Assurance Plan Quality Preservation Plan Miscellaneous Procedures **Risk Management Plan** Risk Management Procedures Risk Register **Assumptions** Commercial Assumptions Technical Assumptions Planning Assumptions Other Assumptions **Dependencies** Buyer Dependencies and Responsibilities Third Party Dependencies and Responsibilities Other Dependencies

Define proposal structure and map it to the solution outputs

The next task is to review any proposal structure mandated by the potential Buyer or to design an appropriate proposal structure. See Chapter 11 for a sample proposal format. Map the solution outputs to the proposal structure and identify any 'gaps'. Solution outputs not reflected in the proposal may be unnecessary, but it is more likely that the proposal structure will require updating. Proposal sections not reflected in the solution outputs indicate the need for additional solution outputs.

Allocate 'owners' for solution outputs and proposal sections and prepare a plan of the solutioning and proposal preparation work. To avoid unnecessary work later, define and distribute a style template so that everyone produces exactly the same look and feel of document – the same headings, the same numbering approach, the same headers and footers, the same paragraph style, bullet style, justification etc.

Instruct the bid team to capture questions and assumptions as they proceed with the solutioning. Assign an overall solution owner and proposal editor. The solution owner is responsible for reviewing solution outputs for consistency and compatibility with other solution outputs, and for ensuring that the total solution 'works' and is elegant. The proposal editor is responsible for ensuring that the proposal comes across as a cohesive and readable document and that there is a balance between the different sections in terms of their size and the level of detail provided.

Prepare high-level design

As we have seen, the level of detail appropriate will be dictated by:

- the nature of the response;
- the size of the deal;
- the scope of the development;
- how much you want to win;
- how much time and resource is available for the bid.

Figure 8.1 indicates some of the design outputs which might be needed:

- Data flow diagrams are an excellent medium for defining and discussing the principal activities or business processes within a system and the flow of data associated with these processes. Data flow diagrams can be understood easily by Buyer staff. They are particularly good for capturing the essence of a new, 'green field' system and the key data entities which the system must be aware of and manage.
- Entity models provide a useful means of understanding and documenting the complex relationships between data entities in a form which is a useful input to logical database design.
- A functional hierarchy or functional decomposition identifies the main functional areas of the system and the individual functions within each area. This is a key input to the process of estimating the effort required to design, build, test and commission the system.

- An application architecture goes a little further than a functional decomposition. It groups areas of functionality together and identifies the packaging of individual programs or classes.
- A high-level interface specification is necessary for each existing or future system with which any form of data exchange is required. It identifies the data which will pass across the interface, volumes, communications protocols, error handling, and how the interface will be tested. Preparing high-level interface specifications will clarify what you *don't* know about the interface and enable you to document some appropriate assumptions.
- Schedules of hardware, system software and Commercial Off-The-Shelf (COTS) applications are required inputs to the estimating process.
- Complex multi-tier architectures will require an infrastructure design to ensure that platforms, operating systems, middleware and networks will interwork to provide a sound and cohesive technical platform to support the applications.

Group the high-level design solution outputs into a high-level design document.

Define project approach

You have already prepared a high-level approach to the delivery of the project. What is needed now is an increased level of definition. Figure 8.1 indicates some of the outputs from the definition of the project approach. These outputs fit very well into the following sections of the PID:

- introduction;
- project mission, goals and objectives;
- scope;
- approach;
- project organisation;
- project management, control and reporting.

The level of detail required is a matter of judgement. For example, it is more important to spend time considering and documenting the project-specific strategy for integration and testing, and how responsibility in this area will divide between Vendor and Buyer, than to define detailed procedures. Your objective is to build up an overall picture of how the project will be managed and delivered. The detail can be added after contract. What is important is to have a complete and cohesive framework in place on Day 1 of the project to support this later detail.

Prepare estimates and plans

As Figure 8.1 suggests, the first task is to specify the work products to be produced by the project team. Work products include the deliverables which you pass on to the Buyer. It is a good idea to propose which deliverables should be milestones. Of course, these should include key deliverables. However, you also need to plan your cash flow, so ensure that payment milestones are evenly distributed across the life of the plan and that they include some deliverables which are not too challenging to produce.

The first plan you need to prepare is the Quality Plan. The reason for this is that the Quality Plan defines, for each work product type (or even for each work product), the Verification and Validation (V&V) activities you intend to use to check that the appropriate level of quality has been achieved. Note that we are not just considering testing here; V&V also covers design, code and document reviews. These software quality control activities must be included in the work breakdown structure, otherwise your estimates will exclude the cost of some of the essential activities required to deliver a successful project. V&V activities can also generate additional work products, which need to be included in the Project Work Products section of the PID. Quality planning is a solutioning activity. It is covered in more detail in Chapter 10, but the time to do the quality planning is while you are defining and refining the solution.

When you have defined the deliverables and other work products, you can define the tasks needed to produce them. A work breakdown structure is a task hierarchy which forms a useful input to the estimating process. Many Vendors have 'standard' work breakdown structures which reflect the different development life cycles used – traditional 'waterfall' software engineering, rapid application development, package integration etc. These provide useful checklists with which to assess the completeness of your task hierarchy. Don't use them to provide a first-cut plan as this approach encourages you to disengage your brain.

You are then into project estimating and planning. These two activities, which go hand in hand, are covered in detail in Chapter 9.

Hold a technical and risk review

At the end of the detailed solutioning and before any final, pre-proposal submission meeting with the potential Buyer, hold a technical and risk review. The objectives of this review are to:

- test the completeness, quality and viability of the solution against the Buyer's requirements and their Vendor selection criteria;
- capture assumptions used in solution definition and any issues arising from these;
- capture any final questions to be put to the potential Buyer prior to proposal submission;
- identify any changes needed in solution outputs, plus any additional solution outputs required;
- present and discuss first-cut pricing;
- update the Risk Management Plan, including the cost of risk reduction measures.

In order to provide added value, the review should include the participation of an independent technical architect or development manager, the production manager in the owning business, and the QA professional. Risk management is covered in detail in Chapter 10.

Buyer meeting #3

Buyer meeting #3 is a bonus. Above all else, it is an opportunity to practise your formal presentation and check that you are 'on message'. You should be, because you have already met the potential Buyer to understand their Vendor selection criteria and 'hot buttons'. You have also met with the Buyer to take them through your first-cut solution and test its acceptability. Thus, meeting #3 is the time to present your solution and explain the benefits it provides to the Buyer. Of course, you need to be sensitive to feedback, but the adjustments you need to make to your solution and proposal should be few.

This meeting is the time to pose your final round of questions, test the acceptability of the assumptions you have used to underpin your solution and estimates, and check that any areas of non-compliance in your solution are not going to exclude you from the competition for the contract. You should also review the Risk Management Plan.

The one potential minefield is the issue of price. You must not formally present your pricing as this will be seen by the Buyer as breaching the procurement rules. Pricing is best discussed informally after the meeting, if an opportunity presents itself.

You then need to hurry back to the office to cut and paste the solution into the proposal and write that Executive Summary.

Remember!

The output of the sales process in NOT a proposal. It is a potential Buyer who wants to buy YOUR solution and YOUR people. Your focus is on:

---

1 The potential Buyer and their requirements

---

2 Your solution

---

3 Your proposal

... in that order.

Chapter 9

PROJECT ESTIMATING, PLANNING, CONTRACT NEGOTIATION AND PRICING

Introduction

> **Troubled project root causes to avoid when estimating, planning and pricing the solution**
> *Be on the lookout for:*
> **RC12** Vendor underestimation of resources (predominantly person-effort) required
> **RC15** Poor project planning, management and execution
> **RC16** Failure to clearly define roles and responsibilities in the contract/ sub-contracts

RC12 – Vendor underestimation of the staff months required to deliver a project – is probably the most common of all the root causes of troubled projects, which makes this chapter one of the most important in this book. RC12 is a special case of RC15 – poor project planning, management and execution. Both root causes are bound up with:

- a failure to define the scope of the project and the work products to be produced;
- a failure to accurately estimate the size or complexity of work products (for example the size of the code; the size of associated artifacts such as requirements, design, test and user documentation; or the number of defects to find and remove);
- a failure to accurately estimate the staff-months required by the project team to produce the work products.

RC16 – failure to clearly define roles and responsibilities in either the Vendor's contract with the Buyer or the Vendor's contracts with subcontractors – is, once again, a special case of RC15. All of these root causes can be avoided if the solution is shaped, developed, defined and documented as described in the preceding chapters.

In Part 2 of this book we have so far discussed:

- the importance of *opportunity qualification* to ensure that bid budget and staff energy is focused only on opportunities which you have a good chance of winning;
- the need to *engage* with your potential Buyer to understand their requirements, business drivers and motivators (or 'hot buttons'), and to enlist their help in solution definition and 'polishing';
- the nature of *a solution*:
  - what – the architecture of the system [technology]
  - how – the approach and plan for the project [process]
  - who – the project organisation [people];
- how to *shape* your solution and use feedback from the potential Buyer to maximise both the fit of your solution to their business requirements and the attractiveness of your proposal to the potential Buyer;
- how to define *solution outputs*:
  - architectural and design outputs, such as data flow diagrams and functional decompositions,
  - project definition outputs, such as a schedule of deliverables and work products, and the definition of the project organisation,
  - outputs associated with the project approach, such as the software development processes, methods and tools to be deployed,
  - planning outputs, such as work breakdown structures to define the activities and tasks needed to create the work products.

This is the starting point for bottom-up (or activity-based) software project cost estimation – the only approach to cost estimation that is sufficiently 'industrial strength' to be used as a basis for contract.

Estimating is not a one-time activity undertaken prior to the start of a software project. Estimates should be refined throughout the project, based on real project data, such as the productivity rates of teams and individuals, and the number of defects discovered and corrected per thousand lines of code (KLOC) or function point. Defects should be categorised as requirements, design, coding, documentation and 'bad fix' defects.

The best book I know in this area is *Estimating Software Costs*[1] by T Capers Jones. In my view, this is essential reading for all project managers, development managers and bid managers.

The power of function points

In the late 1970s, Allan Albrecht of IBM White Plains developed the concept of the function point as a means of sizing the development work associated with substantial software development projects. The work was put into the public domain in 1979. The power of the function point metric is that:

- It does not vary with the development language, the software life cycle approach (software development processes) or the tools used to develop the software. This is due to the fact that the function point count for a software system is derived from a count of the inputs, outputs, enquiries, logical files and interfaces of the system, which are not dependent on implementation detail such as the language used. This has become of even greater significance since the advent of object-oriented and non-procedural languages.

- It is possible to retrospectively convert lines of code into function points for a software project. This means that an organisation, provided it keeps good records of staff-months expended on projects, by activity, can build up a database of historical project performance. This can be used to estimate future software development projects with similar function point counts (the relationship between function point size and development effort required being non-linear).

- Function points can be used as a stake in the ground in cases where the requirements of the system are not well specified. An assumed baseline function point count can be built into the contract between Buyer and Vendor and, if the eventual function point count is higher than the baseline, the price of the contract can be adjusted. Function points are also increasingly being built into application maintenance contracts, the maintenance cost per function point being an effective way of pricing these deals.

- Function points are supported by many commercially available software cost estimating tools. These tools are of value not simply to generate or validate estimates prior to contract, but also to assess the productivity of project teams during delivery.

Function points were not an overnight success, but it was clear that they had an important role to play in estimating software costs. Even in the early days, tables were published which enabled software developers to convert function point counts into lines of code in the target language of their project. Lines of code (LOC) or thousands of lines of code (KLOC) were familiar metrics which development managers could use with some degree of accuracy to estimate the resources required for software projects. In 1986, the International Function Point Users Group (IFPUG) was formed. IFPUG has taken responsibility for publishing function point counting rules, with Version 4 being released in 1994. Unfortunately, several alternative function point standards have been proposed by other individuals and organisations. This means that whenever a function point count is quoted, it is important to understand which type of function point has been used.

I remember being rather sceptical about function points. It just seemed so unlikely that enumeration of inputs, outputs etc could provide anything like as accurate a handle on the size of a software development project as a bottom-up estimate based on a functional decomposition and a schedule of software development activities. However, I used function points myself to good effect when engaged as an expert witness in the UK High Court on behalf of an IT services supplier. The supplier was being sued for failing to produce a system which met the Buyer's requirements. My principal task was to prepare a report to demonstrate that the system did indeed meet the documented user requirements. By doing a manual function point count from the system specification and by 'backfiring' a function point count from the actual size of the code, I was also able to show that the project team had delivered higher than normal productivity. This facilitated the agreement of an out-of-court settlement.

Today, most commercially available software cost estimating tools provide support for function points. If a reasonably accurate function point count can be obtained (for example by backfiring from the code size of a similar project, or by undertaking a function point count from the requirements specification), these tools provide a valuable contribution to estimating precision. It is surprising that only about 30 per cent of commercial IT services Vendors use them. This figure rises to about 50 per cent in the case of Vendors specialising in military or systems software, but approximately 60 per cent of all development projects are still estimated manually.

Getting into the correct ball-park – initial 'guesstimates'

It is advisable for a Vendor to generate an early 'guesstimate' of the scale of a software development, as any mismatch between the Vendor's estimated staff-effort and timescale and any proposed budget and timescale indicated in the Buyer's RFP/ITT is an important consideration during the opportunity qualification process.

The way I generate this guesstimate of project scale is very subjective. I tend to look at the RFP/ITT, gain an impression of the degree and complexity of the functionality and the complexity of the interfaces, search my memory for 'similar projects' and try and recall the timescales of these projects and the approximate size of the team. This is not a good approach, but it often gets me into the right ball-park.

A far better approach is to generate an early function point estimate from the requirements documentation, using skilled resources who specialise in software sizing and estimation. In my view, software sizing professionals are an essential part of a Vendor's capability. The earlier they can be deployed on an opportunity, the better.

I pass on below, with the permission of the McGraw-Hill companies, a very interesting ball-park estimating approach presented by T Capers Jones in his book *Estimating Software Costs*.[1] Jones himself gives this approach a health warning and I will reiterate it! This approach is unsuitable for serious estimating purposes, such as the generation of a cost estimate for contractual purposes. However, it can provide an early guesstimate or be used as a 'sanity check' on a guesstimate generated by other means. This is what you do. Using Table 9.1, select the *scope* of the software item or system which most closely matches the project you are sizing, and write down the number of the item. For example, for a new system, the number is 9.

Next, select the *class* of software system which most closely matches the project you are sizing, and write down the number of the item. For example, for a contract project – civilian, the number is 6. Next, select the *type* of software system which most closely matches the project you are sizing, and write down the number of the item. For example, for a client/server project, the number is 8. Add up the numbers and raise the total to the power 2.35 to produce an estimated size in IFPUG Version 4 function points. For our example of a new client/server system for a commercial Buyer, the total is 23. Raising this to the power 2.35 yields a guesstimate of 1585 IFPUG Version 4 function points.

Capers Jones provides several rules of thumb, several of which are included, with permission from the McGraw-Hill companies, in Table 9.2. These rules of thumb are quite valuable, when used with the best function point count (FPC) you can derive, to provide early project cost estimates or a 'sanity check' on manual activity-based estimates.

A word of warning. According to Capers Jones, the chance of a project being cancelled increases with the function point count. Sixty-five per cent of projects in the 100,000 function point range are cancelled, 48 per cent of projects in the 10,000 function point range are cancelled, and 20 per cent of projects in the 1000 function point range are cancelled.

Table 9.1   *Capers Jones Scope, Class and Type Values*

Scope		Class		Type	
1	Subroutine	1	Individual software	1	Non-procedural
2	Module	2	Shareware	2	Web applet
3	Reusable module	3	Academic software	3	Batch
4	Disposable prototype	4	Single location – internal	4	Interactive
5	Evolutionary prototype	5	Multilocation – internal	5	Interactive GUI
6	Standalone program	6	Contract project – civilian	6	Batch database
7	Component of system	7	Time sharing	7	Interactive database
8	Release of system	8	Military services	8	Client/server
9	New system	9	Internet	9	Mathematical
10	Compound system	10	Leased software	10	Systems
		11	Bundled software	11	Communications
		12	Marketed commercially	12	Process control
		13	Outsource contract	13	Trusted system
		14	Government contract	14	Embedded
		15	Military contract	15	Image processing
				16	Multimedia
				17	Robotics
				18	Artificial intelligence
				19	Neural net
				20	Hybrid: mixed

Table 9.2   *Sizing Rules of Thumb Based on Function Points*

The number of lines of code (assuming a procedural language like C) is of the order of 100 times the FPC. For C⁺⁺, the number of lines of code is of the order of 50 times the FPC, assuming a typical object library	So, in our example, the first-cut estimate of the number of lines of procedural language code is 158,500
The total number of coding defects is of the order of 1.75 times the FPC	So, in our example, the first-cut estimate of the total number of coding defects to be detected and fixed is 2774
The project timescale, in months, is of the order of the FPC raised to the power 0.4 (for commercial projects) or 0.45 (for military projects)	So, in our example, the first-cut estimate of project timescale is 19 months
Productivity ranges from about 4 function points per staff-month for a novice team with poor software development processes, to 18 function points per staff-month for a superior team with excellent software development processes. Average productivity is of the order of 8* function points per staff month	So, in our example, dividing the FPC by 8 gives a first cut estimate of staff-effort required of 198 staff-months * Note: these productivity figures cover the entire software life cycle, not just coding
The size of the project team is of the order of the FPC divided by 150	So, in our example, the first-cut estimate of project team size is 10.5. Multiplying this by the first-cut estimate of project timescale gives a total staff-effort of 200 staff-months
Scope creep (or requirements creep) is typically of the order of 1% – 2% per month. It is prudent to assume that a quarter of this scope creep (0.5% per month) will have to be absorbed by the project at no additional charge to the Buyer	So, in our example, we can expect a 9.5 per cent increase in scope, equivalent to 19 staff-months of effort, about 5 staff-months of which will be unfunded
The number of test cases required is of the order of: unit test: 0.45 times the FPC system test: 0.25 times the FPC acceptance test: 0.20 times the FPC	So, in our example, we can expect to see some 396 system test cases

Manual bottom-up (activity-based) estimating

Accurate software development estimates depend on many factors, including:

- the skill of the estimator. Software cost estimating is not a black art, but it does reside in that hinterland somewhere between science, engineering and an art. There is no real substitute for experience;

- the quality of the requirements;
- the definition of deliverables and other work products;
- the accuracy with which deliverables and work products can be sized;
- the software development processes to be deployed;
- the methods and tools to be deployed;
- the software development environment (the languages, database management systems, and support environments) to be deployed;
- the capability or software process maturity of the Vendor organisation;
- the individual capabilities of the project team members (the effective productivity of individual developers can vary by at least an order of magnitude);
- the availability of historical project data which can be used to underpin the estimates. In an ideal world, historical data would:
  - be detailed;
  - be quantitative (including staff-months by activity and total KLOC produced);
  - reflect the current capability of the Vendor organisation and the project team;
  - include projects from the same application domain;
  - include projects of similar size;
  - include projects using the same software development processes, development environment, methods and tools;
- the inclusion of all necessary activities, tasks and resources;
- the likely degree of scope creep;
- the level of quality targeted – the number of requirements, design, coding; documentation and 'bad fix' defects expected (and the target ceiling for the number of defects per KLOC delivered to the Buyer);
- standard Vendor data on fee rates, fee rate indexation etc;
- assumptions on promotions (leading to increased cost) and staff turnover (leading to training costs, lower than planned productivity during the learning curve of new team members, and higher management overhead);
- assumptions on the number of productive staff-days per month or per year.

Many Vendors have 'standard' work breakdown structures for different types of development (software engineering projects, Rapid Application Development (RAD) projects, object-oriented (OO) projects, packaged software implementation projects etc). However, there is a substantial degree of commonality between these types of development in terms of the underlying activities. Table 9.3 shows a set of activities which can be used as a basis for activity-based estimates. This list is based on one presented in the Capers Jones book and is reproduced with permission from the McGraw-Hill companies. Not all activities will be necessary on every project, but I would make a plea for you to routinely plan to undertake design inspections and code inspections. These are not the province of military and process control software alone. Formal design inspections will typically uncover up to 65 per cent of defects in the design. Formal code inspections will typically uncover up to 60 per cent of coding defects. On the other hand, each wave of testing (unit, module, integration, system etc) will at best uncover 30 per cent of defects.

Table 9.3   *Common Software Development Activities*

1	requirements clarification, baselining and scope creep,	13	configuration management
2	prototyping	14	integration
3	architecture/infrastructure definition	15	user documentation
4	project planning	16	unit testing
5	initial, high-level design	17	module/functional area testing
6	detailed, low-level design	18	integration testing
7	design reviews	19	system testing
8	coding	20	field testing
9	acquisition of reusable artifacts (architectures, designs, code, documentation etc)	21	factory acceptance testing (FAT)
10	purchase of packaged/COTS software	22	site acceptance testing (SAT)
11	code inspections	23	software quality assurance
12	independent verification and validation	24	installation and commissioning
		25	training
		26	project management
		27	project reviews and reporting
		28	subcontract management

Estimating hints and tips

- Use a spreadsheet or an automated cost estimating tool, not the back of a cigarette packet. Estimates need to be maintained and updated in the light of actual productivity, and overlooked activities need to be added. Retain each set of estimates; they provide a vital audit trail.
- Mark up your functional decomposition (or requirements schedule) to show each function/requirement as either simple, average or complex. Work through your work breakdown structure (or activity list). For each activity, review the functional decomposition (or requirements schedule) and estimate the effort associated with each function or requirement.
- Round up individual estimates to the nearest day.
- As far as this is feasible, estimate each activity and task in the knowledge of which member of the team will do the work. Ask the team members for their opinion of the realism of your estimates. If you don't know who will be doing the work, don't assume that you will have a team of super-developers. Rather, assume the average level of skill available in your organisation.
- John Boddie in his excellent book, *Crunch Mode*,[2] advises that when you have prepared a set of estimates you should put them away and go home. Next morning, develop a new set of estimates without reference to the previous set.

If the two sets are wildly different, Boddie advises repeating the process until the correlation improves, and then taking the average of your estimates.

- Always commission two independent estimates, both from experienced developers or development managers. They should both use the same work breakdown structure or activity list, functional decomposition or requirements schedule, and spreadsheet pro forma. They should not confer until both sets of estimates have been completed, at which time they should get together and walk through both sets of estimates, concentrating on the differences and reaching an agreed staff-month figure in every case.
- If you are planning to reuse software assets from previous projects, be conservative about the degree of reuse which can be achieved and realistic about the effort required to modify and integrate the assets.
- Use an automated tool as a 'sanity check' on the manual estimates. It will highlight several things you have forgotten and help you to achieve the correct balance between the several phases and ongoing activities of the project, such as requirements definition, clarification and management; design; coding; testing; integration; change management; configuration management; documentation; project management; software quality assurance etc.
- Alternatively, refer to Capers Jones' book where a table is presented showing the percentage of staff-effort typically spent on each activity for several different types of system development (commercial, systems software, military etc). This is not as elegant a solution as the use of an automated tool because ratios between activities change with the size of the development.
- Use the fee rates of the staff who will work on the project. Add a contingency of (say) 5 per cent to cover promotions and the impact of staff turnover.
- Build contingency into the estimates at the line-item level by defining best case, worst case and likely case resource usage. The reason for this is twofold:
  - some tasks will be new and complex and will require a substantial contingency, whilst others will be familiar and simple and will require very little contingency. The use of 'blanket contingency' hides these realities from view and is unhelpful,
  - the use of these 'three-point' estimates will give you the ability to run a Monte Carlo analysis on the plan, using a risk analysis tool, and obtain project end dates for different confidence levels.
- After you have mapped the estimates onto the project plan, calculate the adjustment required for fee rate increases (unless your price will be tied to an inflation index).

Manual top-down (project-level or phase-level) estimating

This type of estimation can be used as a cross-check on a manual or automated activity-based estimate, but it is unsuitable for use in generating estimates to be used to underpin a contract between a Buyer and a Vendor.

Manual phase-level estimation is the traditional approach to estimating software development. The starting point is an estimate of the size of the code. You divide the estimated code size by the full life cycle productivity rate (LOC/staff-month) which is appropriate to the development language and the skills of the Vendor organisation. For example, suppose you have a C^{++} project opportunity to estimate. A previous project (Project A) generated 32,000 lines of C^{++} code and used 114 staff-months of effort, giving a full life cycle productivity rate for your organisation of 280 lines of C^{++} per staff-month.

Your new opportunity is larger, with more windows, more complexity and more transaction logic. From a comparison of the number of use cases in Project A and the new opportunity, you estimate it will require 80,000 lines of C^{++} code, but you will be using a different class library from that used in Project A, which you believe is more powerful. You decide to bank this possible productivity improvement. The full life cycle estimate is therefore 80,000/280 or 286 staff-months.

You then refer to typical ratios between requirements clarification and management, design, coding, unit and functional area testing, system testing and user acceptance testing for object-oriented development to generate the high-level project plan.

The disadvantages of this approach to estimating are that:

- It is rare for a previous project to match a current opportunity very closely. Often the application domain will be different, the development environment will be different, the design methods and tools will be different, and the team will be different.
- Ratios between activities or phases do not scale with project size. Larger developments require a higher percentage of total project time to be spent on integration and testing, and require higher management overhead.
- Ratios differ between classes of project. For example, COTS application software development projects require a far higher percentage of effort to be expended on help text and user documentation than most other classes of project.
- Ratios differ between types of development (for example, software engineering, RAD and OO projects have different ratios for a given function point count).
- The use of ratios may encourage you to overlook activities such as project planning, subcontractor management, software quality assurance, database administration, configuration management or change management.
- Project development environments are becoming more complex. Often two or three different programming languages will be used, there will be reuse of code and artifacts from earlier projects, COTS products will be integrated, and more than one design technique will be deployed. This degree of complexity requires a detailed activity-based estimating approach.

The use of automated estimating tools

Automated estimating tools typically provide:

- a knowledge base of several hundred projects;
- support for function points and LOC in all common languages;
- the ability to produce initial estimates to phase level based on minimal data (such as an initial function point count);
- standard 'charts of account' or activity schedules for activity-based costing;
- sizing logic for code, specifications, test cases, defects etc;
- support for a variety of software development life cycle processes;
- the ability for the user to set up templates to match particular types of project;
- support for mixed programming languages.

The value of these tools is that they provide more consistent estimates, more easily, than can be achieved manually. For this reason, they are hugely valuable:

- to provide an early sizing;
- to support a detailed activity-based estimate;
- to provide an industrial-strength 'sanity check' on manual activity-based estimates;
- to use throughout a project to provide an ever-improving estimated cost to completion;
- to act as a repository for project metrics to be used for future estimation purposes;
- to provide a means of quantitatively auditing the productivity of projects.

Some leading automated cost estimating tools are:

- ESTIMACS, from Computer Associates International Inc.;
- KnowledgePlan, from Software Productivity Research Inc.;
- SLIM, from Quantitative Software Management Inc.

There are also several estimating tools available based on the COCOMO[3] and COCOMO II[4] constructive cost models developed by Dr Barry Boehm.

Converting the estimates into an inter-locked project plan

The next task is to convert the estimates into a time-line plan (or Gantt Chart) using a project scheduling tool such as Microsoft Project. Another benefit of commercial automated cost estimating tools is that many of them have the ability to export data to Microsoft Project and other project scheduling tools.

Show all dependencies between activities, particularly dependencies on the Buyer, subcontractors and third parties. Some adjustment of estimates is usually necessary to map the activities and tasks of the work breakdown structure onto a team structure, but at the end of this planning session you have the Project Plan section of your PID, and the basis for pricing the project.

The Capability Maturity Model

The discussion of automated cost estimating tools featuring a knowledge base of project metrics probably raised the questions in your mind, 'Yes, but how do I know that the metrics pre-loaded into the tool are representative of the productivity of my people? If the projects in the knowledge base were poorly executed, I'm going to overestimate the cost of my next project and lose the business. On the other hand, if the metrics in the tool were for outstandingly productive and successful projects, I'm going to underestimate the effort needed on my next project and lose money.'

These are very relevant questions. Software development organisations are not equally effective. The more effective and mature your software development processes, the more productive and competitive you will be. This brings us to the Capability Maturity Model (CMM).

The Software Engineering Institute at Carnegie Mellon University started work on defining a framework which would help organisations improve their software development processes – and hence their productivity and software quality – in late 1986. The initiative was in response to a request from the US Department of Defense for a method for assessing the capability of software contractors. The current version of the model was released in 1993, following the release, review and usage of an earlier version of the model in 1991.

The fact that the capability maturity model was conceived within the defence environment – where unusually large projects are the norm and projects are typically implemented using a software engineering or 'waterfall' software life cycle approach – does beg the question, 'Is CMM relevant to commercial organisations?'

The reasons why the answer to this question is a resounding 'Yes!' include:

- The model describes the key components of an effective software development process in general, non-prescriptive terms which do not imply or require a particular design or development method to be followed.
- Five levels of software maturity are defined, providing organisations with a means of assessing where they are on the 'scale' of software process maturity and where to focus their software process improvement initiatives.
- The underlying premise of the model is that a high-quality process will deliver a high-quality result – which is hard to disprove.
- The concept of software process maturity is a valuable one. It implies that processes are defined. It implies that processes are effective. It implies that processes are used. It implies that processes are used by everyone. It implies that processes are managed, measured and improved where necessary. This is a powerful concept. The majority of organisations developing software can

point to documents setting out standard processes and methods. A key differentiator between immature and mature software development organisations is that the mature organisation uses its processes consistently on all projects, while the immature organisation uses its process descriptions predominantly as 'boilerplate' in proposals or as 'shelfware'.

- Moving up the software process maturity levels implies that effectiveness and productivity increase, project cost and timescale become more predictable, and the organisation becomes more competitive.

Characteristics of mature and immature software development organisations

The Carnegie Mellon University Software Engineering Institute has produced an excellent book, *The Capability Maturity Model: guidelines for improving the software process*,[5] to describe the model and advise on its use. In this book is a very telling description of the differences between immature and mature software organisations, which is reproduced here by permission of Pearson Education Inc. Reading this description will undoubtedly remind you of companies for which you have worked!

'In an immature software organisation, software processes are generally improvised by practitioners and their managers during the course of the project. Even if a software process has been specified, it is not rigorously followed or enforced. The immature software organisation is reactionary, and its managers are usually focused on solving immediate crises (better known as fire fighting). These organisations routinely exceed schedules and budgets because they are not based on realistic estimates. When hard deadlines are imposed, they may compromise product functionality and quality to meet the schedule.

In an immature organisation, there is no objective basis for judging product quality or for solving product or process problems. There is little understanding of how the steps of the software process affect quality, and product quality is difficult to predict. Moreover, activities intended to enhance quality, such as reviews and testing, are often curtailed or eliminated when projects fall behind schedule. The customer has little insight into the product until delivery.

A mature software organisation, in contrast, possesses an organisation-wide ability for managing software development and maintenance processes. It accurately communicates the software process to both existing staff and new employees, and carries out work activities according to the planned process. The processes mandated are documented, usable, and consistent with the way the work actually gets done. The process definitions are updated when necessary, and improvements are developed through controlled pilot-tests and/or cost benefit analyses. There is broad-scale, active involvement across the organisation in improvement activities. Roles and responsibilities within the process are clear throughout the project and across the organisation.

In a mature organisation, managers monitor the quality of the software products and the process that produces them. There is an objective, quantitative basis for judging product quality and analysing problems with the product and process. Schedules and budgets are based on historical performance and are realistic; the expected results for cost, schedule, functionality, and quality of the product are usually achieved. In general, the mature organisation follows a disciplined process consistently because all of the participants understand the value of doing so, and the necessary infrastructure exists to support the process.'

To give a 'flavour' of the model, I summarise the key process areas and behaviours at each level of the model in Table 9.4. In doing this, there is a danger that you will say, 'Yeah, we do all that. We must be at Level 5!' To avoid this danger, you really need to read and refer to the Carnegie Mellon University SEI book previously referenced. This contains a full description of each *key process area*, covering:

- a description of the *activities performed*;
- a description of the 'enablers' required to give individuals and the organisation the *ability to perform*;
- a description of the indicators that the organisation has a *commitment to perform*;
- the *goals* of the key process area.

This will enable you to form a better impression of which level of the CMM model your organisation has reached. For an even better fix, please refer to the exercises at the end of this chapter.

For an IT services Vendor, the benefit of achieving higher levels of maturity can be summarised as greater competitiveness. Organisations at Level 3 are about 25 per cent more productive than those at Level 1 and there is some evidence that productivity increases even more dramatically at the higher levels.

Of course there is a cost associated with moving from Level 1 to Level 3, but there is also a return on this investment:

- Hughes Ground Systems Group Software Engineering Division moved from Level 2 to Level 3. They spent approximately $450,000 over a two-year period and achieved a $2 million annual reduction in cost overruns.
- Raytheon Equipment Division's Software Systems Laboratory moved from Level 1 in 1988 to Level 3 in 1991, spending approximately $1 million annually. Rework costs decreased by $15.8 million from 41 per cent to 11 per cent of contract value. Productivity increased by a factor of 2.3, average project costs decreased by 30 per cent, integration effort decreased by 80 per cent, retesting effort decreased by 50 per cent and projects were typically 4 per cent– 6 per cent under budget.

Table 9.4   *Key Process Areas of the CMM Model, by Level*

Behavioural Characterisation	Key Process Areas
Level 5 – Optimising There is a focus on continuous improvement. Software defects are analysed and processes adjusted to improve project and organisational productivity and software quality.	• Defect prevention • Technology change management • Process change management
Level 4 – Managed Process performance and software quality are measured, tracked and maintained within quantitative limits. Project outcomes are quantifiable and predictable.	• Quantitative process management • Software quality management
Level 3 – Defined Standard software development and management processes – including verification mechanisms such as entry & exit criteria and design & code inspections – are consistently used across the organisation. A group is responsible for process improvement. An organisation-wide training programme is in place. Software quality is tracked.	• Organisation process focus • Organisation process definition • Training programme • Integrated software management • Software product engineering • Inter-group co-ordination • Peer reviews
Level 2 – Repeatable Basic disciplines are in place to plan, track and manage projects. Requirements are defined. An effort is made to make realistic commitments based on past organisational and project performance. Projects follow defined processes which are not abandoned when the going gets tough. Processes often differ between projects.	• Requirements management • Software project planning • Software project tracking and oversight • Software subcontract management • Software quality assurance • Software configuration management
Level 1 – Initial Ad hoc, chaotic processes. Fire-fighting style of management. Success depends on the capability and heroics of individuals. Projects are often late and over budget. Successes are hard to repeat.	No key process areas defined at this level

- The Boeing Company has used CMM as the framework for software process improvement since 1991. Over 10,000 staff have been trained in CMM. Over 120 assessments have been conducted during the period 1991–1998 in different software organisations in the company. The average time to achieve movement between levels has been:
  Level 1 to Level 2 – 34 months
  Level 2 to Level 3 – 25 months
  Level 3 to Level 4 – 30 months

Investment information is not available, but the benefits seen include:

Benefit	Level 1 > 2	Level 2 > 3	Level 3 > 4
Defect reduction	12%	40%	85%
Schedule reduction	10%	38%	63%
Schedule variance	8%	35%	75%
Cost reduction	145%	24%	15%

There are other, equally tangible benefits of achieving higher levels of software process maturity, not associated purely with software quality, revenue and profit growth. These include:

- increased employee morale and job satisfaction;
- fewer overtime hours;
- lower staff turnover;
- higher customer satisfaction.

Contract negotiation

This is the activity leading to a contract with terms and conditions and a statement of work which is acceptable to both Buyer and Vendor. It is not about price negotiation. Terms and conditions are usually negotiated by contracts or legal professionals within the Buyer and Vendor organisations. These are usually slightly remote from the Buyer's decision-maker and the Vendor principal. The only piece of advice I want to give is that it is wise for the Vendor principal to ensure that contractual negotiations do not get too 'heavy', too soon. Until the Buyer is showing signs of wanting to buy your solution it is wise to ensure that the contracts professionals are indicating an 'agreement to agree' on mutually acceptable terms and conditions. Failure to achieve this could give the Buyer the impression that you are going to be difficult to work with and this might adversely affect your win chance.

Pricing the deal

Your base cost estimates will require uplift to cater for:

- the anticipated cost of identified, and even unidentified, risks – see Chapter 10;
- the impact of inflation, unless your price is tied to an inflation index;
- your target Gross Profit.

Avoid irritants

My wife runs a training company, *The Learning Works UK*, specialising in achieving real change at personal, team and corporate levels. Every training event or motivational workshop she undertakes is a privilege. I help out in the back office. Every invoice I raise is a joy. It doesn't cost us 10 per cent extra to process expenses, so we don't charge it.

Avoid components of your price which the Buyer may find irritating. For example:

- Don't charge high daily fee rates for business manager or production manager oversight of a project. The Buyer will rightly expect this cost to be covered by the fee rates of the project manager and their team.
- Don't charge for Quality Assurance. This should be part of the service.
- Don't levy additional charges for the use of PCs by team members and consultants. These costs should be covered by fee rates and be invisible to the Buyer.
- Don't charge outrageous mileage rates.
- Don't charge travelling time.
- Don't add a 10 per cent handling charge to expenses.

These things probably won't lose you the business, but why do anything to spoil your win chance?

Summary

Vendor underestimation of the effort required to deliver a project is probably the most common of all the root causes of troubled projects. Activity-based software project cost estimation is the only approach that is sufficiently 'industrial strength' to be used as a basis for contract. Software sizing professionals are an essential part of a Vendor's capability, providing valuable software sizing and estimating support to bid teams. Automated cost estimating tools provide more consistent estimates, more easily, than can be achieved manually. They are very valuable to provide an early sizing of a software project, to support a detailed activity-based estimate, and to provide a 'sanity check' on manual activity-based estimates.

The more effective your software development processes – or the higher the level of the Capability Maturity Model your organisation has reached – the more competitive you will be in the marketplace and the more accurate your estimates will be. Process improvement programmes to move from Level 1 to Level 3 are costly, but there is a substantial and ongoing return on this investment.

Exercises

1. Read *Estimating Software Costs*.[1]
2. If you don't currently have one, set up a small centre of excellence in software development and system integration project cost estimation. Equip the staff with automated software cost estimating tools and charge them with the task of collating historical project productivity metrics.
3. Read *The Capability Maturity Model: guidelines for improving the software process*.[5] Find out where you are positioned on the CMM model. You can do this by hiring a certified CMM assessor to conduct a CMM capability evaluation audit. Or, you can send some of your people on a CMM assessment course and use them to perform an internal process assessment against the model. Once you know which level of the CMM model you are at, you can decide where you want to be and plan a software process improvement programme.

References

1. T Capers Jones, *Estimating Software Costs*, McGraw-Hill, 1998.
2. John Boddie, *Crunch Mode*, Prentice-Hall, 1987.
3. Barry Boehm, *Software Engineering Economics*, Prentice-Hall, 1981.
4. Barry Boehm & Ellis Harrowitz, *Software Cost Estimation with COCOMO II*, Prentice-Hall, 2000.
5. Carnegie Mellon University Software Engineering Institute – Paulk *et al.*, *The Capability Maturity Model: guidelines for improving the software process*, Addison-Wesley Publishing Company Inc, 1995.

Chapter 10

MANAGING QUALITY AND RISK

The synergy between quality and risk

Quality management and risk management are usually a focus for the Vendor's Quality Assurance (QA) organisation. In low CMM (Capability Maturity Model) maturity organisations, quality management and risk management can be regarded by project managers and their teams as boring activities which are peripheral to the real work of running a project and developing software. They are often addressed as an afterthought, once the solution has been developed and the proposal has been written. This is a big mistake, as the key synergy between quality and risk management is that both are major determinants of the approach, software development methods and tools to be adopted for the project. The Risk Management Plan and the Quality Plan should both result in a set of project tasks and activities to be costed and incorporated into the work breakdown structure and plans for the project. These plans are not peripheral to the definition and delivery of a project. They are fundamental to its success.

In general terms, we try to maximise quality and minimise risk and there can be an inverse relationship between them. For example, poor quality software development processes imply the production of poor quality software, which results in schedule delays, increased cost, a dissatisfied Buyer and increased commercial risk for the Vendor. However, there is another side to this coin. Perfection in software – in absolute terms, zero defects per thousand lines of code (KLOC) – is very costly indeed and, if pursued on projects where this level of software quality is simply not required, can result in very high commercial risk to the Vendor, and even project failure.

Troubled project root causes to avoid when managing quality and risk
Be on the lookout for:

RC01 Project based on an unsound premise or an unrealistic business case

RC03 Project based on state-of-the-art and immature technology

RC05 Buyer's funding and/or timescale expectations unrealistically low

RC06 Buyer failure to break a complex project into phases or smaller projects

RC07 Vendor setting unrealistic expectations on cost, timescale or Vendor capability

RC08 Buyer failure to define and document requirements (functional and non-functional)

RC10	Vendor failure to invest enough resources to scope the project prior to contract
RC12	Vendor underestimation of resources (predominantly person-effort) required
RC13	Vendor failure to define project tasks, deliverables and acceptance processes
RC14	Failure to actively manage risks and maintain robust contingency plans
RC15	Poor project planning, management and execution
RC16	Failure to clearly define roles and responsibilities in the contract/ subcontracts
RC17	Full-scope, fixed-price contracting (requirements, design and development)
RC19	Poor choice of technical platform and/or architecture
RC21	Poor choice of design/development method
RC23	Vendor lack/loss of skilled resources
RC24	Poor Vendor standards deployment (design, coding, testing, configuration management etc)
RC26	Buyer retains design authority with right to approve/reject low-level designs
RC32	Lack of a formal, 'engineering' approach to integration and testing by Vendor
RC33	Insufficient attention paid by Vendor to non-functional requirements

The majority of these generic root causes of troubled projects have already been referenced in Part 2 of this book, the implication being that they will have been sensed and addressed by the bid team during the bid process. The inclusion of these generic root causes in this chapter underlines the valuable role of QA as a safety net for the Vendor.

Some root causes of troubled projects have not been mentioned previously:

- RC07 is a frequent root cause of troubled projects. Bid teams often have an unrealistically high view of Vendor capability and can be influenced by Buyer expectations to propose costs and timescales which are too low. QA professionals, being independent of the bid team, are well placed to detect this problem and ensure that plans are adjusted appropriately.
- RC10 and RC23 are root causes easily spotted by QA. They are typically manifested by a lack of completeness and detail in the solution and a poorly prepared proposal. Sometimes, it will be necessary for QA to insist on a 'no bid'.
- RC14 – the failure to manage risk – is evidenced by the lack of a risk register and the view expressed by the bid team that this is a 'low-risk' or 'risk-free' project. This chapter covers risk management in some depth. It is important to note that risk identification must be undertaken early in the bid phase as the majority of risk reduction actions need to be undertaken *before* the proposal is submitted.

- RC24, RC32 and RC33 are all associated with failure to plan for, or deliver, the required level of quality. Quality planning is also covered in some detail in this chapter.

What *is* quality?

ISO 8402 defines quality as 'the totality of features and characteristics of a product, process or service that bear on its ability to satisfy stated or implied needs.'

Put simply, quality is the balance of cost, timescale, functionality, reliability and performance which works for the Buyer. The Buyer wants the right level of quality – no better (unless the extra quality comes free of charge) and no worse – at the right price.

This sounds subjective, and it undoubtedly is. However, quality cannot be treated as an abstract, illusive and impossible-to-document attribute of software and systems. The Buyer's subjective expectations of quality can and must be captured and expressed in tangible, measurable, real-world terms, as the challenge for all Vendor project managers is to deliver software and systems which demonstrably meet the requirements of the Buyer. These requirements include the level of quality needed.

Quality covers functional requirements and non-functional requirements such as performance, reliability, availability, usability, maintainability, portability, level of defects and many others.

How are quality requirements specified?

We can expect, and should ensure, that all functional requirements are documented in one or more requirement specifications. These specifications will often also attempt to set out non-functional requirements such as response times and workload handling requirements. Some non-functional requirements, such as those relating to availability, may be expressed in the contract between the Buyer and the Vendor. Others, such as the required timescale, are implicit in the project plan presented in the proposal and often embodied in the contract. It is the project manager's responsibility to ensure that these requirements are clearly referenced in the Quality Requirements section of the Quality Plan. Also to be captured and documented in this section of the Quality Plan are the key quality attributes of the software or system – more of this later.

How is quality delivered?

Most, but by no means all, Vendors will have established a Quality Management System (QMS) to ensure that all projects can access and use a common set of software development processes and standards. A QMS is required in order for a Vendor to achieve registration under their appropriate national standards – ISO

9001 and 9000-3 for the UK. ISO 9001/9000-3 defines 20 key requirements of a QMS as shown in Table 10.1.

The QMS typically contains or references a comprehensive set of Vendor standards (such as a Visual Basic coding standard), methods (such as the Vendor's methods for rapid application development or COTS (Commercial Off-The-Shelf) software implementation) and procedures (such as a document review procedure). It also requires a Quality Plan to be prepared for each project.

The key objectives of the Quality Plan for a project are to define:

- the quality requirements, in a tangible and measurable form;
- the methods the project team will use to attain the required level of quality;
- the quality control methods the project team will use to verify and validate the quality delivered by these attainment methods;
- the quality assurance activities the Vendor's independent QA professionals will use to confirm that quality attainment and quality control plans are being followed and are indeed resulting in software or a system of the required quality.

It is clear from the above that a good Quality Plan provides a multi-level defence against poor quality. A good analogy is the medieval castle, as shown in Figure 10.1. The illustration is reproduced by permission of Kingfisher Publications plc.

As we saw in Chapter 9, low CMM maturity organisations tend not to follow their own QMS very consistently. It is also the case that low CMM maturity organisations:

- do not consistently prepare Quality Plans for projects;
- do not consistently prepare *good* Quality Plans for projects;
- do not consistently *action* Quality Plans when they are prepared.

Table 10.1   *Key QMS Requirements (ISO 9001/9000-3)*

- Management responsibility
- Quality system/quality plan
- Contract review
- Design control
- Document and data control
- Purchasing
- Control of customer-supplied product
- Product identification and traceability
- Process control
- Inspection and testing
- Control of inspection, measuring and test equipment
- Inspection and test status
- Control of non-conforming product
- Corrective and preventive action
- Handling, storage, packaging, presentation and delivery
- Control of quality records
- Internal quality audits
- Training
- Servicing
- Statistical techniques

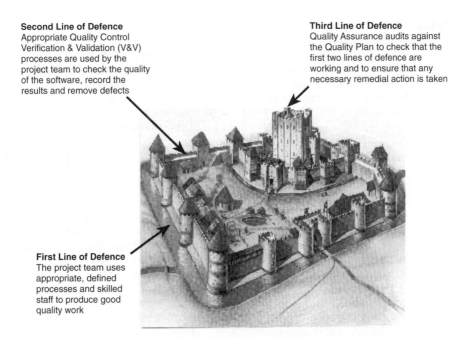

Second Line of Defence
Appropriate Quality Control
Verification & Validation (V&V)
processes are used by the
project team to check the quality
of the software, record the
results and remove defects

Third Line of Defence
Quality Assurance audits against
the Quality Plan to check that the
first two lines of defence are
working and to ensure that any
necessary remedial action is taken

First Line of Defence
The project team uses
appropriate, defined
processes and skilled
staff to produce good
quality work

Figure 10.1   *The Three Lines of Defence against Poor Quality Software*

What makes a good quality plan?

A suggested format for a Quality Plan is shown in Table 10.2 and described below.

Section 1 – introduction

The objectives of the Quality Plan are to define:

- Buyer and Vendor responsibilities for quality management;
- the quality requirements for the software or system being developed/integrated as part of the project;
- the software development methods and tools to be used to achieve the required level of quality;
- how quality control will be applied within the project (by work product) to ensure that the required level of quality is achieved;
- how quality assurance will be applied to the project to ensure that quality control is being undertaken in accordance with the Quality Plan;
- how quality will be preserved throughout the project and when the software or system enters its operational and support phase.

The subsection regarding the maintenance of the Quality Plan is important. It sets out how the plan will be updated during the project. It is important to note

Table 10.2   *Suggested Quality Plan Format*

1 INTRODUCTION	4.3 The development and test
1.1 Objectives of this quality plan	environment(s) to be deployed
1.2 Contents of this quality plan	4.4 The target environment
1.3 Maintenance of this quality	(hardware and software)
plan	4.5 Training to be given to project
	team members
2 QUALITY MANAGEMENT	
2.1 Vendor quality organisation	5 QUALITY CONTROL PLAN
2.2 Vendor quality management	5.1 Schedule/matrix of V&V
system	methods to be used by work
2.3 Project quality organisation	product type
2.4 Project manager quality	5.2 Design review procedure
responsibilities	5.3 Code inspection procedure
2.5 Project quality assurance	5.4 Document inspection procedure
manager responsibilities	5.5 Automated inspection tools to
2.6 Business quality manager	be deployed
responsibilities	5.6 Integration and testing strategy
2.7 Buyer quality assurance	(or reference to section of
responsibilities	Product Initiation Document
2.8 Maintenance of quality records	(PID))
2.9 Capture and analysis of	5.7 Integration and testing plan
metrics	5.8 Quality control of COTS
	products
3 QUALITY REQUIREMENTS	5.9 Quality control of subcontractor
3.1 Description and characterisa-	software/services
tion of the system/software	
3.2 Key quality attributes required	6 QUALITY ASSURANCE PLAN
of the system/software	6.1 Project quality audit (against
3.3 Schedule of work products, by	the quality plan) procedure
type	6.2 Project quality audit schedule
3.4 Applicable standards by work	6.3 Ad hoc project quality audits
product type	6.4 Deliverable/Release review
3.5 Applicable specifications	procedure
3.6 Precedence of contractual	6.5 Deliverable/Release review
documents with regard to	schedule
quality	6.6 Project delivery review
	procedure
4 QUALITY ATTAINMENT	6.7 Project delivery review
PLAN	schedule
4.1 Software development	6.8 Ad hoc project delivery
processes and methods to be	reviews
used	
4.2 Automated tools to be	
deployed in support of the	
processes and methods	

(*continued*)

Table 10.2   *Suggested Quality Plan Format (continued)*

7	QUALITY PRESERVATION PLAN	7.6	Defect reporting, analysis, correction and clearance procedure
7.1	Configuration control procedures	7.7	Process improvement plan
7.2	Requirements clarification procedure	8	MISCELLANEOUS PROCEDURES
7.3	Change control procedure		
7.4	Security procedures	8.1	Purchasing procedures
7.5	Back-up, restore and archive procedures	8.2	Goods-in inspection procedure
		8.3	Dispatch procedure

that the Quality Plan is a living plan, just like the project plan, and will develop and be updated throughout the project. It is *not* shelfware.

Section 2 – quality management

This section describes the Vendor's corporate QMS and the QMS for the project. Quality responsibilities of the project manager, the quality assurance manager on the project (one will be required for a large project), the QA manager in the Vendor business unit 'owning' the project, and the QA manager within the Buyer organisation. It also sets out what quality records will be maintained and what metrics will be captured during the project (particularly with regard to defects).

Section 3 – quality requirements

Subsection 3.1 contains a brief description of the system/software including a characterisation of the type of system or software. For example, is it a military real-time operational system, a retail banking system, an E-commerce system, a COTS package for managing hazardous chemicals, or a system to store and retrieve optical images of purchase orders and invoices? The purpose of this is to make clear the intended business use of the system or software, as this informs the quality attributes required.

Non-functional requirements should be summarised in subsection 3.2 of the Quality Plan as these require additional focus to ensure that they are met in the delivered system or software. Care must be taken to ensure that non-functional requirements are quantitative. For example, if 'ease of use' is a requirement, then this would typically be expressed in a form such as:

> 'It must be possible for a new user with good MS Windows skills to operate transactions A, B, L and M following X hours of training with an achieved transaction throughput of Y and an error rate of less than Z.'

Note that this simple example illustrates the precision required in definition of terms. We would need to define very precisely what we mean by 'good MS Windows skills', 'training', and 'error rate'.

How would we plan to deliver this level of 'ease of use' quality? Well, we might consider designing the key (A, B, L and M) transactions with 'no frills' to make them simple to operate, providing field-level validation so that users will know which inputs are causing trouble, context-sensitive help, or even an irritating animated paper clip. The point here is that defined quality attributes allow us to make appropriate design decisions and embody these in the requirements and design specifications. These specifications will themselves be work products produced by the project team and subject to review to ensure that as many requirements and design defects as possible are removed before coding commences.

Another example of a key quality attribute:

> 'The switch must operate without data loss at rated output and latency at a continuous data input rate of X Mbps on each input channel.'

This quality attribute might require us to model the performance of the design to ensure that the target platform is capable of supporting the maximum continuous load. It might also require us to prepare a performance model and allocate maximum timings to key software procedures or threads. The point here is that defined quality attributes allow us to modify the software development process (and the project plan) to ensure that the required level of quality can be delivered. This example also introduces the concept of 'quality factoring' – the breaking down of an overall quality attribute into requirements for component work products of the software or system.

Subsection 3.3 of the Quality Plan sets out a schedule of work products to be produced by the project team and categorises them by type. The schedule is one of the outputs produced by the detailed solutioning process, as described in Chapter 8. Note that there's an apparent chicken and egg situation here. We need to define the quality requirements for each type of work product, but we can't logically define these work products until we have determined the methods and tools to be used – which we do in the Quality Attainment Plan section which follows. In reality, these sections of the Quality Plan are worked on in parallel.

The objective of identifying work product type is to allow us to define, in subsection 3.4, the standards which should govern the production of each work product of a given type. A project typically utilises more than one development language and appropriate coding standards will need to be referenced for each language.

The functional (as opposed to non-functional) quality attributes should be documented in the set of requirements specifications which govern the contract and reference must be made to these in subsection 3.5 of the Quality Plan.

Subsection 3.6 sets out the precedence of the documents which define quality, for use in the event of a conflict between them.

Section 4 – quality attainment plan

This section of the Quality Plan sets out the software development processes to be used to develop the software and perform systems integration. Once again, different processes might be needed for different work product types. These are likely to be a subset of the Vendor's standard processes and methods as contained in the QMS, but they might also reference processes and methods not previously used by the Vendor – perhaps dictated by the Buyer or by the type of software/system being developed. Any automated tools to be used should be defined, as should the development, test and target environments. Trained staff are needed to produce quality software. The types of training required should be specified. This might include induction training, domain/application training, standards training and methods training.

Section 5 – quality control plan

This section of the Quality Plan defines the quality control or Verification & Validation (V&V) processes to be used for each work product type to ensure that the Quality Attainment approach specified in Section 4 of the Quality Plan has indeed produced the required level of work product quality. Typically, a matrix will be presented showing the V&V methods to be used for each work product type. These might include design reviews, code inspections (Fagan inspections), document reviews and software testing. The procedures to be used for these different types of V&V activity are referenced. Any automated inspection tools to be deployed – such as a complexity analyser capable of identifying unnecessary complexity and redundant code – are defined. The integration and test strategy is set out, or a reference made to the PID which contains this information. The integration and testing plan is presented or a reference made to the project plan. The quality control to be applied to COTS products and subcontracted services is also defined.

Section 6 – quality assurance plan

This section of the Quality Plan first sets out the procedure and plan for QA audits. These are compliance audits, checking that the project is following the processes defined in the Quality Plan. The procedure and plan for deliverable/release reviews are also defined. Deliverable/release reviews assess the level of readiness of a deliverable or release, again by means of checking that appropriate quality attainment and quality control processes have been followed and that required quality records exist. Finally, the procedure and plan for project delivery reviews are presented. These are discussed in detail in Part 3 of this book.

Section 7 – quality preservation plan

The objective of this section of the Quality Plan is to define how quality will be maintained throughout the project and throughout the life of the software/system.

The configuration control procedures define how configuration items will be identified and controlled, and how baselines will be managed. The requirements clarification procedure details how the Buyer and Vendor will collaborate to resolve unclear, conflicting or missing requirements. The change control procedure defines how the same parties will collaborate to identify, analyse and cost changes to requirements. The security procedures cover physical and system security requirements. The back-up, restore and archive procedures set out how the project will protect the Buyer and Vendor from the loss of software, documentation or data. The defect reporting, analysis, correction and clearance procedure describes the processes which the Buyer and Vendor will follow to raise defect reports, analyse the defect reports to establish the type (requirements, design, code, test case etc) and severity of each defect, correct the defect, and establish that the defect removal has been successful. The final subsection of the Quality Preservation Plan covers how software process improvement opportunities will be identified, documented and progressed.

Section 8 – miscellaneous procedures

This section defines purchasing, goods handling and logistics procedures.

> It is vital to ensure that all activities arising from the Quality Plan are reflected in the work breakdown structure, estimates and project plans, otherwise the Quality Plan **will** be shelfware and the required software/system quality **will not** be delivered.

The role of QA

We have just covered the role of QA in auditing the project during delivery for compliance with the Quality Plan, checking deliverable/release readiness, and undertaking project delivery reviews.

QA also has a key role to play during the opportunity selection and bid phases. This role covers:

* the provision of an independent opinion on whether an opportunity should be selected;
* a review of solutions and proposals to ensure that potential projects are likely to:
  * deliver the targeted levels of revenue and gross profit (*commercial assurance*),
  * provide software or a system which will meet user requirements (*technical assurance*),
  * be deliverable (*project assurance*).

QA must have the power of veto if it is to be effective. The QA professional must also act as, and be seen as, a member of the Vendor's business unit rather than as an external 'enemy of sales'.

Risk management

During the acceptance testing of a database system for which I was project manager, a random user terminal would occasionally 'hang' for no apparent reason. The error occurred once or twice a day but could not be created at will. We could locate no obvious application error, but we were able to establish that, when the process thread for that terminal crashed, the application had just made an Operating System (OS) call to write a block of data to disc. After two weeks of 12-hour days, we were able to create a test which would always cause several terminals to hang. The test required 10 fingers to press the ENTER key on 10 terminals to send 10 full pages of data to the system for validation and storage. We found that every process thread which crashed had just made an OS call to write a block of data to disc. After trying for a further two weeks to discover the cause of the problem, we decided to dismantle the application, piece by piece, until the problem went away. We found that if we removed a process which logged after images of screens to magnetic tape, the terminals no longer hung. We built the logging process back into the system and investigated its status at the point of the terminal process crashes. We found that it too had crashed, just after issuing an OS command to read a block of data from disc. We had stumbled over a bug in the real-time OS. We placed a simple semaphore into the code to ensure that no write block command could be issued while a read block command was outstanding (and vice versa). It solved the problem. The bug had cost us a delay of four weeks and about £50,000 in staff effort.

Risk management is about planning for the 'bad things' which might happen during a project. Some of these are generic, ever-present risks, such as the risk that skilled staff might leave the project. Others, like the example above, can never be foreseen. In general terms, the more likely a risk is to occur, the easier it is to foresee and manage.

The goal of risk management

The goal of risk management is to preserve the quality and integrity of a project by reducing cost escalation and project slippage. In broad terms, this is achieved by identifying the foreseeable risks, taking risk reduction actions to reduce the likelihood of each risk materialising and/or the impact if it does, and setting out a contingency plan to be followed if each risk does materialise. The theory is that the overall cost of a project which manages its risks is lower than the cost if risks are unmanaged. This is illustrated in Figure 10.2, which is reproduced, with the permission of John Wiley & Sons Limited, from Martin Ould's book, *Managing Software Quality and Business Risk.*[1]

It is important to remember that risk planning is an ongoing activity, not just something we do at the bid stage of a project. The Vendor's project manager must review and update the risk register regularly and discuss a version of the risk register with the Buyer. The two versions of the risk register will not be identical, as there will always be some risks which the Vendor will wish to keep private.

Risks, issues and opportunities

Risks are 'bad things' which *might* happen. Issues are 'bad things' which *have* happened – risks which have materialised or have such a high probability of materialising that they demand the triggering of the contingency plan. Opportunities are 'good things' which might be beneficial to the project if we can make them happen. All are managed in a broadly similar way:

- identification;
- analysis, including consideration of probability and impact;
- planning;
- implementation of the plans.

Risk planning takes the form of defining the most effective risk reduction/ mitigation actions to reduce the probability of each risk materialising or the impact when it does (preferably both). Risk planning also defines the actions to be

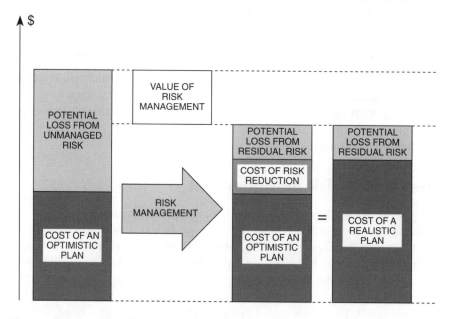

Figure 10.2   *The Value of Risk Management*

taken if a risk does materialise, and what event will trigger the execution of the contingency plan.

Issue planning concentrates on understanding the impact of the issue, its root causes and how to deal with it cost-effectively and with minimal impact on the project.

Opportunity planning takes the form of setting out the actions which can be taken to take advantage of an opportunity to improve the software/system or to reduce project cost or timescale. For example, in the early stages of an SI project to integrate several COTS packages, one of the COTS suppliers may release a new version of their package which provides enhanced data import and export facilities. The Buyer and Vendor could decide to adopt the new release immediately, with some potential saving in bespoke coding but some exposure to the possibility that the package may contain some serious bugs. Alternatively, they might decide to adopt the release as a post-acceptance enhancement, by which time any serious bugs in the release should have been detected and fixed.

Opportunities are the risks which are worth taking, once you have fully thought through the potential up-side and down-side consequences.

Risk identification

Risk identification is best undertaken in a workshop, the objectives of which are typically to:

- review and analyse the issues and risks facing the project;
- identify risk reduction actions, timescales, costs and ownership;
- quantify residual risk remaining (after risk reduction actions);
- draft contingency plans for the key risks;
- consider worst-case scenarios and strategic options;
- consider likely scenarios and plan future checkpoints.

Risk analysis

A classic paper by Erik Clemens[2] identifies five types of risk:

- Financial – causing unacceptable financial exposure or reducing business benefits and thereby prejudicing the original business case for the software/ system.
- Technical – risks that the chosen technology will not support the system.
- Project – risks that the Vendor will be unable to deliver against the contract.
- Functional – risks that the system as delivered will not meet user requirements due to incorrect requirement definition, incorrect delivery of requirements, or changes in the environment and business needs.
- Systemic – risks that the system will have such a large impact that it will alter the environment and all assumptions about costs and benefits.

Risks can also be characterised as 'binary' or 'scalar' risks. A binary risk can either materialise or not. For example, a Vendor might identify a risk that their dotcom Buyer might go out of business. This risk will either materialise or it won't. A scalar risk can materialise to a greater or lesser degree. For example, a Vendor might foresee a risk that the project will slip due to the inability of the Buyer's team to complete acceptance testing in the allotted time. This risk may or may not materialise (like a binary risk) but if it does, the slippage could be insignificant or substantial.

When analysing the risks faced by a project, it is helpful to characterise them using this taxonomy. Analysis of a risk must also identify the root cause, as this might prevent a recurrence of the risk on this or a future project.

Risk probability can be expressed as a qualitative likelihood of the risk materialising (very likely, likely, unlikely, very unlikely) or as a quantitative percentage probability. Some feel that the use of percentage probabilities gives a spurious sense of precision which is unjustified. My own view is that their use is helpful as they give a better feel for the 'shape' of a risk than the use of words such as 'quite likely'.

Risk impact can be expressed using a qualitative scale ranging from 'negligible impact' to 'life-threatening'. We also need to express the impact more tangibly. For example, if it is very likely that a software component is of poor quality (because it was coded and unit tested by an indifferent developer), we could foresee some cost and time penalty. The module might need a thorough code review, a full retest and substantial remedial work. At worst, we might have to re-code the entire module. We need to generate the best estimate we can of the cost and timescale impact of each risk.

Risk reduction

The objective of risk reduction is to change the risk profile. The focus is initially on very likely, high impact risks and the objective is to transform these risks into less likely risks or risks with lower impact (or both). The Probability-Impact matrix is illustrated in Figure 10.3, which is reproduced, with the permission of John Wiley & Sons Limited, from Martin Ould's book, *Managing Software Quality and Business Risk*.[1]

The diagram shows a 'danger zone'. If risks fall within the danger zone, they are prime candidates for risk reduction action planning. The danger zone itself will differ between projects, very few software systems having the potential to threaten life. Our objective in risk reduction is to shift the risks down and left, out of the danger zone.

Risk reduction can be achieved by:

- information gathering – experimentation, measurement, prototyping, etc to reduce the probability or impact of the risk, or simply to demonstrate that there isn't a problem;

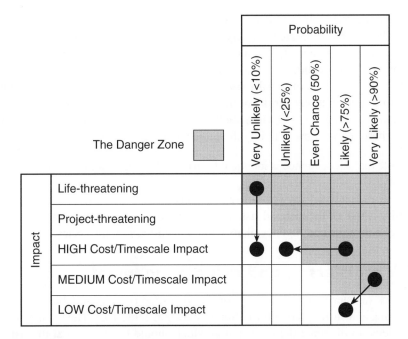

Figure 10.3   *The Probability-Impact Matrix*

- risk influencing – doing something proactive to reduce the probability of the risk or its impact;
- changing the process to reduce the risk probability or impact;
- contractual transfer – passing the risk to someone else better able to handle it in order to virtually eliminate the risk (usually at a cost).

Risk reduction actions cost money. Those undertaken prior to contract are bid costs. Those to be undertaken after contract must be costed and potentially built into the price (see later).

Strategies, contingency plans and scenarios

The risk remaining when all risk reduction actions have been defined is the 're-sidual risk' for the project. This is made up of individual risks, each with a (hope-fully reduced) probability of materialising and a (hopefully reduced) impact. Con-tingency planning involves:

- identification of the options likely to be available if, despite our best risk re-duction efforts, the risk materialises;
- analysis of the options using the SWOT (Strengths, Weaknesses, Opportuni-ties and Threats) technique to identify the option with the best balance be-tween cost and beneficial impact;

- planning, to set out the bones of a contingency plan to address the risk when it strikes, and to estimate the likely cost of plan implementation;
- allocation of ownership and the definition of the 'triggering event' which will initiate the execution of the contingency plan. Definition of the trigger is important. Risks can materialise slowly, with more and more evidence accumulating. It is tempting for the project manager to hold back from taking action in the hope that the risk will actually go away. Defining a trigger which is one of these 'early signs' will buy the project manager a little extra time.

Note that the sequence is identical to that used for the initial risk management activity.

It is prudent to set out worst-case and likely-case scenarios. In each case, these identify which of the residual risks will materialise, what the impact will be and how effective the contingency plans will be in addressing the issues.

Risk registers ... and risk management

The risk register is the repository for the identified risks. A suitable format for capturing and storing risk information is shown in Table 10.3. The form has been completed to illustrate the information which should be captured at the risk reviews.

Risk registers are, like Quality Plans, only of value if the plans within them are followed. This implies that the project manager regularly reviews the status of risk reduction actions and regularly reviews and updates the risk register.

Automated risk register tools such as *Predict! Risk Controller*, marketed by Risk Decisions Limited in the UK, provide many powerful facilities to help the project manager and the Vendor to proactively manage risk. These include:

- management of the risk of the Vendor's portfolio of projects, by business unit;
- risk tracking and automatic e-mailing of reminders to risk action owners;
- powerful reporting features;
- audit trail functionality.

The cost of residual risk

The cost of risk reduction actions is usually easy to estimate. Risk reduction actions may be funded by the bid budget, for most risks identified prior to contract, or by the project budget. Estimating the likely cost of residual risk is more complex. One way to do it is to identify a number of scenarios – best-case, likely-case, worst-case – and sum the cost impact of the risks materialising in each scenario. Note that the best case would normally assume that some risks materialise, and the worst case would not normally assume that all risks materialise.

The traditional way of calculating what residual risk contingency should be set aside for risk is to put the probabilities and cost impacts of the risks into a

Table 10.3   *A Risk Register Form*

Risk Number 04			Risk Type Financial/Scalar	
Risk Description There is a risk that the tracking module will require a total rewrite.				
Root Cause/Contributing Risk Number(s) The existing least-squares algorithm is too processor-intensive and does not give an acceptably stable prediction vector (See Risk #02.).				
Probability 70%				
Impact 1 Slippage of Factory Acceptance Test (FAT) start by circa four months 2 Staff-effort cost of about £180,000 3 Possible triggering of £50,000 of liquidated damages				
No	**Risk Reduction Action**	**Owner**	**Cost (£K)**	**Target Date**
1	Investigate proposed damping algorithm	JGB	4.0	17/8
2	Investigate software tuning possibilities	JGB	6.0	10/9
3	Measure performance on 900MHz card	JGB	1	13/9
Residual Risk Quantification Risk reduction actions will inform whether a rewrite is necessary. Current view is that the rewrite is the preferred option.				
No	**Contingency Actions**	**Owner**	**Cost (£K)**	**Trigger**
1	Find out the size of the track module on the ZAP and ALERT projects	JGB	0.5	Damping algorithm does not give Buyer-acceptable display effect
2	Determine whether it will be cost-effective to port code from Ada to C	JGB	5.0	Ditto
3	Estimate total size of code and degree of reuse	JGB	3.0	Port study complete
4	Prepare detailed cost/time estimates	JGB/CK	6.0	–
Issue No 1	Completed by CK	Date 3/8/2004		Review Date 3/9/2004
Notes				

Table 10.4   *Traditional Calculation of Residual Risk Contingency*

Risk #	Probability (%)	Cost Impact (£)	Probabilised Cost (£)
1	5	1,000,000	50,000
2	10	300,000	30,000
3	20	120,000	24,000
4	30	80,000	24,000
5	60	100,000	60,000
			Total 188,000

spreadsheet, multiply each individual risk probability by its impact, and sum the probabilised impacts, as shown in Table 10.4.

We can immediately see the problem with this simplistic approach. A risk will actually either materialise or it won't, giving a range of cost impacts from £0 (if no risks materialise) to £1,600,000 if they all materialise. There are 2^5 possible cost outcomes, because there are five risks in this simple example. The sequence commences: £0, £80,000, £100,000, £120,000, £180,000, £200,000, £220,000 … etc.

A residual risk contingency of £188,000 will give excellent protection if the most likely risks (Risks 4 & 5) materialise, but wholly inadequate protection if, against the odds, Risks 1 & 2 materialise. To feel comfortable with the business risk we are taking, we really need to set the residual risk contingency at a level which gives us (say) 90 per cent confidence that it will cover the actual cost of risk.

This can be achieved using a risk analysis tool. Plugging the risks into the *Predict! Risk Controller* risk register and analysing the risks using the Monte Carlo facility in *Predict! Risk Analyser*, yields the probability distribution shown in Figure 10.4.

The tool predicts that, for a confidence level of 90 per cent, a residual risk contingency of £413,000 should be set aside – rather more than the traditional calculation would suggest.

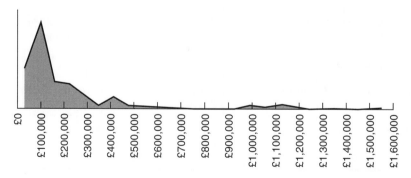

Figure 10.4   *Probability Distribution of Risk Cost using Monte Carlo Analysis*

Table 10.5   *Defining the Bounds of Cost Impact for Each Risk*

Risk #	Probability (%)	Minimum Cost Impact (£)	Likely Cost Impact (£)	Maximum Cost Impact (£)
1	5	800,000	1,000,000	1,200,000
2	10	200,000	300,000	350,000
3	20	100,000	120,000	150,000
4	30	75,000	80,000	100,000
5	60	50,000	100,000	120,000

These tools can do a little more for us. If we have a feel for the 'shape' of each risk, particularly for the likely cost impact, the analysis tool can apply a probability distribution to the impact of each risk. With a little extra discussion at the risk review, we can probably set out minimum, likely and maximum cost impacts for each risk as shown in Table 10.5.

The tool now produces the probability distribution shown in Figure 10.5. The tool predicts that for a confidence level of 90 per cent, a residual risk contingency of £367,000 should be set aside – again rather more than the traditional calculation would suggest. The tool also shows that there is only a 70 per cent confidence that the cost of risk could be held to £188,000.

The message is clear. The traditional method of residual risk calculation does not provide sufficient protection. Automated tools provide a better feel for the size of the commercial risk.

Who should fund residual risk contingency?

On a Time & Materials project, the Buyer will generally fund any additional cost caused through the materialisation of one or more risks. The production of a risk register, containing risk-reduced residual risks is therefore of key importance to the Buyer. The Buyer will be keen to establish that the risk register excludes any

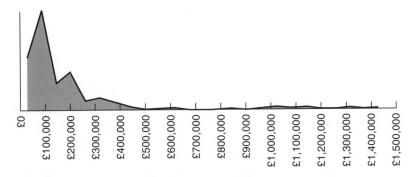

Figure 10.5   *Probability Distribution of Risk Cost using Monte Carlo Analysis and a Triangular Distribution for the Impact of Each Risk*

risks and cost impacts which are not a direct result of the project work and are really the Vendor's responsibility. A typical example would be the risk that staff will leave the Vendor's organisation and replacement staff will require training. The Buyer cannot avoid the impact of the learning curve of these staff, but the Buyer should not be charged for the training courses.

On a fixed-price project, the Vendor has traditionally been expected to quantify the cost of residual risk and charge the Vendor a fixed fee. If few risks materialise, the Buyer still pays the full fee and the Vendor makes additional profit. If more risks materialise than those for which the Vendor has made provision, then the Vendor's profit is hit and the Buyer's 'insurance policy' can be seen to have paid off.

The lottery evident on fixed price projects is very unsatisfactory and many contracting Vendors and Buyers are now managing risk jointly to ensure that neither party wins or loses and that costs are borne by the appropriate party.

Summary

Up with Quality! Down with Risk!

Quality Plans and Risk Management plans *must* result in project tasks to be actioned, tracked and managed to completion, otherwise the Vendor's quality plans and risk management plans are simply shelfware.

One of the biggest causes of troubled projects is Vendor over-confidence in their abilities. A vital role of an independent QA organisation is to detect this problem and ensure that plans are realistic and achievable.

Quality is delivered through:

- specifying quality requirements in tangible, real-world terms;
- defining *and using* appropriate software development processes;
- controlling quality through the use of appropriate V&V processes;
- independent QA reviews to ensure that quality attainment plans and quality control plans are being executed;
- defining *and using* appropriate processes to preserve quality throughout the life of the software.

All of the above are defined in the Quality Plan, a crucial input to project estimation and planning.

The goal of risk management is to reduce project overspend and slippage, and thereby to maximise quality. Risks must be identified and analysed to determine their probability and impact. Risk reduction actions can then be defined to re-engineer the risk profile. What is left is the residual risk. Residual risk can be examined using best, likely and worst case scenarios, and appropriate contingency strategies and plans defined. Automated statistical tools can indicate the residual risk contingency which should be set aside to provide the desired confidence level that the contingency will not be exceeded.

Exercises

1. Undertake a short study in your organisation to determine:

   - what percentage of your projects have Quality Plans;
   - what percentage of projects with Quality Plans have tangible quality requirements, a clear quality attainment plan, a defined quality control plan, a quality assurance plan and a quality preservation plan;
   - what percentage of projects are actually following their Quality Plan.

2. If your organisation does not use a company-wide risk register, giving visibility of risks at project, business unit and business levels, visit a few risk tool vendors to see how such a tool could improve your risk management performance and provide more visibility of the commercial risks of each potential project.

References

1. Martyn A Ould, *Managing Software Quality and Business Risk*, John Wiley & Sons Ltd, 1999.
2. Eric K Clemens, *Evaluation of Strategic Investments in Information Technology*, Communications of the ACM, Vol 34, No 1, January 1991.

Chapter 11

WRITING AND PRESENTING THE PROPOSAL

Introduction

In a police system proposal, I devoted an early chapter to describing how the system would be used to support the Force's fight against crime, right from the time the officer logged in with his collar number and password. I described how the system would provide rapid direct retrieval by name or vehicle registration mark to support beat officers radioing-in for online checks. I described how the system could be used to search for crime suspects on the basis of a particular modus operandi or conviction history. I went on to describe how the search results could be refined by restricting the search to particular geographical areas, or by restricting hits by imposing an age or height range on the suspect, or by adding an additional search parameter such as a red car. I didn't describe any functionality that wasn't explicitly requested in the Invitation to Tender (ITT). I simply explained how the system met those requirements by reference to representative policing situations and in words a police officer could relate to. We won the business and I asked for a de-brief. The Home Office representative told me that what had swung the decision was the chapter in the proposal describing the system in use. The Chief Superintendent had apparently said, 'That's the system I want.'

Proposals must be focused on the potential Buyer and on how your solution will help them to meet their business challenges. The focus must *not* be on you – the Vendor – and your superior capabilities.

The purpose of your proposal

The purpose of your proposal is to convince the potential Buyer that:

- you understand their business and the challenges they face;
- you have appreciated their objectives for the project and tailored your solution to meet these objectives to the highest degree possible;
- your people are professional and capable of delivering a high-quality system;
- giving you the business will spell 'low risk' to them;
- even though you may not be the cheapest, your price represents excellent value;
- their project is important to you.

If you have been able to engage the potential Buyer during the bid phase, you will already have achieved much of the above. The proposal will simply confirm what the Buyer already knows about your solution, your company and your people. However, it is also the vehicle by which your message reaches others in the Buyer's business with whom you have not been able to engage during the bid.

The proposal also provides the means for the Buyer to compare competitive solutions with each other and with the Request For Information (RFI)/Request For Proposals (RFP)/Invitation to Tender (ITT)/Statement of Work (SOW). Even when the Buyer wants to buy *your* solution, a formal evaluation must still be done and be seen to be done. This means that the proposal structure and content must be designed for ease of evaluation.

Proposal content and format

In broad terms, the proposal should set out the *what? how? when? who? how much?* and *why me?* of your offering. This is a very close match to the content of your detailed solution. This means that it is generally possible to cut and paste into the proposal skeleton much of the material you have already produced for your high-level design and project initiation document.

Often, the format will be mandated by the potential Buyer. If it is, comply with it, as it is an irritant to the potential Buyer if you do not. If the mandated format omits a topic which you believe is very important – like acceptance testing, for example – then explain this in the executive summary or introductory section and add material on the topic as an annex to the proposal.

If the format is not mandated, consider not writing a conventional proposal at all but using a presentation format. This can be very effective. It's easy to read and forms an excellent basis for the post-submission presentation to the Buyer. Check the acceptability of this approach with the potential Buyer first!

Sample proposal format

Executive Summary

1. Introduction
2. Your business challenges/our understanding of your business requirements
3. Outline of our solution
4. The system architecture (this can be an annex to the proposal)
5. Our proposed approach and plan
6. Project management, control and progress reporting
7. Our team/project organisation
8. Quality management
9. Risk management
10. Assumptions and dependencies

11.   Costs

Annexes, as appropriate. For example:

> Statement of compliance
> Vendor financial results
> Terms & conditions
> Product documentation
> Detailed schedules of deliverables, plans and design documents
> CVs of key members of the project team
> Reference clients/systems

A word or two on each section of the proposal

1. Introduction

Include a brief background to the proposal, a 'thank you' for the opportunity to propose and a very short explanation of the structure of the document. That's all. There's no 'selling' to be done here.

2. Your business challenges/our understanding of your business requirements

Demonstrate that you understand the Buyer's marketplace, the competitive pressures and business challenges they face and their objectives for the project. Replay the Vendor selection criteria and particular 'hot buttons' which you have elicited from the Buyer during the shaping and refining of your solution. There's no 'selling' to be done here. Concentrate on the Buyer, not on yourself or your solution.

3. Outline of our solution

The proposal may be read by many individuals. They won't all be technically literate, so don't use any jargon at all in this section. They won't all be familiar with the requirements either. This section should set out the broad 'shape' of your solution. By the time they have finished reading this section they must have a clear appreciation of what you are offering and why. Include:

- the strategy or rationale underpinning your solution;
- a diagram of the building blocks of the system;
- the key deliverables;
- how you propose to structure the project into phases and activities, and why;
- the timescales, presented in a very high-level plan;
- any options;
- the Buyer's role and responsibility in the project;
- why this solution is optimal for the Buyer.

There's no heavy 'selling' to be done here. The solution, which has been developed to match the Buyer's needs, will sell itself.

4. The system architecture (this can be an annex to the proposal)

Describe the architecture and why it was selected. Describe how it supports the Buyer's business requirements and all benefits which accrue to the Buyer. Describe each building block of the system, covering key features or strengths, the resulting benefits to the Buyer and all 'uniques' of your architecture. This is a 'selling' section but don't be heavy-handed.

5. Our proposed approach and plan

Describe your approach to requirements clarification, design, development, integration, testing, acceptance, implementation and support. Include a short description of the methods, standards and tools you will use. Set out the key deliverables of the project, by phase, and the activities required to create them. Present a plan showing these, together with milestones, key review points, internal dependencies between activities and external dependencies on the Buyer and third parties. Describe why you have taken this approach – for example, to minimise risk or provide early business benefit.

6. Project management, control and progress reporting

Describe how the project will be managed. Mention a specific project management method by all means, but make it clear that there is more to successful project management than the deployment of a method. The Buyer will rightly be more interested in the track record of your project manager than in the use of a particular project management method. Set out what will be required from the Buyer in terms of people, skills, resources and time. Mention the importance of scope and change management and the processes which will be used.

7. Our team/project organisation

Describe your team structure, the Buyer's team structure and the several interfaces between them. Introduce the key members of your team and why they are well suited to their assigned roles.

8. Quality management

Describe your quality objectives for the project. Using an extract from the quality plan, describe how quality will be controlled during design and development, and how quality assurance will be provided. This needs to be project-specific. Finally, state the level of quality accreditation that the Vendor organisation holds.

9. Risk management

Describe how risks will be assessed and managed during the project and set out the current content of your risk register. Show individual risks, their likelihood, their impact, containment actions being taken currently, and mitigation actions to be taken in the future if the risks materialise.

10. Assumptions and dependencies

List the commercial, technical, project and other assumptions which you have used in order to scope, size and cost the project. List all dependencies on the Buyer, third parties, and external products or events.

11. Costs (not 'your investment')

Present cost information clearly so that the Buyer does not have to undertake a set of calculations to arrive at the total price. Be clear about which costs are fixed and which costs are budgetary estimates. Be clear about fixed costs which are tied to an inflation index. Be clear about T&M rates, which might vary when Vendor fee rates change or when staff are promoted to a higher grade. Make a clear statement about expenses, giving an estimate if possible.

The statement of compliance

Many Buyers require a Statement of Compliance to simplify the task of evaluating the proposals of competing Vendors. This can be a simple matrix showing, for each essential/mandatory, highly-desirable and desirable requirement whether a Vendor's solution is fully compliant (FC), partially compliant (PC) or non-compliant (NC). However, it tends to be a more wordy section, as Buyers generally want to see some tangible evidence of compliance. They need to see, for each requirement, a statement showing *how* the Vendor's solution meets the requirement.

From experience of undertaking proposal evaluations, I can tell you that, even with this descriptive text, it is very difficult to establish the true level of compliance a Vendor's solution has to any or all of the requirements. And in reality, the statement of compliance is seldom the deciding factor in Vendor selection. However, the Statement of Compliance has to be completed. Here are a few hints and tips:

- above all else, your statements must be honest and truthful;
- you do need to demonstrate a high degree of compliance;
- presentation is the key;
- if you are wholly non-compliant with both the letter and the spirit of a requirement, your solution simply does not support the requirement and you are unable or unprepared to offer what is required, then give a response of NC. Note that some requirements will relate to contractual matters and NC will not be an unexpected response. If, in your view, the requirement is non-essential to the Buyer's outcomes for the project, or can be achieved in a different manner,

then say so. Of course, if it is a mandatory requirement, you need to establish with the Buyer whether an NC response, even when coupled with your alternative approach, will cause your proposal to be discarded;

• If you are NC with the letter of a requirement but your solution supports the spirit of the requirement such that your solution provides a usable level of support for the business, then:

FC – Our solution supports the underlying business requirement as follows …	is better than …	NC – Our solution does not support this specific requirement but does provide an equivalent function by means of …

Do's and don'ts of proposal writing

Do!	*Don't!*
• make the proposal Buyer-focused and business-focused,	• focus primarily on your solution and how great you are!,
• thank the Buyer for the work they have put in to help you develop the best solution you can,	• criticise the Buyer's requirements,
	• be heavy-handed in your 'selling',
• follow the Buyer's proposal format if one is provided,	• make the proposal longer than it needs to be,
• make the proposal personal. Use 'you' and 'we' rather than <buyername> and <vendorname>,	• pad out a proposal with product brochures or white papers,
• write in a friendly, conversational, positive, persuasive, crisp, clear and business-like style,	• use general-purpose 'boilerplate' with the exception of standard material covering such things as Vendor financial results. It is very hard to decide what is relevant and often quicker to write an incisive paragraph or two from scratch. Boilerplate is a world-class material for constructing boilers; it is *not* a good material for constructing proposals,
• ensure that your proposal is logically sequenced, starts with an overview and progressively presents more detail,	
• describe the benefit to the Buyer of every feature list you include – to avoid the 'so what?' syndrome,	• disclose your estimating or risk contingency. The Buyer will consider it negotiable,
	• use jargon. If you have to, define what it means,
• intersperse text with diagrams,	• use clip art. It adds little value and can irritate,
• allocate an editor to ensure that the proposal flows well and is consistent in style,	• denigrate or discredit the opposition.

- hold a 'red team' review to read the whole proposal through from the Buyer's perspective,
- highlight features of your solution which are of substantial business benefit to the Buyer and which other Vendors cannot offer,
- let the Buyer know how much you value their business.

The Executive Summary

The importance of the Executive Summary is probably overstated, but it is worth doing well. It is the section of the proposal viewed by the Vendor's sales executive as their responsibility and the place to 'sell'. Well, it *is* a place to 'sell', but it's by no means the only place; the whole proposal speaks volumes about the quality of your organisation, your solution and your people. Unfortunately, not all sales executives have the gift of writing, and a poorly written Executive Summary gives a very negative initial impression to the potential Buyer. The Vendor business manager who will own the profit & loss (P&L) for the project must ensure that the best person for the job writes the Executive Summary. That may not be the sales executive. The person assigned as editor for the whole proposal should also edit the Executive Summary, both to ensure consistency of style and achieve accuracy of content.

Equally importantly, the 'sell' in the Executive Summary has to be subtle and effective. Like the proposal itself, the Executive Summary must be focused on the Buyer, their business requirements, and how your solution meets the Buyer's objectives for the project. It must demonstrate business understanding by the Vendor, and business benefit to the Buyer. It must portray professionalism of approach, a low risk solution, and how much you want the business and are excited by the project.

As a consultant acting for clients over many years, I have read many proposals and many executive summaries. I continue to be amazed at how many executive summaries major on how big the Vendor's company is, how they dominate their marketplace, and how their products are better than those of every other Vendor. This is not an effective 'sell'. It comes across as arrogance.

Here is an example of an Executive Summary. See if you agree with me that it's a good one! I've included the text of the Executive Summary and some notes to illustrate what is likely to be going on inside the head of the executive reading it.

Introduction

Fulcrum Digital Archiving Incorporated (FDAI) would like to thank the Washington National Library of Commerce (WNLC) for the opportunity to bid to become your technology and services partner for the design, integration and commissioning of a Digital Archive System.

They're thanking me for the opportunity to bid.

Our team would like to thank your staff at all levels for their full co-operation and for their substantial investment of time. This has enabled us to fully understand your business requirements and explore alternative solutions and implementation approaches.

They're thanking all my folks for their time and effort.

This close co-operation between our teams has been outstandingly productive and has prepared a firm foundation for future partnership.

We've worked well together – a good omen for the future.

This proposal sets out in detail our proposed architecture for the system (Section 3), our proposals for supporting the system in live operation (Section 4), and our plans and approach to project management (Sections 6 and 7).

This is the shape of their proposal.

The proposal is necessarily very detailed and technically complex. Therefore, in this Executive Summary we provide an overview and rationale for the approach we have taken.

They're going to explain the rationale for their approach.

They sound friendly!

Your business challenges

Mankind has literally thousands of years of experience of the storage and stewardship of manuscripts, books and other hard-copy documents. In contrast, information has been available in digital form for less than two generations and it is only since IBM invented the personal computer in 1982 that the generation, storage and exchange of digital information has become pervasive.

What we are doing is relatively new – there's not much experience to call upon.

Technology is changing at a vast pace. Many of us have learned to use three or four different word

Technology is changing fast (tell me about it!).

processing systems during our careers. Some of us have 5¼" floppy discs stored away containing word processing documents and spreadsheets which will never be retrieved and used again, as the programs do not run on modern PCs. This is a microcosm of the challenge you face as you prepare to become long-term custodians of the nation's digital assets.

Long-term custody of national digital assets will be challenging.

Many of the challenges are technical:

- the very long-term storage of digital information;
- finding robust solutions to the application, operating system and hardware dependencies of digital information;
- ensuring that the encoding and indexing structures used from Day 1 will be capable of migrating to new generations of hardware and software platforms – potentially many times;
- providing scalability in an environment where accurate prediction of future volumes is simply not possible.

Challenge #1 – Yeah

Challenge #2 – Yeah

Challenge #3 – Yeah

Challenge #4 – Yeah. OK, they understand the issues, but what does all this mean to me?

We believe that these challenges demand that you select a supplier which is an established, specialist company and which is likely to be still trading in 10, 20 and 50 years' time.

Ah! It means that I need to choose the company very carefully.

We believe that FDAI is that company.

FDAI perhaps!

Our credentials as a technology and services partner

FDAI is committed to providing technology, solutions and services to support the management of collections in the world's leading libraries, museums and archives. We have been in the forefront of digital archive technology since 1993. Our commercial archive customers include the California State Patent Bureau, the French National Library of Commerce, the UK National Records Office and the Berlin Library of Mankind.

They specialise in digital archiving. They've been in the market for a long time. They've got some high-profile clients.

We are continuing to develop our digital archive software platforms. Over the same period, the FDAI product set has been ported to every major version of the UNIX operating system. We have the most comprehensive range of tools available to enable worldwide, pay-per-view web access to our clients' collections.

They invest in the product.
They support open platforms.

They've got good tools to build just what I need.

What this means to yourselves is that we have a track record in digital archive systems which we believe no other supplier can match. We also have all the proven building blocks we need to design and build a state-of-the-art digital archive system for WNLC, within your target timescale and with a minimum of bespoke development.

So what? What's the benefit to me?

Reduced risk!
Yes, that's important!

Our proposed solution for the digital archive system

WHAT they are proposing

Section 3 contains a full and necessarily quite technical description of our proposed architecture for your system. Underpinning the architecture are the following, simple design principles:

These are the principles on which their solution is based.

- Standard, open products should be used wherever possible;
- 'bespoke' coding should be minimised;
- experience and solutions from other, successful digital archive solutions and projects should be reused;
- the architecture should conform to the OAIS model, exploit the CORBA standard, and feature a browser-based user interface;
- the architecture should be modular and flexible, to facilitate migration to next generation hardware in due time, to support new object types and to interface to future WNLC systems;
- the design must be extraordinarily scalable;
- data integrity must be guaranteed, with comprehensive logging of every system and user activity.

Principle #1 – openness

Principle #2 – quick?
Principle #3 – cheap?

Principle #4 – ?!@*?

Principle #5 – future-proof

Principle #6 – a safe bet
Principle #7 – the data is safe too. Good principles, but so what? What's the benefit to me?

These principles have been chosen to ensure a rapid, low-risk implementation of the WNLC system with no compromise whatsoever of long-term durability and robustness.

Ah! Rapid delivery, low risk!

Our Proposed Approach to Implementation

HOW they will deliver

High-level requirements for the system exist and our two teams have worked together very productively to gain a joint appreciation of the business processes to be supported.

However, there *is* a need for the requirements to be clarified and captured formally, together with 'non-functional' requirements – such as performance, availability and scalability – in a requirements baseline. In order to achieve this, we propose an initial, fixed-price design phase of just under four months.

Requirements clarification and design phase.

During this phase, our two teams will work together, predominantly in requirements and design workshops, to document and agree this requirements baseline. This will be achieved about eight weeks into the study. Our team will then prepare the detailed design for the system, the acceptance test strategy, and the detailed plans and fixed-price for the Build and Delivery phase.

Workshops.

The Build and Delivery phase will be split into two main sub-projects:

Build phase.

- the customisation of ingest;
- the customisation of remaining functions and interfaces.

So what? What's the benefit to me?

This will give early proving of the architecture and early visibility of function. This approach offers important advantages over what has become known as a 'big bang, full-scope development' in which a supplier gives a fixed price for requirements definition, design, development and implementation of a system. Such an approach is often successful in delivering a system the client does not want at a

Ah! Early proof of concept!

price they can't afford. We believe that the phased approach offers scope for:

- rigorous definition of requirements up front;
- the ability for our teams to prioritise requirements in such a way that the initial 'go live' system can be tailored to meet your budget;
- lower risk for us, which means a lower price for you.

These guys tell it like it is. I could work with these guys!

Our team

WHO will deliver our project

Jay Henshaw is our client executive responsible for the FDAI/WNLC relationship. Jay is our nominated point of contact for commercial issues prior to contract.

Carl Collins Jnr will act as our project manager, responsible for the project in delivery. Carl has extensive experience of managing systems integration programmes for commercial and public sector clients. He managed the delivery of the California State Patent Bureau system to time and budget.

A Vendor project manager with a proven track record – that's a plus!

The Benefits of FDAI's Proposal

Go on then. Tell Me.

We offer you the following important benefits:

- A 'heavyweight' technology partner, committed to your marketplace and likely to be able to support your business into the next century and beyond.
- A track record in providing technology, solutions and services to support the management of collections in the world's leading archives, libraries and museums.
- A low-risk solution, based on advanced yet proven products, featuring a minimum of custom development.
- Compliance with your timescale imperatives.
- A low-risk, two-phase implementation approach which allows our two teams to

Benefit #1 – Muscle

Benefit #2 – Pedigree

Benefit #3 – Low Risk

Benefit #4 – Timeliness
Benefit #5 – Control

work together to define a system which can
be built to a budget.

- An experienced and committed team.

Benefit #6 – Passion
Good. What's the
punchline?

We believe that these advantages will actively
support you in your mission to be the leading
national library of commerce in the world, for
both hard-copy and electronic collections,
deliverable to a global audience.

FDAI will help me
achieve my Mission!

We very much look forward to working with
you on this exciting project.

Good summary, Dick!
FDAI sounds like a
strong contender!

Dick F Johnson
Chief Executive Officer – Fulcrum Digital Archiving Inc.

The presentation

If you reach the shortlist, you will probably be invited to give a formal presentation to a selection panel. This is often the final hurdle. If your solution and proposal are good, the Buyer will be expecting your presentation to be good also. I
am not going to cover presentation skills in this book in any detail, but some Do's
and Don'ts are given below.

Do's and don'ts of presentations

Do!	*Don't!*
• ask the Buyer several days beforehand how long you have for the presentation, excluding questions;	• just turn up and busk with no visual aids. You are at least 20 per cent more likely to achieve your out- comes with good visual aids;
• define measurable outcomes and the impression you wish to make;	• use purely textual material. It's boring; use a mix of bullet points and diagrams;
• break your presentation into a number of mini-presentations by key members of your team. This maintains the interest of the audience;	• use overly 'busy' or detailed foils; the audience will be reading ahead and will miss what you are saying;

- define 1–2 'must remember messages' for each mini-presentation;
- practise the whole presentation at least twice, in front of a live audience of Vendor staff, and act on the feedback you receive;
- take hard copy back-up foils in case the overhead projector or your Notebook PC fails;
- go around the Buyer's team before you present, shaking hands;
- let your project manager take the lead role in the presentation and in chairing your team during the question and answer session;
- maintain eye contact and smile;
- act confident, even if you are not;
- encourage questions and encourage interaction;
- conclude by summarising the 'must remember messages'.

- use too many foils; you will rush them and your presentation will lose its impact;
- read the foils; the audience can do this faster than you can; use the foils to reinforce your verbal message;
- read from detailed notes; practise until you can deliver the presentation with only key 'prompts' on a few cards to jog your memory;
- hand out copies of the foils until after the presentation; the audience will flick through them and miss some of the 'must remember messages'.

Negotiating the deal

I am not going to cover negotiation in this book as there are a number of excellent texts on this subject. See the references section at the end of this chapter.

The de-brief

Always ask for a de-brief, whether you win or lose. The purpose is to gather information on what you did well and what you did less well compared with the competition. You need this information in order to improve your qualification, solutioning and bidding skills.

Arrange for a 30-minute de-brief, 2–3 weeks after the decision has been announced so that everyone's emotions have settled down. Ask open questions, take notes, and prepare a report for your business manager and the marketing/sales team. Maintain the relationship with the Buyer, even if you lose.

Postscript to Part 2

Part 2 of this book has been about reducing the risk of a troubled project during the planning or bid phase. In many ways, it's the most important part of this book. Reducing risk at the bid stage will result in increased sales, more profitable business and fewer problems to manage during project delivery.

Part 2 is less about 'selling' than it is about engagement with the potential Buyer. Sometimes, potential Buyers do not want to engage with Vendors. Often, they feel that it is inappropriate or too early in the procurement cycle. Sometimes, they don't see the benefit and feel that they will be subjected to a 'hard sell' from several Vendors. Sometimes they just don't want to make the necessary investment of time. Sometimes you will be unable to persuade the potential Buyer to meet with you. But do try, as engagement of Vendor and Buyer is a powerful recipe for an effective and trouble-free project.

References

1. Jane Hodgson, *Thinking on your feet in negotiations*, Pitman, 1996.
2. Donald & Rebecca Hendon, *How to negotiate world-wide*, Gower, 1989.
3. Roger Fisher & William Ury, *Getting to Yes*, Business Books Limited, 1991.
4. Robert B Cialdini, *Influence*, Longman, 1992.
5. Genie Z Laborde, *Influencing with Integrity*, Syntony Publishing, 1984.
6. Dan S Bagley III & Edward J Reese, *Beyond Selling*, Meta Publications, 1988.
7. Stephen R Covey, *The Seven Habits of Highly Effective People*, Simon & Schuster, 1992.

Part 3

REVIEWING TROUBLED PROJECTS IN DELIVERY

Chapter 12

PROJECT DELIVERY REVIEWS

I once took over the management of a programme containing two application development projects. One was the development of an accounting package, the other the development of a spare parts sales system. When I joined the project I initiated a review of both projects, covering all the 'focus areas' introduced later in this chapter. The review included the technical architecture and the way in which it had been implemented. I discovered that the spare parts sales system had some unusual features.

Record locking had not been fully implemented and it was possible for two operators to allocate the same instance of a part to two different customers. Also, transaction management had not been implemented at all, which meant that there was no way of rolling back an incomplete transaction that had failed. It also meant that, in the event of a serious failure of the system, all sales transactions completed since the previous dump of the database had to be re-entered manually before normal customer service could be resumed. It was not possible to recover automatically to the point of failure using the last dump of the database and the day's transaction log file.

Most project teams are under pressure. No matter how talented the team members are, they can overlook important business or technical aspects of the software they are developing or integrating. One of the main benefits of project delivery reviews is that external and impartial reviewers can often bring such issues to light.

Introduction to Part 3

Part 3 of this book covers how to plan and conduct project delivery reviews during the system design and system development stages of the project life cycle. My assumption is that the delivery reviews are undertaken by an IT services Vendor and that the project is being run for an external Buyer. However, exactly the same principles apply in the case of a project being run by an IS/IT unit within any organisation for an in-house customer.

Chapter 12 covers the objectives of delivery reviews and lists a number of 'focus areas' for these reviews. The focus areas cover all the important aspects of projects in delivery and are based on substantial experience. I have found the approach described to be very effective at uncovering project issues and their root causes.

Chapter 13 sets out the Terms of Reference for two types of project delivery review and advises how to determine which depth of review is appropriate.

Chapter 14 covers the conduct of the review and the preparation of the report or presentation.

Chapters 15–19 cover, for each review focus area, the key questions which need answering during the review, together with some common issues for which reviewers should be on the look out. A detailed list of actual questions is not given as:

- most reviewers will be experienced project managers, technical architects, consultants or Quality Assurance (QA) professionals, who do not need this level of guidance;
- the use of standard checklists and questionnaires in reviews is not as effective as asking a few open questions about a focus area, listening carefully to the answers, and then pursuing the lines of inquiry which are suggested by the answers.

I refer to a number of roles in this part of the book. As different IT services organisations use different job titles, I have described the roles in Table 12.1, below. One individual may have more than one role.

The objectives of delivery reviews

The example given at the beginning of this chapter illustrates the need for delivery reviews. It is very hard for those engaged at the work-face of a project to see the wood for the trees. An independent and informed opinion on the health of a project from outside the project team is essential.

In addition to regular, formal progress meetings with the Buyer, it is normal for most professional services organisations to hold regular, internal progress reviews. These might be fortnightly or monthly. They provide an opportunity for the production manager to be briefed by the project manager. These regular reviews typically include a review of progress against the plan, a summary of what has been achieved since the previous review, the outlook for the period up to the next review, discussion of issues and risks, and the state of the project's financials.

The delivery reviews described in Part 3 of this book do not replace these internal progress reviews; rather, they complement them. They are more in-depth reviews than the regular progress reviews and occur less frequently, perhaps every six months for a project which is performing well and every three months for a project which is troubled. The delivery reviews might be the responsibility of the QA department or they might be carried out by the owning business using senior project management or technical staff.

The objectives of delivery reviews are to:

1. Ensure that projects are well scoped, planned, resourced and equipped with all the management systems required to meet the commitments made to the Buyer at a cost that is within the financial budget signed off by the Business Manager.

Table 12.1 *Description of Roles used in Part 3*

Role	Description
Project Manager (PM)	The project manager of the project to be reviewed. Large projects may be run by a project director or programme manager
Client Manager	The sales executive, principal or partner responsible for ongoing development of the business relationship with the Buyer
Production Manager	The manager in the owning business responsible for the health of the project portfolio, achieved through regular reviews with PMs
Business Manager	The director or executive in the business who owns the profit and loss
Management Accountant	The management accountant or financial controller who is responsible for maintaining accounts for projects in the owning business
Contracts Professional	The professional representing the business on all matters concerning contract terms and conditions
QA Professional	The Quality Assurance professional responsible for reviewing the original bid and for undertaking delivery reviews after contract
Requirements Manager	The market sector specialist, business analyst or subject matter expert responsible for defining/ maintaining the requirements baseline
Technical Architect	The designer or technical design authority responsible for the solution architecture/design baseline
Development Manager	The manager or team leader responsible to the PM for the development, testing and integration of application software
Test Manager	The manager or team leader responsible to either the PM or the development manager for system testing. They may also be responsible for integration testing
Buyer Representative	The PM's opposite number in the Buyer organisation

2. Detect problems early in the life of a project in order to prevent it from becoming troubled, thereby saving substantial sums of money and providing the means to keep the project on track in terms of progress, quality, commercial performance and Buyer satisfaction.

3. Investigate the causes of an already troubled project in order that a 'Turn-around Plan' can be prepared.
4. Review project risks and containment plans.
5. Capture any 'lessons learned' (more accurately, *learning opportunities*) which might avoid similar problems on other projects.

The essentials of a project delivery report

The report must reach the required audience in the Vendor organisation. This includes managers in the branch or vertical market sector of the business owning the project. It also includes managers at a higher level in the business who need sight of project performance and project issues across the whole project portfolio of the business.

To facilitate the tracking of a project's state of health, a 'marking' scheme is helpful. It is appropriate to give ratings for:

- the commercial health of the project compared with the original budget (cost, price and gross profit) signed off at contract award;
- the extent to which the project is meeting its plans;
- the quality of work being produced;
- the level of Buyer satisfaction.

The report must identify a short set of key findings. If the quality of the work being produced is excellent, the report must say so; it is dispiriting to a project team when a review team's focus is purely on what is bad or what can be improved. The report must also set out clearly any underlying troubled project root causes.

The report must contain clear, practical and achievable recommendations, making it clear who is responsible for undertaking them and the time-scale allowed for their completion. Brevity is good. Concentrate on the key issues and what must be done to address them. Here is a suggested structure for the report:

- introduction (project name, review date, names of reviewers, distribution etc);
- state of health of the project;
- key findings;
- recommendations;
- project financials;
- detailed findings by focus area;
- status of recommended actions from previous reviews.

Qualities required in a project delivery reviewer

A project delivery reviewer or trouble-shooter requires:

- the ability to command the respect of the project manager and the team. This requires the reviewer to have solid experience of running projects at senior level;
- the confidence and presence to let the project manager know immediately that here is someone who punches with equal or greater weight than themselves;
- the ability to build rapport and put the project manager and the team at ease;
- an open mind, with an absence of preconceptions and pet theories about what is likely to be wrong with the project;
- the ability to ask probing questions;
- good secretarial support, or (preferably) excellent keyboard skills;
- above all, good listening skills.

You may be asked to undertake a project delivery review by yourself. For large projects, and particularly for in-depth trouble-shooting reviews, support is needed. In these cases, define the skills you need to complement your own. The type of skill to use may depend on where the project is in its life cycle. You are unlikely to need a team of more than three reviewers.

The focus areas of a delivery review are quite wide-ranging; you will need to form a team with members who can conduct meaningful conversations on these. Those who should be able to provide valuable contributions include experienced:

- project managers;
- technical architects, particularly if the project is technically complex;
- software development managers or team leaders;
- testing team leaders;
- business sector specialists or subject matter experts.

Review focus areas

Table 12.2 lists the focus areas for a project delivery review and shows in which chapter of this book they are covered.

The review report and/or presentation should include a summary of the findings under each of these focus areas. It provides a structured overview of the state of health of the project and an excellent means of tracking progress as a project improves or deteriorates from one review to the next.

Other types of project review

It is advisable for both Buyer and Vendor to review projects at all stages of the project life cycle, as shown in Table 12.3.

During the Project Conception stage, the main responsibility for project reviews must rest with the Buyer. The principal focus of reviews at this stage is to ensure that the business case is realistic and that the overall shape of the project is such as to minimise risk – for example, by breaking the project into phases and tackling one phase at a time. I remember the time when business cases for UK

Table 12.2   *Focus Areas for a Project Delivery Review*

Chapter	Focus Areas
15	Clarity of the requirements baseline
	Quality/completeness of the architecture and design
16	Stability and realism of the project plan and resource estimates
	Progress against plan
17	Development approach
	Integration and testing strategy
	Quality plan compliance
	Project initiation document compliance
18	Project structure
	Clarity of project roles and responsibilities
	Staff motivation and morale
19	Project management system • project planning • project resourcing • project information management • progress monitoring and control • financial monitoring and control (including financial accounting, and billing and credit control) • contract management (including change control/and subcontract management) • buyer relationship management • issue management • risk management • quality of monthly reporting

Table 12.3   *Project Review Responsibility, by Project Stage*

Project Stage	Reviews	
	Buyer	Vendor
Project Conception	Essential	–
Project Initiation/Mobilisation	Essential	Essential
System Design	Valuable	Essential
System Development	Essential	Essential
System Implementation	Essential	Valuable
System Operation, Benefit Delivery, Stewardship and Disposal	Essential	Valuable

Government IT projects were constructed principally by calculating the number of civil servants that the new system would release from their posts. Little consideration was given to the value of improved customer service. The same approach would be taken when the time came to replace the system – still more posts were required to be saved. I have often mused that the logical outcome of this strategy would be, eventually, to have no civil servants at all. Thankfully, the focus in government has changed radically to one of providing better, faster service and more service offerings.

During the Project Initiation/Mobilisation stage, reviews by the Buyer will concentrate on the budget, the proposals/tenders from vendors and on the selection of the successful supplier. Reviews by the Vendor will focus upon the bid/no bid decision and reviews of the solution, proposal and pricing.

In the System Design and System Development stages, the Vendor has a clear need to manage progress to the plan and budget. Delivery reviews play an important role in keeping Vendor and Buyer senior management informed of project progress and issues. Early reviews will focus on ensuring that the solution will meet the needs of the Buyer and that project start-up has been undertaken successfully, with required management systems and procedures in place. Often, the Buyer relaxes somewhat during these stages and waits for the Vendor to deliver against the contract. This is a missed opportunity; if the Buyer stays close to the project, they can detect Vendor problems early and keep Buyer senior management informed. The Buyer must also be prepared to adjust the scope or the timescale (and, by implication, the contract) in order to retain control over the destiny of the project. The Buyer must also be vigilant for signs that the business case is coming under threat. If the project becomes seriously troubled, the Buyer must work with the Vendor to establish whether there is a viable turnaround strategy, as detailed in Part 4 of this book. If turnaround is not possible, the Buyer must have the courage to terminate the project rather than pouring good money after bad until the project fails.

During the System Implementation stage, the onus is on both parties to review progress, even in cases where the Buyer is responsible for implementation. It does the Vendor no credit when a system they have designed and built fails to deliver looked-for business benefit. And Vendor participation in project reviews at this stage, even when their contract with the Buyer is complete, provides scope to maximise the success of the project and undertake on-going business development.

During the System Operation, Benefit Delivery, Stewardship and Disposal stage, the principal responsibility for project review lies with the Buyer. Once again, there are tremendous advantages to be gained by the Vendor in staying close to the project and being part of ongoing reviews of benefit delivery and performance.

Summary

The key objective of project delivery reviews is to provide ongoing project health assessment, enabling problems to be detected early, before the project becomes troubled. Clear and crisp findings and recommendations are required.

Reviewers must be experienced, senior people who are independent of, and respected by, the project team.

Reports must be visible to senior management in the Vendor organisation.

A set of 'focus areas' has been presented which will enable you to detect the majority of the root causes of troubled projects during the system design and system development life cycle stages.

Exercises

1. Prepare a cross-reference table mapping the roles defined in Table 12.1 with those in your own organisation. Are there any missing roles in your organisation?

Chapter 13

REVIEW PLANNING AND PREPARATION

Good planning and preparation for a project delivery review is essential because:

- if you don't tailor the review to the project you risk either wasting the time of the project team or failing to uncover issues/troubled project root causes,
- if you don't understand the issues of concern to the people commissioning the review, you are not focusing on the needs of your customer,
- if you don't agree the Terms of Reference with the project manager, you won't be in command of the agenda during the review,
- if you don't bring yourself sufficiently 'up to speed' by reading certain documentation, you won't earn the respect of the team,
- you will probably need to arrange for some specialist help. This takes time to achieve as the best people are always busy.

Determining the depth of the review

You will need to exercise professional judgement regarding the breadth and depth of a project delivery review. Your decision will depend on where the project is in its life cycle, how large the project is, and the extent to which it is troubled. Intuitively, high-value projects and projects which are troubled require more thorough review than others. Also, projects in start-up probably require more attention than when they are ticking over in delivery and in a good state of health.

Pursuing the medical metaphor, there are two categories of project delivery reviews:

- a project health check;
- an in-depth project investigation (or trouble-shooting review).

The project health check

This type of project delivery review is typically conducted every six months for a project in 'good health' and more regularly for a project which is troubled. It requires you to spend one or two days on site and a further day to finalise the report. The review features the full range of focus areas but the depth of investigation of focus areas is varied to investigate fully only those areas where issues are apparent.

Exactly as for the in-depth project investigation, and perhaps even more important as you will spend less time on site, you must do your homework thoroughly before attending on-site for the review. This is covered later in this chapter.

The review starts with an interview with the project manager. This is followed by a number of one-on-one interviews, including a discussion or telephone call with the Buyer representative. The report is drafted and reviewed with the project manager. Any errors of fact are corrected and other small changes are made to satisfy the project manager, provided they do not dilute the findings and recommendations. A short presentation of the report to the management team of the project may be given and, following any minor adjustments which might be appropriate, the report is then distributed.

The total effort required on your part is of the order of four days in total. More importantly, the impact on the project is low as you are conducting one-on-one interviews most of the time.

The in-depth project investigation or trouble-shooting review

This type of project delivery review is needed when:

- a troubled project has not responded positively to the recommendations of regular project health check delivery reviews;
- project health is deteriorating;
- the management of the owning business requires an independent, expert opinion in addition to the ongoing project health check delivery reviews;
- a crisis has occurred which calls the future of the project into question and the business needs to consider its options.

This type of project delivery review features the full range of focus areas and a full depth of investigation of all focus areas. For this type of review, you need to deploy a small team of 3–4, including yourself. Your team will need at least half a day to complete its homework before the review and will then spend 3–4 days on site. The investment required by the project manager and the team is much higher than for a health check review, but the return on this investment can be enormous if the project turns the corner as the result of following your recommendations.

The review begins with a workshop with the project manager and their management team, during which the project team presents to your review team. This may take half a day or even a whole day, given that there will be discussion of each topic. Topics covered in the presentation would typically include:

- the Buyer's business requirements;
- the history of the project;
- the contract;
- the project organisation;

- the technical architecture/design or solution;
- the development approach and life cycle;
- the original baseline estimates and plans;
- current plans and progress against them;
- the financials;
- the relationship with the Buyer organisation;
- a summary of issues and risks.

Your review team then sets out an interview schedule and, over 2–3 days, conducts a series of one-on-one or two-on-one interviews to investigate focus areas in depth. A Buyer representative is interviewed. You then gather your team to pull the information together, extract findings, brainstorm recommendations, and assemble the bones of the report/presentation.

Most projects which have contributed this level of time and energy to the review expect the review team to give a presentation of their findings, ahead of the release of the formal report.

You leave the site with a set of comments from the project team and, over the next 1–2 days, you finalise the formal report. If the project is sufficiently troubled for a turnaround strategy and plan to be required, this work would be undertaken as a subsequent exercise, fully engaging the Vendor and Buyer project teams. This activity is described in Part 4 of this book.

Setting expectations – the terms of reference

About six weeks before a project delivery review is due, speak with the production manager in the owning business and make a note of any particular issues or concerns they have. Review the latest internal and external monthly progress reports. The internal report should show the financial performance of the project against the budget signed off at project start. Review the findings and recommendations of any previous reviews. Speak to the project manager to discover how they believe the project is progressing. Then you are in a position to determine the type of review that is appropriate. Unless project health is deteriorating, a project health check review is likely to be required.

If you operate as a trouble-shooter, you will have been called in to look at a particular troubled project. All of the above advice still applies.

About four weeks before the review, contact the project manager to:

- inform them of the type of review (project health check or trouble-shooting review) you are going to undertake;
- discuss the Terms of Reference so that they can brief their team;
- ask them to provide project organisation charts, telephone lists, copies of recent monthly reports, copies of the contract and any other documentation you feel it appropriate to study ahead of the review;
- book the review in their diaries and ask them to confirm that all key members of the project team will be available;

- ideally, plan key interviews in advance;
- ask them to advise the Buyer representative that you will be calling to arrange a time for a meeting or telephone call;
- in the case of a trouble-shooting review, outline the topics you would like them to cover in the initial workshop;
- ask them to arrange accommodation (ideally a conference room) for use by the team for the duration of the review.

The Terms of Reference for a project health check review are shown in Table 13.1. Those for a trouble-shooting review are shown in Table 13.2.

Doing your homework

If you are planning to conduct a project health check review of a project which is unfamiliar, ensure that you read enough documentation ahead of the review to give you a good feel for the nature of the project. This would typically include the Buyer's requirements specification, the proposal and the contract.

Setting the ground rules and responsibilities

Whatever type of review you are undertaking, I suggest the following ground rules for you and your team:

- You are not policemen or judges; your job is to add value and provide recommendations to the project and the business, which, if followed, will materially improve the state of health of the project.
- You should call out good points as well as weaknesses.
- You need to keep an open mind and not pre-judge issues or their solution using 'pet theories'.
- Focus on the big issues.
- Be sure of your findings and able to defend them if challenged. All findings must be based on factual evidence and cross-checked with several members of the project team.
- You need to ask many insightful questions (open questions mainly) and do a great deal of listening.
- Don't use long checklists of standard questions. You may fail to pick up on a vital cue if you are thinking about the next question to ask.
- Nothing you hear should be directly attributed to an individual.
- Ask everyone about project issues and risks, and team morale.
- Record the name and role of everyone you speak with.
- Make a note of all documentation you see.
- Be strong in your recommendations.

Table 13.1   *Terms of Reference for a Project Health Check Review*

Objectives:
- to determine whether the project is well scoped, planned, resourced and equipped with all the management systems required to meet commitments made to the Buyer and to deliver within the financial budget signed off by the Vendor;
- to assess the overall health of the project;
- to review project risks and containment plans;
- to present findings;
- to make recommendations to address the issues highlighted in the findings;
- to capture 'lessons learned'.

Approach:
- the review team reads key project documentation ahead of the review;
- reviewers interview project staff, covering all aspects of the project;
- a report is prepared and distributed;
- actions are followed up.

Project documentation required to be available for review if requested:
- request for proposal (RFP)/invitation to tender (ITT)/statement of requirements (SOR);
- proposals;
- contracts, side letters, letters of intent, authorisation to proceed letters, contract variations;
- previous review reports;
- correspondence files;
- original project budget (costs, price to Buyer and gross profit);
- project definition report or project initiation document;
- functional specification;
- system and program design documentation;
- integration and test strategy and plans;
- acceptance test criteria/acceptance test specification/acceptance test plan;
- original and current resource estimates;
- original (baseline) plans;
- current plans, showing planned and actual activities, milestones, deliverables and major internal and external dependencies;
- project quality plan;
- project safety plan;
- project standards (documentation, coding, testing, configuration management etc);
- change request log;
- issue/problem log(s);
- risk log/management plan;
- progress reports (internal and external);
- project accounts showing budgeted and actual costs to date and predicted costs to complete;
- billing and credit control information;
- project organisation chart and telephone list.

Table 13.2   *Terms of Reference for a Trouble-shooting Review*

Objectives:
- to thoroughly investigate the state of health of the project;
- to review project risks and containment plans;
- to present findings covering issues and their root causes;
- to make recommendations to address the issues;
- to capture 'lessons learned'.

Approach:
- the review team reads key project documentation ahead of the review;
- the project team presents to the review team on the first day, covering all aspects of the project;
- reviewers interview project staff, covering all aspects of the project;
- a report/presentation is prepared;
- the review team may advise of the need for a subsequent 'turnaround' strategy/planning session;
- actions are followed up.

Project documentation required to be available for review:
- request for proposal (RFP)/invitation to tender (ITT)/statement of requirements (SOR);
- proposals;
- contracts, side letters, letters of intent, authorisation to proceed letters, contract variations;
- previous review reports;
- correspondence files;
- original project budget (costs, price to Buyer and gross profit);
- project definition report or project initiation document;
- functional specification;
- system and program design documentation;
- integration and test strategy and plans;
- acceptance test criteria/acceptance test specification/acceptance test plan;
- original and current resource estimates;
- original (baseline) plans;
- current plans, showing planned and actual activities, milestones, deliverables and major internal and external dependencies;
- project quality plan;
- project safety plan;
- project standards (documentation, coding, testing, configuration management etc);
- change request log;
- issue/problem log(s);
- risk log/management plan;
- progress reports (internal and external);
- project accounts showing budgeted and actual costs to date and predicted costs to complete;
- billing and credit control information;
- project organisation chart and telephone list.

Summary

Two types of project delivery review have been outlined:

1. The project health check is a routine review which requires you to spend one or two days on site. The review features the full range of focus areas, but the depth of investigation is varied to investigate fully only those where issues are apparent.
2. The trouble-shooting review is needed when a project is in serious difficulty and the business needs to consider its options. The full range of focus areas is investigated in depth. For this type of review, you need the support of a small team. Your team will need at least half a day to complete its homework before the review and will then spend 3–4 days on site.

You need to decide what type of review is appropriate and provide Terms of Reference to the project manager and the team. You are then in charge of the agenda. Sample Terms of Reference have been given.

You and your team need to undertake sufficient 'reading into the project' to avoid wasting the project's time, to establish credibility with the project team, and to help you to identify the focus areas which most need investigation.

You need to remember that you are doing the review to add value. You are not sitting in judgement on the project.

Chapter 14

CONDUCTING THE REVIEW AND PREPARING THE REPORT

Introduction

This chapter presents some hints and tips on how to conduct trouble-shooting reviews and project health check reviews, and how to prepare the review report or presentation as efficiently as possible.

Trouble-shooting reviews

Initial workshop with the project manager and the team

Make sure that the format of the room is appropriately informal – not set out like a parole board, with the review team sitting in judgement on the project team.

Take control of the session by taking the project manager and the project team through the Terms of Reference for the review and the approach you intend to take.

Then sit back and listen to the project team's presentation to the review team. A list of suggested topics for this presentation is given in Chapter 13. Ask plenty of questions to build rapport, to promote discussion and to achieve maximum value from the presentations. Ask for hard copies of all the slides presented by the project team. Find out who the 'experts' are on each topic as an aid to interview planning.

Interview planning

Meet with your review team after the presentation. While you are going to cover all focus areas anyway, it is worth brainstorming the areas where particular focus is required. You then need to prepare an interview schedule. You would typically wish to interview those with the following roles:

- project manager;
- production manager;
- business manager;
- client manager;
- requirements manager;
- technical architect;
- integration manager;
- a cross-section of developers and testers, chosen at random;
- management accountant or business office manager;
- contracts professional;

- development manager;
- test manager;
- quality assurance professional;
- Buyer representative.

Interviews with the business manager, the contracts professional and the Buyer representative might be conducted over the telephone, but face-to-face interviews generate more rapport and more information.

Report skeleton preparation

Before you arrive on the first day of the review, you should have decided whether to present your findings in the form of a report or as a presentation. Reports are to be preferred for project health check reviews as standardised reports provide a clear audit trail of the state of health of the project. A suggested outline structure is given in Chapter 12. For a trouble-shooting review, it might be appropriate simply to provide a presentation of your findings and recommendations to the senior management of the company. Remember that a trouble-shooting review will typically be followed up by a turnaround strategy/planning study which will plan the actions needed to turn around the project. My recommendation is to provide both a presentation and a report for a trouble-shooting review.

Prepare the skeleton of the report and presentation before you arrive on the site.

Conducting the interviews

For most interviews, the subject area will be defined as one or more of the focus areas of the review. Start with some open questions and selectively probe different aspects of the focus area. Ask to see relevant documentation and ask for a copy of any document which you feel you need to study in depth.

If you are a good typist, it is a really effective use of your time to type your notes directly into a Notebook PC. This saves the hassle of having to type up your notes later which is a huge benefit; you know when you go home at night that you have a day's worth of report 'in the bag'. You can also use your Notebook PC to prepare some questions ahead of time, providing space under each question for the answer. Ideally, type text straight into your skeleton report. An alternative approach is to have a colleague typing up the interview while you ask the questions, but this is a far less efficient use of resources.

I can't stress sufficiently just how liberating this 'paper-less' approach can be. I have worked on IS/IT strategy studies for a 'Big 5' management consulting firm. Typically, the study is planned assuming a certain number of interviews per team member per day. As resources are expensive, team members are expected to undertake three or even four interviews per day and type up their notes. This means a working day stretching from around 8 am to very late in the evening. If you fall behind with the typing up of your notes, you are dead in the water. It's not fun.

If your assistants take the same approach, a draft report can be created very rapidly indeed by cutting and pasting. While you won't have to type up manuscript notes, you *will* want to spend some time massaging your typed interview notes into candidate findings under the several focus areas of the report. Your assistants should do the same.

Daily round-up sessions with the review team

At the end of each day, or first thing next morning, get together with your review team to share what each member of the team has found out, and to check whether you have all gained a similar overall impression of the project. Feel free to vary the interview schedule to spend more time on focus areas where you have uncovered serious problems.

Workshop to agree findings and recommendations

Get together with your review team on the afternoon of the penultimate day to pull together your findings, by focus area, and to brainstorm and 'test drive' your recommendations.

Prioritise your findings to identify the 'big hitters' and the root causes behind them. Anticipate challenges from the project team and be ready to support your findings with factual back-up material. If gaps are apparent in the team's coverage of the focus areas, or review team members have different views regarding the findings, you have time on the following day to complete your research and achieve review team consensus on the findings.

Recommendations must be clear, practical, auditable and have an assigned owner. A flipchart is invaluable for this workshop activity. Identify no more than a handful of key recommendations; too many recommendations and your audience will not know which ones to focus on. It is unlikely that you will have sufficient time in a trouble-shooting review to develop a detailed turnaround strategy and plan. What you should do is to:

- present the options to be considered in the turnaround strategy/planning study which should follow;
- set out the objectives, approach, deliverables, participants, timescale and plan for this study.

Presenting back to the project team

If you are presenting to several members of the project team, take the project manager through the slides ahead of the presentation. This is a courtesy and should ensure that the presentation does not turn into a heated debate.

Normal advice regarding presentations applies:

- visual aids do not have to be world-class, but they should be tidy and readable;
- be friendly, confident and professional;

- maintain eye contact with your audience. You will come across with more authority and receive instant feedback on whether your findings and recommendations are being accepted or challenged.

As to structure:

- present the project health assessment up front. If there is bad news to be given, it is best to give it right up front rather than building up to it at the end. In your assessment of project health, cover:
  - the commercial health of the project compared with the original budget (cost, price and gross profit) signed off at contract award,
  - the extent to which the project is meeting its plans,
  - the quality of work products and deliverables being produced,
  - the level of Buyer satisfaction;
- present a clear summary of findings by focus area, highlighting the 'big hitters' and the troubled project root causes which you have detected;
- set out your key recommendations;
- outline the objectives of the turnaround strategy/planning study and describe the process (this is covered in Chapter 20).

The report

If you and your assistants have followed the advice above and typed your notes directly into a report skeleton, the mechanics of putting the report together is simple. Read the whole report through to ensure that it is clear and conveys the right messages. Check any assertions or findings that you are unsure about. If you are still unsure, edit them out. A weak finding or recommendation can be used by a project team which is resistant to the need for change to discredit your entire report. Beware of emotive wording which you might have used in the heat of the review but which adds no value and might cause offence.

Try to complete the report and forward a draft to the project manager for comment within 2–3 working days. If you leave it longer than that, the review becomes history and you have lost the momentum leading up to the turnaround strategy/planning study. Remember that you are seeking comments on matters of fact from the project team, not necessarily concurrence with your findings and recommendations.

Arranging the 'turnaround' strategy/planning study

Meet with the business manager and production manager (and probably the client manager) to brief them on the results of the review and obtain concurrence on the next steps.

Project health check reviews

Much of the guidance given above also applies to project health check reviews.

Spend a couple of hours with the project manager on the morning of the first day to:

- review the objectives, approach and outputs of the review;
- understand and document the background and current status of the project;
- discuss and document the project manager's view of the key issues and risks;
- go briefly through each focus area and capture the project manager's view of the current status;
- understand the project organisation, and obtain a telephone list;
- ask them who they think you should talk to, but use the list in this chapter as a starter. Obtain the telephone number of the Buyer representative and ask the project manager to telepone the Buyer to advise them that you will be calling.

Plan your interviews, including a session towards the end of the review to take the project manager through your findings and recommendations.

Next, conduct the interviews, typing directly into the appropriate section of the skeleton report which you have prepared before arriving on site. Highlight candidate findings and recommendations as you go. Make a note of further questions which you need to ask individuals, and things you want to cross-check with people you have already seen or are yet to see.

At the end of the interviews, prepare the detailed findings of the review, by focus area. During this task you may uncover areas where you need further information or facts that you need to check. It may also be your view that there are sufficient serious issues to require a further, trouble-shooting review or a detailed and independent technical review of some aspect of the project. If you are conducting a project health check review with an assistant, the advice given above with regard to round-up sessions and a workshop to brainstorm findings and recommendations all applies.

Refine your findings and recommendations and give the project manager a debrief of these and your overall project health assessment. These are all the tasks you need to do on site. When the report is complete, forward a copy to the project manager for comment.

Summary

Decide ahead of the review whether you will produce a report or presentation or both. Prepare a skeleton report or presentation on your Notebook PC before you arrive on site. Type your notes directly into your PC.

Start trouble-shooting reviews by holding a workshop with the project manager and project team leaders.

If using colleagues to assist with the review, hold regular round-up sessions to share findings and candidate recommendations.

Be sure of your findings, as a weak finding or recommendation can be used by a project team which is resistant to the need for change to discredit your entire report.

In the case of a trouble-shooting review, brief the business manager who has commissioned the review and plan the turnaround strategy/planning study.

Chapter 15

REQUIREMENTS AND DESIGN BASELINES

Clarity of the requirements baseline

When leading an IS Strategy Study for the Overseas Trade Divisions of the Department of Trade and Industry I was interested in the success of existing strategic business systems. The most strategic of all was the flagship system, BOTIS (Board of Trade Information System). Advisors in the Overseas Trade Divisions provided a service to small and medium sized enterprises (SMEs), helping small businesses to find potential customers in overseas markets. A businessman could telephone with a request like 'what is the size of the market for ball bearings in Taiwan, what are the issues facing UK exporters in this market, and can you give me some contacts in local companies?' The DTI advisors would contact the Foreign Office post in the target country and the 'Post' would use their network of contacts to answer the query. BOTIS was developed as a repository of useful information for the DTI advisors. Data entry staff prepared and keyed in information on different market sectors and countries. Also stored was advice given to SMEs in response to particular queries. At the time of the study, charges had just been introduced for this service and the DTI collected the charges and forwarded them to the Foreign Office.

Consideration was being given to leveraging BOTIS by selling information lodged as a result of previous enquiries to new enquirers. This seemed like a sound business proposition. When I visited offices in the Department to see the advisors at work, the BOTIS terminal was seldom being used. Quite often, it was powered off. A few staff did not know what the terminal was for. I asked several staff to demonstrate the most useful aspects of the system. I received a consistent message that the system was seldom used because the quality of the information was poor. Advisors questioned the concept of charging for BOTIS information as their experience indicated that an SME enquiry seldom matched a previous enquiry and that SMEs wanted up-to-the-minute information. In our report we recommended that BOTIS should be decommissioned, as it was not delivering business benefit commensurate with the expense being incurred. It was a bold recommendation. I was impressed that it was boldly received and acted upon immediately. The system was withdrawn and support staff were redeployed. Substantial savings resulted.

The above is an example of Root Cause RC01 – a project based on an unsound premise or an unrealistic business case. The idea of intellectual capital storage and reuse was laudable but what the end customer actually wanted was current information, specifically tailored for them by the Foreign Office 'Post'.

Sources of information

The RFI/ITT/SOR, the proposal, the functional specification, the project manager, the requirements manager, the technical architect, the development manager, the test manager and individual team members are good sources of information on this focus area.

Root Causes
Be on the lookout for:
RC01 Project based on an unsound premise or an unrealistic business case
RC08 Buyer failure to define and document requirements (functional and non-functional)
RC17 Full-scope, fixed-price contracting (requirements, design and development)
RC18 Failure to 'freeze' the requirements baseline and apply change control
RC20 Vendor starting a phase prior to completing a previous phase
RC25 Poor Vendor requirements traceability (requirements > design > code > test)
RC33 Insufficient attention paid by Vendor to non-functional requirements

---

The key question you must answer

'Are the system requirements defined with sufficient clarity and in sufficient detail to provide a sound foundation for the development and implementation of the solution?'

(Requirements include 'functional requirements' which define what the system must do to support the business process, and 'non-functional requirements' which define such issues as response times, availability, data integrity and systems management.)

Full-scope, fixed-price projects

By definition, these projects commence *without* a detailed statement of system requirements. However, there will be some very high-level statement of the business processes that the system must be designed to support. The first task is for the Vendor and Buyer teams to collaborate, often by means of requirements workshops, to capture and document the requirements.

Fixed-price projects which commence with only a high-level, 'cardinal point' requirement specification are close to full-scope, fixed-price and must be managed accordingly.

Check that:

- Buyer and Vendor staff are working together collaboratively and well;
- Buyer staff are providing authoritative information on requirements;
- there is a low level of re-work on requirements already captured;
- the scope of the system is not expanding beyond that implicit in the high-level statement of business processes against which the Vendor's tender was constructed;
- each party is meeting the timescales defined in the contract for commenting on work products produced by the other party.

Check for contract clauses which give the Buyer the right to set aside pre-contract requirements information, such as business process models, and effectively start with a blank piece of paper.

'Traditional' projects

Often, the Buyer will have prepared a statement of requirements, perhaps issued as part of the ITT. In other cases, a Vendor project team will have analysed the Buyer's requirements and prepared a requirements or functional specification.

Check that a requirements specification exists, that it is under configuration management, that it is being maintained in line with agreed change requests, and that it *has been signed off by the Buyer*. Typically, the requirements specification will form part of the contract between the parties. Check that there is an empowered person on the Buyer side who is actively engaged with the Vendor on requirements issues.

Often, and particularly in cases where the Buyer's requirements are expressed at a high level, the Vendor project team will have prepared a more detailed, Functional Specification. Check that this specification:

- exists;
- is stable (i.e. new requirements are not emerging from the woodwork during the system design phase or, worse, during the development and testing phases). If this is happening, it may indicate that the project has been attempting to speed up delivery by performing analysis, design and development in parallel. This is seldom effective at actually accelerating a project (RC20);
- is being maintained up-to-date (particularly if the specification is not a paper document, but contained on a systems analysis and design 'workbench' tool);
- is sufficiently detailed to provide a sound basis for the design and development, and for the preparation of system, integration and acceptance test specifications. For most applications with a Graphical User Interface (GUI), this implies the inclusion of window designs and the specification of the business

rules or logic behind the windows. Report formats should also be defined. Check that there is requirements traceability from the contractual requirements specification to the functional specification;

- is explicit about which requirements in the Buyer's requirements specification are included and which are not. If a requirements or functional specification is silent about a common requirement, it generates scope for the parties to argue over whether the specification *implies* that a particular function will be provided;

- does include, or expressly excludes, non-functional requirements. If functional requirements are excluded, check that they are specified elsewhere, such as in a non-functional requirements specification. It is not possible to design the infrastructure to support a set of applications without a crisp definition of non-functional requirements.

While Terms & Conditions for IT services contracts generally exclude a 'fitness-for-purpose' clause, Buyers do expect that systems will support their business and this view is likely to be supported by a Court in the event of litigation. This means that, as a responsible and experienced IT supplier, the Vendor will be expected to ensure that appropriate non-functional requirements are defined. This would include the ability of the system to support the intended and specified workload. It would also include the provision of an appropriate level of data integrity. In a typical business application, this would include 'transaction management'. This ensures that, in the event of a hardware/software failure or user error, either *all* or *none* of a business transaction is completed. It also provides the ability to recover business transaction data in the event of the software or computer platform 'crashing'. It would also typically include 'concurrency management' to prevent two users from updating the same piece of information and believing that their update has been successful.

Check the contractual status and 'pecking order' of the requirements documents. Sometimes, the contract will state that the Buyer's requirements document shall take precedence over any other document; in this case requirements traceability is essential. In this situation, it may *not* be in the Vendor's interests to seek Buyer sign-off of lower-level requirements and design documentation, such as the functional specification, as this could limit the Vendor's freedom with regard to *how* the project team chooses to deliver the contractual requirements. Generally though, if the Vendor can achieve Buyer buy-in to the Functional Specification, this will, effectively, become the governing requirements document.

Determine whether the contract contains clauses covering the process to be followed to resolve any dispute between the parties over the interpretation of requirements. I have seen contracts which specify that, in the event of any dispute over the interpretation of requirements, the Buyer's interpretation shall prevail. This type of clause does provide the Buyer with some protection, but it does not encourage both parties to take a reasonable position and is therefore an unhelpful clause, in my view.

Rapid application development (RAD) projects

RAD projects will not have detailed requirements and functional specifications. However, there should be a Feasibility Report, which should define the objectives, scope and business processes at a high level. There should also be a Business Area Definition document, which is effectively a high-level requirements document.

Detailed requirements are typically elicited during a functional prototyping stage and embodied in a functional prototype.

Things to look out for in RAD projects include:

- fixed-price and RAD do not make good bedfellows, particularly if the Vendor is required to fix the price before the feasibility and business study phases;
- RAD projects should *not* have detailed functional specifications, as the basic premise is one of eliciting the detailed requirements by means of user workshops and then delivering core, prioritised functionality within fixed time-boxes;
- active user participation is essential;
- the user representatives must be empowered to make instant decisions;
- strong project management is needed to control the project to time;
- the Buyer must be controlled to prevent 'galloping elegance' – the RAD equivalent of 'scope creep'. The key focus must be on satisfying core business requirements rather than on achieving the ultimate user interface.

Quality/completeness of the architecture and design

I was once responsible for evaluating and selecting a compiler for use on a real-time software development project. At that time, there were only two compilers in the frame, one developed and marketed by AERE Harwell and the other by a commercial supplier. The software to be developed was to control a radar in real time. It had to be efficient.

I wrote a simple test program containing a FOR loop of 10,000 iterations. I timed it at X seconds using a stopwatch. I was then able to place scraps of code into the test program, such as a procedure call with two parameters, or code to initialise to zero all elements of a two-dimensional array. The program was timed again, at Y seconds. The run time of the compiled scrap of code could then be calculated as (Y-X)/10 milliseconds. I did this for a few programming constructs for each compiler. I found that the object code created by the Harwell compiler ran, on average, some 20 times slower than that created by the commercial compiler.

I queried this with Harwell and found that their compiler was based on a pre-existing Fortran compiler. The compiler produced code which executed on the processor stack and did not capitalise on the registers available in the machine. Harwell admitted that the compiler was not really suited to real-time applications. This was bemusing, as the language would only be of interest to developers of real-time, process control software.

The above is an example of Root Cause RC19 – Poor choice of technical platform and/or architecture. The fundamental requirement of a real-time compiler is that the object code it produces should run very efficiently.

Sources of information

The system and program design documentation, the technical architect, the development manager and individual team members are good sources of information on this focus area.

Root Causes
Be on the lookout for:
RC03 Project based on state-of-the-art and immature technology
RC19 Poor choice of technical platform and/or architecture
RC26 Buyer retains design authority with right to approve/reject low-level designs
RC27 Delays cause the project to be overtaken by advances in technology
RC28 Vendor failure to 'freeze' the design (and technical platform) and apply change control

---

The key question you must answer

Is the underlying architecture and design of the system sound, and is it documented such that it can form a firm foundation for development?

If you are conducting the first of a series of project health check reviews, it is likely that the project is still in the design phase and that the detailed design documentation is not yet complete. If this is the case, then conventional wisdom states that development (programmers 'cutting code') should *not* have started. If development has started, typically 'in order to meet the tight contractual milestones', then investigate with the development manager and individual programmers whether they believe they have enough design information with which to make meaningful progress. Ask them what is missing.

Unless you have quite a deep technical background, you will not be equipped to undertake an in-depth technical assessment of the quality of the architecture/ design. But you don't need to. Your skill is to discover, through conversations with technical staff at all levels in the project (and 'techies' are famous for their indiscretion) what they feel the strengths and weaknesses of the design are. If you discover that there is widespread discontent with the quality of the architecture/ design, you might recommend an independent technical review.

The documentation of the architecture and design may take many different forms, depending on the size, complexity and type of the project. These forms may include one or more of the following:

- a business system design/template for a packaged software implementation;
- a design overview document or system context diagram;
- a detailed system design specification;
- a set of logical data and process models on paper or contained in a data dictionary or an analysis/design workbench tool;
- an application architecture, showing the hierarchical structure of the programs in the system;
- for an objected-oriented (OO) development, a set of models, a class catalogue, use cases and class specifications on a workbench such as Rational Rose or Select OMT;
- design deliverables from Structured Systems Analysis and Design Method (SSADM) or a proprietary design method (which might also be on a workbench tool).

Key questions to answer include:

- is the project based on state-of-the-art technology? This is not necessarily a show-stopper. However, it might be if the technology or tools are immature and 'flaky';
- has the project been overtaken by technological advance? This could well be a show-stopper or at least point to the need for a fundamental re-think on the part of Buyer and Vendor;
- is the design documented? (be on the lookout for solutions based on a previous project, which may not have completed yet and which may not have a well-documented or stable architecture/design – or which may even have failed);
- is the documentation being maintained?
- is the form of the architecture/design information appropriate to the type of system?
- is the design information in a form which the Buyer could be taken through in order to ensure that both parties have a common understanding of the solution?
- is there too much or too little design information? It is possible to over-use a method and drown in a sea of paperwork or tool-hosted models;
- is the architecture/design information complete, coherent and consistent?
- is the design stable and baselined or is it being continuously 'tweaked'? (This might indicate inherent weaknesses, 'galloping elegance', 'scope creep', or an excessive degree of change requests.)
- is it possible to trace individual requirements down into the design documentation?

- are non-functional requirements, such as performance, reliability, availability, security, systems management, transaction management and concurrency management addressed appropriately in the design?

Summary

Clarity of the requirements baseline

Fundamental to the success of an application development and systems integration project is the existence of a stable set of detailed system requirements. For this reason, full-scope, fixed-price projects are risky.

The 'pecking order' of requirements documents must be defined to provide both Buyer and Vendor with clarity on what functionality will be delivered. Non-functional requirements are an essential prerequisite of infrastructure design.

RAD projects require tight management to avoid 'galloping elegance'.

Quality/completeness of the architecture and design

Also key to the success of an application development and systems integration project is the correct choice of technical platform or architecture. The next key requirement is that the design should be documented, 'frozen' as a baseline for the development, and subject to change management.

Chapter 16

PROJECT PLANNING AND PROGRESS AGAINST PLANS

Stability and realism of the project plan and resource estimates

One of the key opportunity qualification criteria discussed in Chapter 5 is the quality of the r*elationship* which the Vendor enjoys with the Buyer. The better the relationship, the better placed is the Vendor to e*ngage* the Buyer and win the business – another key qualification criterion. Sales professionals often talk of this in terms of 'an inside track'.

When reviewing a troubled project, I spoke to several current and former project team members to build up a picture of the bid phase of the project. I found that the Vendor had an inside track to die for. The Vendor had delivered a previous project to the Buyer in the same application domain, at a modest profit. The system was in use and giving every satisfaction. The Buyer now wanted a substantial enhancement, the contract for which was to be put out to open tender. The Vendor was awarded a study contract to prepare the ITT for the main development contract. The Vendor also drafted the tender evaluation criteria. This work, coupled with the Vendor's unrivalled knowledge of the internals of the application, gave the Vendor a unique opportunity to develop a winning solution and a cast iron set of estimates. It was payback time!

Unfortunately, the staff with experience of the application domain were all fully committed to other projects and unable to help the bid team to fully understand the complexity of the business requirements. The salesperson's relationship with the Buyer was good, but the Buyer was not about to divulge that there were no other bidders. The Vendor priced aggressively to blow the competitors out of the water. This, coupled with estimates which were too low, sowed the seeds of a troubled project. An inside track is unfortunately not enough. You still have to run around it.

The above is an example of root cause RC10 – Vendor failure to invest enough resources to scope the project prior to contract. It led, inexorably, to root cause RC12 – Vendor underestimation of resources (predominantly person-effort) required.

The most common reason why plans are unrealistic is that they are based on unrealistic estimates. Often the Vendor is influenced by the Buyer's timescale and budget expectations and, as root cause RC05 tells us, the Buyer's funding and/or timescale expectations can be unrealistically low. Once poor estimates are enshrined in a plan which has been presented to the Buyer, a troubled project is more or less inevitable. I can't emphasise enough the need to manage the bid stage of a project with total professionalism – as set out in Part 2 of this book – to avoid this lethal root cause of troubled projects.

Sources of information

The proposal, the contract, original and current resource estimates, original and current plans, the project manager, the development manager, the test manager, the quality assurance professional and individual team members are good sources of information on this focus area.

Root Causes
Be on the lookout for:
RC05   Buyer's funding and/or timescale expectations unrealistically low
RC10   Vendor failure to invest enough resources to scope the project prior to contract
RC12   Vendor underestimation of resources (predominantly person-effort) required
RC13   Vendor failure to define project tasks, deliverables and acceptance processes

---

The key question you must answer

Do time-line and resource plans exist, are they complete in the sense of covering all project tasks required, and are they realistic and achievable?

All projects should have a time-line/Gantt chart project plan, showing the several activities of the project, the milestones and the internal and external dependencies. A picture tells a thousand words, and Gantt charts are the best medium for describing the complexity of a project. Things to look for include:

- the master project plan should be produced using an appropriate project planning and scheduling tool such as Microsoft Project, PMW or Artemis. Planning should be undertaken at the level of activities of 5–50 days' duration. Producing a more detailed master project plan is unhelpful – the plan becomes unwieldy, clarity is lost, and it is impossible for one person to keep a detailed plan for an entire project up to date;
- all contractual milestones should be shown on the master project plan. Similarly, all internal milestones (for example, the production of work products) should also be shown on the master project plan;

- a very high-level plan, showing phases and milestones, is very useful for explaining the overall approach being taken. This is probably best created with a graphics package such as Lotus Freelance or Microsoft Powerpoint, rather than by 'rolling up' the master project plan. The existence of a very high-level plan *only* is evidence that there is no real planning going on;
- separate low-level plans should be produced for each area of project activity. These can be created either using a project planning tool or a spreadsheet tool. Planning should be undertaken at the level of tasks of between ½ a day and five days' duration. Team leaders and individual project team members should use these plans to schedule and control their work. Planned and actual resource usage can be maintained at the task level using a simple spreadsheet, as can the estimated resource needed to complete the task;
- a resource plan should be produced to show the staffing profile and the planned number of person-days needed to complete the project. Ideally, the spreadsheet hosting this resource plan will also hold the daily cost and/or fee rates appropriate to each team member, enabling the predicted cost of the project to be maintained;
- be on the look out for a plan which is shaped primarily by contractual dates for key deliverables rather than by realistic estimates of the tasks to be completed to generate these deliverables. Failure to meet contractual milestone dates may result in liquidated damages or breach of the contract. It is not unusual for a project manager to show the key milestones at the end of the project, have detailed plans for the immediate future and for there to be a large planning void in the middle;
- all deliverables and all activities required to provide them (including testing, defect removal and re-testing) need to be included in the plans. Also to be included are such things as data migration, cut-over to live operation, training, help text generation, user and system documentation, training material development, support etc;
- the project manager should be able to identify the critical path through the plan.

Having established that time-line and resource plans exist, the key questions to answer are:

- are the plans visible to, and being used by, team leaders and developers as the basis for their own detailed plans?
- what underlying assumptions have been used and are they reasonable? For example, do estimates include a provision for 'learning curves', coaching other staff, and management overhead? Do the time-line plans allow for sickness, holidays, training courses etc?
- are the plans viewed as realistic and achievable by team leaders and developers? If not, there will be no ownership of the plans by the team;
- are the plans appropriate to the skills of the staff on the project, or do they assume higher skill levels?

- is the project manager under pressure from the Buyer or from Vendor management not to declare slippage and to continue to work to an unrepresentative plan? Call this situation out, as it is seldom in the interests of either the Vendor or the Buyer to withhold 'bad news' of this type;
- is the master project plan baselined and is there an audit trail of baselined plans going back to the plan shown in the original Proposal?
- is there a high degree of 'churn'? For example, is there constant re-planning going on in order to avoid slippage? Re-planning in order to achieve recovery in a troubled area of the project is to be encouraged, but constant re-planning backwards from an 'immovable' milestone or end date is likely to lead to unrealistically compressed timescales for activities/phases and inappropriate parallelism of activities/phases. A high degree of plan churn is a clear indicator of a project in difficulty.

To form a qualitative view of the realism of the project plans and estimates it can be instructive to plot the project manager's 'estimated cost at completion' against time using information in the monthly progress reports. An example is shown in Figure 16.1.

The closer you get to the end of a project, the more accurate the project manager's estimated cost at completion should be. Most of the problems have emerged and been solved, and tasks yet to be started or yet to be completed can be re-estimated based on real productivity metrics on the project. The estimated cost at completion versus time graph should show an asymptotic approach to a final cost, approximating a $(1-e^{-x})$ curve. The graph will also make visible the major re-plans and 'glitches' which have taken place on the project.

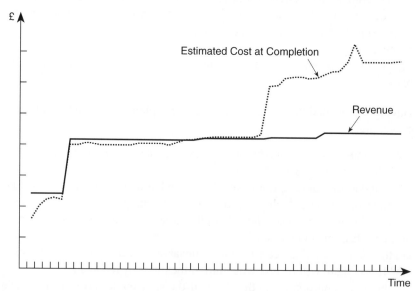

Figure 16.1   *Estimated Cost at Completion v Time Example*

Progress against plan

> When working as a production manager in a software house, I reviewed a number of projects every month. One of these projects was developing about half a dozen COBOL programs, each program being developed by a single project team member. Some of these programs were huge. One of them was over 70 pages of listing paper in length. I found it hard to believe that this was the best structure for the application but was assured that it was. All of the programs were nearly complete, several of them 90 per cent complete. And yet, every month, there was little tangible evidence that we really were drawing closer to our goal. I was reduced to the 'How's it going then?' technique of progress monitoring and was given the 'It's coming along fine' technique of progress reporting.

I'm unsure whether the above is an example of root cause RC21 – poor choice of design/development method, or an example of root cause RC15 – poor project planning, management and execution. It's probably both. Even if there are no architectural/technical reasons to break a project into small deliverables, there is certainly a project management reason to do so. Project managers need a quantitative means of tracking progress at the micro level as well as at the macro level. A project must not just have milestones; it must have 'inch-pebbles' as well.

Earned value analysis is becoming increasingly popular, particularly on large projects, as a means of monitoring progress and productivity.

Sources of information

Internal and external progress reports, the project manager, the production manager, the development manager, the test manager, team leaders and individual developers are good sources of information on this focus area.

> **Root Causes**
> *Be on the lookout for:*
> **RC15** Poor project planning, management and execution
> **RC20** Vendor starting a phase prior to completing a previous phase

The key question you must answer

> Is the project achieving, over-achieving or under-achieving its plans, and what is the likely impact on the completion date, Buyer satisfaction and project profitability?

Clearly, this focus area is tightly linked to the previous one, and the answer to the above question will be clear once you have researched the stability and realism of the project plans. Also, a plan without a project control system (the means by which past and current performance is fed back into the plan to yield schedule and cost variance figures) is not an effective controlling device. See the Progress Monitoring & Control section of Chapter 19.

If the project is *not* delivering to plan it could be for a number of reasons, including:

- poor requirements definition, or poor definition of the architecture and design (Chapter 15);
- an unrealistic plan (already covered in this chapter);
- inadequately skilled or experienced staff at working level, team leader level or project manager level (Chapter 17);
- a flawed development, integration or testing approach (Chapter 17);
- non-adherence to project quality standards (Chapter 17);
- unclear definition of project scope, objectives, approach, deliverables, organisation etc (Chapter 17);
- lack of project infrastructure such as PCs, servers, tools, space etc (Chapter 17);
- insufficient staff resources (Chapter 18);
- lack of engagement and leadership from senior management in the Vendor organisation (Chapter 18);
- inadequate project management system (Chapter 19).

Many of these issues can be fixed and must be covered in the recommendations of your project delivery review. Call out unrealistic and unachievable plans as they point to the need for urgent re-planning. Continual failure of a project to meet its plan causes:

- the plan to become ineffective as a controlling device. People give up trying to hit impossible targets and the project ceases to be merely 'challenging' and becomes a 'death march' for the team;
- the team to cut corners. Deviation from the project's software development processes often compounds the timescale problem;
- poor morale. The corollary is that a project which is consistently meeting its plans has high morale and a sense of getting somewhere.

Summary

Stability and realism of the project plan and resource estimates

The most common reason why project plans are unrealistic is that they are based on unrealistic estimates.

All projects require a master project plan, prepared using an appropriate project planning and scheduling tool. The master project plan should be constructed at activity level. A plan constructed at a very detailed level cannot be maintained by one person and the plan rapidly becomes out of date.

Separate low-level plans must be prepared for each area of project activity. These should be constructed at the task level and used to control progress.

It is vital to establish whether the plans are being used to control the project. It is also important to establish whether the team members regard the plans as realistic and achievable.

Progress against plan

Establish whether the project is failing to meet its plans. Investigation of other review focus areas will identify the reasons for the slippage. A plan which is unachievable causes poor morale and ceases to be an effective controlling device. The team will cut corners to attempt to stay on track, causing secondary problems.

Chapter 17

THE DEVELOPMENT LIFE CYCLE

Development approach

I once managed the development of software for an advanced secondary surveillance radar (SSR) station. An SSR ground station has a narrow-beam antenna rotating at 10 rpm and broadcasting some 440 'interrogations' every second. Black boxes called transponders on civil aircraft respond to an interrogation with their identity or height. The ground station receives the replies and establishes the angular position (azimuth) of each aircraft. Range is determined by the delay between the interrogation and the reply. Increasing air traffic was filling the ether with SSR replies, many overlapping each other. It was becoming difficult to establish the position of aircraft accurately.

The advanced SSR system dramatically reduced the number of interrogations and replies. The ground station tracked the position of aircraft and sent a single interrogation to every aircraft just as the antenna began to sweep through it. An identity code was included in the interrogation. Several transponders might receive the interrogation, but only one would respond – with its identity and height.

At the heart of the software was a task scheduler, which endlessly cycled through a set of procedure calls. If a procedure had no work to do, it returned control to the scheduler. The last procedure in the list (BINBCD) performed a binary to BCD conversion and updated a display showing the azimuth of the antenna. Nobody ever looked at the display, as it changed too quickly for the human eye to follow.

When the station was operational, I undertook a study to determine whether the aircraft handling capacity could be increased. I was able to find a number of 'hot spots' in the system. The most significant saving was achieved when I established that the task scheduler cycled round its loop of procedure calls about 4000 times during a 6-second rotation of the antenna and that the BINBCD procedure took 1mS to execute. This meant that about 65 per cent of the power of the processor was dedicated to updating the azimuth display. Inserting three lines of code to call the procedure on every 10th pass through the scheduling loop more than doubled the aircraft capacity.

The above is an example of Root Cause RC30 – Inadequate Vendor review of designs/code/documentation by team leaders. I had reviewed every single line of code in the system, but the significance of this virtually irrelevant procedure executing once every cycle of the task scheduler had eluded me.

Sources of information

The Quality Plan, the proposal, project plans, the project manager, the technical architect, the development manager, the test manager, team leaders and individual developers and testers are good sources of information on this focus area. You need to ask them to describe the development environment and the development life cycle (including integration and testing).

Root Causes
Be on the lookout for:
RC21 Poor choice of design/development method
RC29 Inadequate Vendor training and supervision of junior staff
RC30 Inadequate Vendor review of designs/code/documentation

The key questions you must answer

Is an appropriate and professional approach to software development being taken? Are the software development processes documented and are they being followed?

Compliance with the Quality Plan is covered later in this chapter. In the Development Approach focus area, you are not checking for compliance with a particular design and development method; rather, you are establishing whether the approach being taken to design and development is sensible, will result in high-quality work products, and will ensure that the project meets its timescale targets. Things to look out for include:

- are analysts and designers maintaining contact with developers to ensure that the coders understand the business processes which the code must support?
- is development uncovering issues which should have been fully defined during the analysis phase (for example, new requirements, or requirements which are poorly defined)?
- is the development environment unduly complex, with multiple programming languages being used?
- what are the programmers working from? Clear program specifications (ideally), a clear functional specification defining windows and business logic, backed up with design documentation (OK), or an incomplete and woolly set of user requirements (dangerous, even for a RAD development)?
- can developers test their code? Do they have access to test harnesses and test data, adequate de-bugging tools etc?
- are requirements and design documents being updated to reflect changes made to the code?
- is code being commented to ease subsequent maintenance?

- are team leaders taking an active role in design reviews, code inspections and the verification of unit test plans and results?
- do developers have adequate hardware and software to enable them to work with maximum efficiency?
- is all code and documentation being held under configuration management?
- have developers seen the system test specification or the user acceptance test specification (the ultimate definition of the software under development)?
- what corners are being cut? Watch out for poor-quality code being passed to the test team as a result of pressure to meet development timescales;
- is sufficient user participation built into the development process? This is essential to avoid divergence between Buyer and Vendor expectations.

Integration and testing strategy

I once reviewed a project which was planned to include an integration stage of three months, followed by a system testing stage of two months. Due to time pressure, the integration stage was virtually omitted. The system was built and system testing commenced. System testing occupied an elapsed time of 27 months.

If you don't approach the integration of a complex system carefully, formally and professionally – by building trusted building blocks and assembling them, a few at a time, until you have a working system – you will store up enormous grief for later. Time invested at the integration stage pays enormous dividends later on.

Figure 17.1 shows the conventional approach to the integration of complex software.

Sources of information

The proposal, the contract, the Quality Plan, the Project Initiation Document (if available), the technical architect, the development manager, the test manager, and individual developers and testers are good sources of information on this focus area.

Root Causes
Be on the lookout for:
RC32 Lack of a formal, 'engineering' approach to integration and testing by Vendor
RC33 Insufficient attention paid by Vendor to non-functional requirements

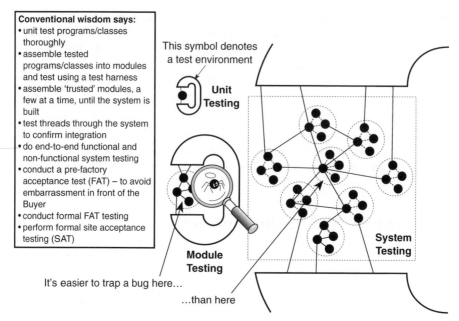

Figure 17.1   *Integrating Complex Software*

The key questions you must answer

> How will the individual hardware and software building blocks of the system be assembled, tested and contractually accepted? Are Buyer and Vendor responsibilities clear? Is testing of non-functional requirements included in the test plans?

The acceptance process should be defined in the contract. Otherwise, the ITT/RFP/SOR or proposal is likely to define the process.

The integration and testing strategy should be defined early in the project. When you do your first project health check review, the project team should be able to describe in broad terms how the system will be assembled and tested. Ideally, there will be an integration and testing strategy document defining the types of testing to be undertaken. The actual test plans and test scripts will not be available until later, but their preparation should not be left until nearly the end of the development phase.

Things to look out for include:

- who is responsible for integration? Often testers are given this responsibility, but integration is a complex task, best undertaken by development staff;
- has an integration test specification been prepared? This is often a subset of the system test specification, used to confirm that building blocks of the system are inter-operating correctly;

- is a system test specification available? It should be possible to prepare this quite early in the project. System testing should be a comprehensive test of the functionality of the system, ideally structured as a set of business scenarios to test the end-to-end functionality of the system. It should be cross-referenced to the governing requirements document to ensure that all functional requirements are tested;
- are non-functional tests planned, even if there is no contractual requirement to meet specific non-functional requirements? It is not unusual to find a project team which assumes that the dbms will take care of transaction management and that there is no need to test database recovery;
- are contractual acceptance criteria clearly defined?
- who is preparing the user acceptance test (UAT) specification? If it is the Buyer, does the project team have a copy? If the Vendor is preparing the test specification, has it been signed off by the Buyer? Some projects might feature a factory acceptance test (FAT) and a site acceptance test (SAT). The SAT test might be a simple re-run of the FAT test or, more commonly, SAT might be a subset of FAT;
- have test databases been prepared to support testing? These should contain some 'live data' provided by the Buyer. The team should also have access to a representatively sized test database for performance testing purposes;
- does the Vendor have sufficient access to live systems in order to fully test interfaces to external systems?
- is appropriate configuration management of code under test in place? No 'patching' of the build of code under test should be allowed, as it frequently has unforeseen effects on functionality already tested;
- has the team considered the use of automated test tools? These are particularly valuable when the nature of the project requires substantial regression testing, for example in projects with a multi-drop delivery approach;
- how many passes of UAT has the team assumed? Most project plans show one pass, the implication being that there will be no defects, no re-testing and no impact on the project plan. Does the team know how long a complete UAT will take?
- is any form of user trial anticipated? If so, the ground rules and completion criteria must be defined;
- are tools and processes in place to support defect reporting, analysis, removal and re-testing?

Quality Plan compliance

Sources of information

The Quality Plan, the ITT/RFP/SOR, the contract, the proposal, the quality assurance professional, the project manager, the development manager, team leaders and individual team members are good sources of information on this focus area.

Root Causes
Be on the lookout for:
RC24 Poor Vendor standards deployment (design, coding, testing, configuration management etc)

The key questions you must answer

Is there a Quality Plan? Does it contain a clear definition of quality requirements, a description of the software development processes (a quality attainment plan), a quality control plan, a quality assurance plan and a quality preservation plan? Is the project following the Quality Plan?

Check that:

- project quality requirements are understood and documented;
- the software development processes (which will include integration and testing), defined to meet the specific quality requirements of the project, are documented;
- the quality control or Verification & Validation (V&V) processes to be followed for each work product type are defined;
- team members have a copy of the Quality Plan and are familiar with its contents;
- in addition to gaining familiarity with the software development environment, project team members have been trained in the project software development processes, standards and quality control processes;
- project team members are clear regarding their individual responsibilities with regard to following the defined processes;
- team members are complying with the Quality Plan and not taking short cuts due to pressure of work. Do this by asking to see:
  - the unit test plan, unit test script and unit test results for a particular program or class, chosen at random,
  - the minutes of the review of a particular design specification, chosen at random,
  - evidence that a particular program or class, chosen at random, has been code-reviewed, that the class specification exists, is consistent with the code, and that both are under configuration control;
- there is effective in-project quality assurance to encourage Quality Plan compliance and ensure that appropriate quality control records are maintained;
- the Quality Plan is being updated as a result of experience and that process improvement changes are being promulgated to all project team members.

Project Initiation Document (PID) compliance

Sources of information

The PID, the proposal, the contract and the project manager are good sources of information on this focus area. Even if no PID or project definition document has been prepared, use the headings in Table 8.1 to explore the extent to which the project team understands these important elements. As a number of these are focus areas in Part 3 of this book, the PID compliance focus area should concentrate on:

- the project mission (or charter);
- the project scope;
- the project approach;
- planning assumptions and dependencies.

Root Causes
Be on the lookout for:
RC01 Project based on an unsound premise or an unrealistic business case
RC02 Buyer failure to define clear project objectives, anticipated benefits and success criteria
RC05 Buyer's funding and/or timescale expectations unrealistically low
RC06 Buyer failure to break a complex project into phases or smaller projects
RC07 Buyer's funding and/or timescale expectations unrealistically low
RC10 Vendor failure to invest enough resources to scope the project prior to contract
RC13 Vendor failure to define project tasks, deliverables and acceptance processes

---

The key questions you must answer

Are the Buyer's business goals, objectives and project success criteria documented and realistic? Is the project scope well bounded? Is the overall approach being taken to project delivery sensible? Have all assumptions and dependencies underpinning the planning, control, organisation and funding of the project been documented?

Check that:

- the Buyer's business goals and project objectives are documented in the PID or in a project charter. They are also likely to be summarised in the original RFI/ITT/SOR. Certain project objectives will also be quality requirements, which should be included in the Quality Plan;

- the Buyer's business goals and project objectives are realistic. Subject them to a 'sanity check' by comparing the Buyer's expectations with the outcomes of similar projects in the same market sector;
- the project's timescale targets are defined and realistic, again in comparison with similarly-sized projects in the same market sector;
- the project manager is keeping the Buyer's business goals, project objectives and timescale expectation under review and engaging the Buyer if these aspects of the project come under threat;
- the project scope is clearly defined. We have already considered the need for a clear requirements baseline. However, scope is wider than this, covering such things as who is responsible for preparing test data, constructing and testing interfaces, undertaking data migration, preparing acceptance test scripts, undertaking maintenance when the system is in live use etc;
- the project approach, particularly the manner in which the project is divided into stages, is sensible and efficient;
- the assumptions and dependencies used when constructing the project plans are documented;
- the PID, or the set of documents covering the areas set out in Table 8.1, is being maintained.

Summary

Development approach

Good communication between subteams is essential. Analysts and designers must maintain contact with coders and testers to help them to understand the business processes the system must support. Participation in testing by end users from the Buyer organisation is of similar value. Developers benefit from early sight of the system and user acceptance test specifications.

During design and development, requirements should be stable. Coders should be working from clear program/class specifications and not from an assortment of requirements documentation.

Team members should have access to sufficient development and test hardware and software to enable them to achieve high productivity.

Work products should be inspected by peers and/or team leaders.

Integration and testing strategy

The project team should have a clear, preferably documented, view on how the individual software components of the system will be integrated and tested.

System testing should include both functional and non-functional testing. Test data should include some 'live data' supplied by the Buyer. A fully populated test database should be available for load testing.

Establish whether the master project plan embodies realistic assumptions on the duration of defect removal and re-testing activities.

Quality plan compliance

The Quality Plan must define the quality requirements of the system. It must set out the software development processes to be used to attain the specified level of quality. The quality control to be applied to each work product type must also be defined.

The Quality Plan should be a living document, used by project team members on a regular basis to inform their low-level planning of design and code inspections. Team members must receive training on the software development processes.

Compliance with the Quality Plan is crucially important. If the team is not following the Quality Plan, then either the Quality Plan is flawed and requires urgent amendment, or the project is suffering from a fundamental quality problem.

Project initiation document compliance

The Buyer's mission, objectives and project success criteria should be visible to the Vendor's project team. Determine whether the scope of the project is well-bounded, with Vendor and Buyer responsibilities and dependencies clearly defined. Is the approach being taken to phasing the project sensible?

Chapter 18

PROJECT ORGANISATION

Project structure

> I once reviewed a project where a large number of inexperienced developers had been brought onto the project without:
>
> - a formal induction process;
> - any instruction on software development processes and standards;
> - any review by team leaders of low-level designs, code and unit test plans/results prepared by the new joiners;
> - mentoring and coaching of the new joiners.
>
> The problem was that team leaders did not have time to give the new joiners this level of support. The team leaders were too busy developing code themselves, so the new joiners had to sink or swim. Inevitably, the result was a lapse of quality control and a large quantity of poor quality code which had to be reworked later in the project.

The above is an example of Root Cause RC29 – Inadequate Vendor training and supervision of junior staff.

Sources of information

The proposal, the Project Initiation Document (PID), the Quality Plan and the project manager are good sources of information on this focus area.

> **Root Causes**
> *Be on the lookout for:*
> **RC29** Inadequate Vendor training and supervision of junior staff

The key questions you must answer

> Is the project team structure appropriate to the approach being taken to delivery (the manner in which the project is broken down into phases, and the software development processes being deployed)? Is the size of the project team optimal and likely to allow contractual timescales to be met?

A key factor influencing the size of a project team is the project timescale. It is a great temptation for a project manager to build a large team so that the project can be compressed into a short time period. Similarly, if a project is slipping badly, adding people to the team so that the slippage can be pulled back appears to be a sensible tactical move. Unfortunately, timescale (T) cannot simply be calculated as the required effort (E) in person-years divided by the number of people on the team (N). If T=E/N were true, the plot of team size against project timescale would be a true hyberbola.

I have a hypothesis that T as a function of N is more likely to be $T=E/N +aN^2$ as shown in Figure 18.1. This is because, as teams become larger:

- more complex management structures become necessary;
- communication within the team becomes more difficult;
- individuals have a smaller span of comprehension and influence, so more communication becomes necessary.

If the hypothesis is true, there comes a point when adding extra team members will actually *increase* the timescale. I believe that every project has a 'natural' team size (see Table 9.2.). In general, small is beautiful and no team should be larger than the number of Stone Age men required to kill a mammoth!

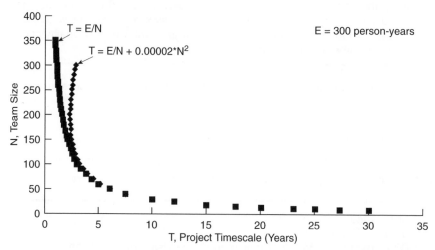

Figure 18.1   *The Diminishing Returns of Additional Team Members*

Things to look out for when reviewing the project organisation include:

- the lack of an up-to-date project organisation chart;
- the project organisation should suit the processes being used to generate work products so that responsibility for work products is clear;
- does the team include all necessary skills and experience? A key role in a software development project is the software development manager (or team

leader). A good project manager and an excellent technical architect cannot normally compensate for the lack of a good development manager;

- does the team have sufficient resources to enable it to meet its plans?
- is the project in danger of deploying too many resources and reaching the point of diminishing returns on the hypothetical curve above? If so, is there potential for:
  - increasing the number of teams, rather than making existing teams larger,
  - splitting the project into subprojects with an over-arching programme manager,
  - phasing the work to allow a slightly smaller team to efficiently deliver drops of software over a rather longer time period;
- does the organisation structure show the Buyer's project organisation and interactions between Vendor and Buyer teams at different levels? All Vendor staff with legitimate roles to play should be shown, including those outside the project team such as the production manager, the business manager, the client manager, the contracts professional and the QA professional. Is there any evidence that the incumbents of these roles are not 'pulling together' in support of the project?
- does the project have the active support and engagement of senior management in Vendor and Buyer organisations? Is there a 'single responsible owner', or project sponsor, in the Buyer organisation?
- does the organisational structure take account of the differing levels of experience on the team and recognise that less experienced staff require more supervision than experienced staff?
- if the project organisation is staffed with Buyer and Vendor staff, are their terms of reference clear and is the team operating as an integrated one? If not, then there may be culture change and team-building challenges to be addressed.

Clarity of project roles and responsibilities

Sources of information

Project, team and individual terms of reference, the project manager, team leaders and all individual team members are good sources of information on this focus area.

Root Causes
Be on the look-out for:
RC16 Failure to clearly define roles and responsibilities in the contract/ subcontracts

---

The key questions you must answer

> Does everyone with a role in the project – in Buyer, Vendor and subcontractor organisations – know what they are responsible for and what other peoples' responsibilities are? Is there any unnecessary duplication of activity? What activities and work products are 'falling through the cracks'?

During interviews it is easy to establish whether people are clear about who they report to and what is expected of them. However, look out for:

- the lack of formal terms of reference;
- the lack of a 'new joiner pack' to introduce new team members to the project;
- poor communication within the team. There should be regular, informal briefing sessions for the whole project team, weekly meetings of the project manager with team leaders, and weekly meetings of team leaders with their team members;
- the lack of defined 'owners' of key documents such as the requirements document, the functional specification, design documents and the master project plan;
- individual subteams or functions within the project 'going native' and acting as 'fiefdoms', more interested in meeting their specific responsibilities and timescales than worrying about the good of the project as a whole. I have sometimes seen an individual team leader, keen to be seen to be achieving his plans, driving the team to pass poor quality or incomplete work to other teams;
- invalid assumptions being made about who is responsible for testing interfaces, shared procedures, middleware etc. These items may be being tested twice or not at all;
- project managers who delegate the management and control of the project to their team leaders, the project office or an administrator, while they concentrate on the Buyer relationship;
- square pegs in round holes.

Also include consideration of Buyer and subcontractor roles:

- are Buyer and subcontractor roles and responsibilities defined in the contract/subcontracts?
- are Buyer and subcontractor dependencies and milestone dates clearly defined?
- are failures by Buyer and subcontractor staff to meet their responsibilities being documented and managed?

Staff motivation and morale

Sources of information

The project manager and any member of the project team are good sources of information on this focus area. You might also speak with managers in resourcing or human resources functions who are likely to have been consulted by any staff wishing to leave the project.

Root Causes
Be on the lookout for:
RC23   Vendor lack/loss of skilled resources

The key questions you must answer

Are team members happy in their work and giving of their best? What are the underlying reasons for any low motivation or morale?

In all your conversations with team members, try to establish:

- the general level of team morale, and whether there are individual teams within the project suffering from poor morale or particularly high levels of stress;
- the quality of the project's social life and what might be done to improve it;
- the frustrations individuals have within the project. These might be due to pressure of work, boredom, fears about the impact of a long or troubled project on their careers, inadequate infrastructure, lack of communication, ill-defined targets or roles, poor management etc;
- whether team members are coasting or really giving of their best;
- whether any member of the project team appears not to be coping with the stress of the job.

You must make it clear to members of the project team that none of their remarks will be directly attributable to them.

Summary

Project structure

It is counterproductive to deploy a team substantially larger that the 'natural' size for a project in an attempt to compress the project timescale.

The team structure should be documented and should suit the approach being taken to project delivery. An experienced software development manager or team leader is key to success. New joiners and less experienced staff require substantial supervision and coaching from their team leaders.

There should be a single responsible owner of the project within the Buyer organisation.

Clarity of project roles and responsibilities

Each team member should have documented terms of reference and be given appropriate induction training upon joining the project.

There must be good communication within the team, both vertically and horizontally.

Establish whether some team members are being asked to shoulder substantially more responsibility that their terms of reference require.

Staff motivation and morale

Determine the general morale of the team and whether there are islands of higher or lower morale within the project. Establish the underlying causes of any morale problems and capture suggestions from team members on how morale could be improved.

Chapter 19

PROJECT MANAGEMENT SYSTEM

Introduction

> I once walked past a project area several times a day on my way to the coffee machine. After a while, I realised that the project manager spent most of his time in front of his PC, working with Microsoft Project. When I reviewed the project a few weeks later, my suspicions were confirmed. The project faced very challenging timescale targets. The project manager was spending a great deal of time feeding in the results of the previous week's progress, re-scheduling, and determining the apparent impact of the previous week's work on the overall plan. The plan was regularly published to the Buyer. Predicted milestone dates were fluctuating wildly from week to week and the Buyer was wondering what was going on. The project manager was 'monitoring the project' or 'steering by the wake', rather than controlling the project.

The above is an example of Root Cause RC15 – Poor project planning, management and execution. More specifically, it is an example of a common misapprehension – that projects are managed using a project planning and control tool or a project management method. They are not. A tool such as Microsoft Project is a valuable aid to generating and presenting project plans, but it is basically a graphics tool with some scheduling capability. Open methods such as PRINCE and proprietary methods such as GS Method from IBM and SUMMIT from PricewaterhouseCoopers provide a useful support structure for project management. But it is the project manager who plans, controls and manages the project, by:

- setting firm milestone dates;
- energising the team and giving them self-belief;
- driving for milestone achievement;
- sensing and managing issues;
- making necessary mid-term corrections to the plan;
- managing and communicating with the Buyer at every step; and
- rewarding the team for commitment and achievement.

Sources of information

The production manager, the project manager, the development manager, the test manager, the project office manager, the project administrator, the management accountant, the contracts professional, the Buyer representative and individual team members are good sources of information on the several focus areas considered under the general heading of the Project Management System.

The key questions you must answer

> Is an effective project management system in place, and is the project under control? Is the project manager 'grasping nettles', taking hard decisions, and dealing firmly and effectively with issues, the project team, subcontractors and the Buyer?

Project planning

> **Root Causes**
> *Be on the lookout for:*
> **RC15**   Poor project planning, management and execution

The key questions you must answer

> Is the need for plans and for ongoing refinement of plans recognised by the project manager and the team? Is planning being done effectively?

The need for time-line (Gantt chart) project plans and resource plans has already been stated in Chapter 16. We have also looked at the need for plans to be realistic and the need for plans to be used to control the project.

Things to look out for include:

- are plans being baselined and filed in the project filing system?
- are all versions of plans being retained to form an audit trail of the project? These may be useful later in the project to demonstrate any slippage caused by the Buyer or third parties not meeting their delivery commitments;
- who is doing the planning? The mechanics of updating plans can be left to administrative staff in the project office, but the intellectual work should be undertaken by the project manager and the team leaders;
- is planning being done only in a 'top-down' manner? It is often tempting for a project manager to develop the master project plan by regarding the timescale

and the team size as givens, and fitting all necessary project activities to the time and effort available. Such a plan is unlikely to be representative of reality. Find out whether team members and team leaders are being encouraged to participate in the planning activity by preparing low-level plans, i.e. a 'bottom-up' approach. Both approaches have value; one can be used to provide a 'sanity check' of the other;

- does the planning horizon cover the whole project timescale, or are activities and work products beyond (say) 3–6 months undefined?

Project resourcing

> **Root Causes**
> *Be on the lookout for:*
> **RC23**   Vendor lack/loss of skilled resources

The key questions you must answer

> Does the project have the staffing, skill and experience profile it needs to deliver to plan and budget? Are key skills being lost? Is the project receiving adequate support from the Vendor's resourcing and human resources (HR) functions?

When there are competing demands for staff within the Vendor organisation, many projects find it hard to obtain the ideal staff. When a project is troubled, staff will be tempted to leave, and potential replacement team members will be wary of joining.

Things to look out for include:

- is there a high level of staff turnover on the project? If so, establish the underlying causes;
- are more experienced – and more expensive – staff being used than budgeted in the original estimates/pricing model, perhaps due to the non-availability of more junior staff? If this is the case, the GP of the project will probably be affected, as more senior staff are not necessarily more productive than junior staff;
- are less experienced staff being used than planned, for example staff with no experience of the software development processes used on the project? Learning on the job can be very expensive in terms of both team leader supervision and the amount of re-work necessary until the new staff become fully effective;
- is the project manager receiving adequate support from production management, resourcing and HR functions within the Vendor organisation?

- is the project dependent on one or two key resources? If so, have these staff committed to stay on the project for defined periods?
- is the project manager taking effective action to obtain necessary resources? If staff cannot be obtained from within the Vendor organisation, the project manager should use available channels to obtain contract staff.

Project information management

> **Root Causes**
> *Be on the lookout for:*
> **RC24** Poor Vendor standards deployment (design, coding, testing, configuration management etc)

The key questions you must answer

> Is the project filing essential information and is an appropriate system – electronic or paper-based – being used? Is personal information being handled with appropriate security?

Information which should be filed includes:

- all RFP/ITT/SOW documentation;
- all Vendor proposals;
- all estimates, pricing models and formal price releases from the business;
- all costs incurred by the project, by accounting period, together with all invoices submitted and payments made;
- all contracts, subcontracts and contract amendments;
- all change control information;
- all quality plans and project initiation documentation, including copies of the standards, processes and procedures specified therein;
- all QA reports and risk assessments;
- all versions of all project plans;
- all documentation work products produced by the project team, including requirements and functional specifications, designs, models, source code, test plans, test scripts, test results, fault reports, build documentation etc;
- all Vendor-internal correspondence, including e-mails;
- all correspondence with the Buyer, including e-mails;
- all progress reports, internal and external;
- all internal and external meeting minutes;
- all project organisation information;
- all staff-related documentation, including terms of reference and appraisal data;

- all project risk logs;
- all issue logs;
- all quality control information, including work product inspection reports, release notes and acceptance documentation.

There are many 'alls' in this list, and deliberately so. It is important to have an audit trail for each type of information. If the project throws away the old version of a document every time it is updated, then reviewers and trouble-shooters lose a vital view of where the project has come from and only have access to information showing where the project thinks it is.

Things to look out for include:

- projects are increasingly using computer-based approaches to project information management. Technology such as Lotus Notes can be used to provide secure document filing and management, information interchange between team members and shared 'project workrooms'. If the project is using a computer-based information management system, check that regular back-ups are being taken and stored in a fire-proof safe;
- ensure that project correspondence – likely to include many e-mails – is being retained. As our mail files expand, most of us are subject to strong pressure from the CIO to jettison old correspondence or delete attachments. It is crucial that projects ensure that all working papers and correspondence are filed. This must include bid-stage documents, especially estimates and estimating assumptions;
- if the project is troubled, it is valuable for the project manager to maintain a log of all contact with the Buyer, subcontractors and third parties. This should include a log of each letter sent and received (including important e-mails and faxes) and a short note summarising the substance of important telephone calls;
- is the filing system being maintained?

Progress monitoring and control

Root Causes
Be on the lookout for:
RC22 Failure to undertake effective project reviews and take decisive action

The key question you must answer

Is progress being *monitored*, or *controlled*?

There is a distinction here! Simply collecting timesheets and updating the plans to show actual effort expended, by activity, is *passive monitoring*. *Active control* requires a feedback loop; it means that the project manager, the development manager and team leaders:

- compare expected progress with actual progress, normally on a weekly cycle;
- identify areas of the project, teams or individuals (including Buyer or subcontractors) which are not delivering to plan;
- clarify the issues;
- take action to address the issues, including those which require the Buyer or a subcontractor to take action or do something differently;
- as a last resort, rather than as an initial response, vary the plans and estimate-to-complete numbers to ensure that time-line and resource plans remain realistic.

Financial monitoring and control

Root Causes
Be on the lookout for:
RC12   Vendor underestimate of resources (predominantly person-effort) required

Financial accounting

The key questions you must answer

Do the project manager, the production manager, the management accountant and the owning business have an accurate view of project financials to date, and a realistic model of revenue, cost, GP and cash flow to project completion? Is GP being monitored or managed?

Projects with good resource planning spreadsheets and processes will maintain their own revenue and cost forecasts. The cost forecast provides a valuable means of confirming the accuracy of charges reported to the project manager from the time recording system and ledgers. Other projects leave the financial monitoring and control to the management accountant within the business. Either approach is acceptable, provided that:

- accurate revenue and cost information is maintained;
- regular checks are made to ensure that only valid charges are accepted by the project manager or management accountant against the project's accounting code;

- the project manager's resource plans are realistic and reflected in the financial forecasts;
- GP is monitored and profit improvement plans put in place if the project fails to meet its GP targets;
- project contingency is being managed and not released into the project's revenue line more quickly than real progress is being made.

Many of the delivery review focus areas are of great interest to the Buyer. This is a prime example; the Buyer must maintain similar financial forecasts of budgeted and anticipated cost.

Billing and credit control

The key questions you must answer

> Is the project manager initiating billing for completed work in a timely fashion and ensuring that the Buyer is meeting the payment terms specified in the contract? Is there any evidence of late payment, which might indicate a Buyer satisfaction issue?

The project manager should have a file of all invoices raised and be able to identify which have been paid. Things to look out for include:

- milestones which are 'complete' but have not been billed due to the Buyer withholding approval of deliverables;
- high-value milestones which cannot be billed due to minor outstanding work;
- credit notes being raised in response to Buyer complaints about quality or timeliness;
- invoices unpaid due to a Buyer satisfaction issue.

Contract management

Root Causes
Be on the lookout for:
RC18 Failure to 'freeze' the requirements baseline and apply change control
RC28 Vendor failure to 'freeze' the design (and technical platform) and apply change control
RC31 Poor Vendor management of subcontractors

Change control

The key question you must answer

> Is the Vendor project manager controlling scope creep and ensuring that all changes requested by the Buyer (and any additional cost resulting from Buyer non-performance) result in chargeable contract variations?

Change management can be a cause of conflict between Buyer and Vendor. In general terms, minimising change is beneficial to both parties. Fewer changes imply lower cost to the Buyer, faster project delivery and less re-work of project work products. Rather than requesting substantial change to a software release in development, Buyers should postpone all non-essential changes until a later software release.

The project manager should have a file of all change control requests (CCRs) and be able to identify the status of each CCR. The project manager should also have a file of contract changes, which will include accepted CCRs. Look out for:

- the lack of 'frozen' requirements and design baselines. Change management is impossible if requirements and design specifications are fluid;
- zero-cost, increased-scope changes. The Vendor project manager has to adopt a robust position and negotiate reasonable additional funding for every CCR;
- the cost of investigating change requests (whether proposed by the Vendor or the Buyer) is legitimate project work and should be charged to the Buyer;
- the project manager must negotiate an extension to all milestone dates affected by each change. This might appear to be unnecessarily confrontational, but it is absolutely vital, particularly for projects which include provision for liquidated damages and/or the possibility of contract breach for failure to meet contractual milestone dates;
- if there is a large number of change control requests, or if some of the changes are substantial (for example, representing 10 per cent or more of the original project revenue), check that the project manager is building enough funding into the pricing of the CCR to fund the management and infrastructure overhead of running the project for (say) 10 per cent longer;
- check that the project manager is obtaining appropriate release approvals from QA, the contracts professional and the business.

Subcontract management

The key questions you must answer

> What is the Vendor's dependency on third parties, and are any key exposures or issues likely to impact the success, timeliness or profitability of the project?

Things to look out for include:

- work having started on the project, probably under a letter of intent (LOI) or an authorisation to proceed (ATP) from the Buyer, but no subcontract signed with one or more subcontractors;
- poorly defined subcontract Statements of Work (SOW) which do not include a schedule of deliverables or do not map clearly onto the requirements documents governing the Vendor's contract with the Buyer;
- subcontracts not 'flowing down' the Terms and Conditions of the Vendor's contract with the Buyer, particularly in the area of liquidated damages;
- the Vendor doing business on fixed-price terms with the Buyer and Time & Materials (T & M) terms with any subcontractor;
- do the subcontractors have quality systems in place and do the subcontracts give the Vendor sight of quality plans and controls, and access to appropriate metrics indicative of progress?
- subcontracts should have a defined subcontract manager on the project team (not necessarily full-time). A subcontractor management system should be in place, with baseline documentation, deliverable approval procedures, formal progress reporting, issue management, change control and contract variation procedures – a microcosm of the project's own management system;
- are the subcontractors' invoices being checked and paid in a timely manner, in accordance with the payment terms defined in the subcontracts?
- reliance on immature hardware or software products developed by a subcontractor. An appropriate escrow arrangement is required, plus a contingency plan indicating how the project will recover from subcontractor failure to deliver;
- reliance on internal, Vendor 'subcontractors'. These can be treated less formally than external subcontractors. This is unwise. Detailed statements of work are needed, and documents of understanding (the equivalent of a subcontract but, unfortunately, not legally binding when the parties are both within the same organisation) should be prepared and signed. Executive-level contact between the owning business and the internal 'subcontractor' must also be established.

Buyer relationship management

Root Causes
Be on the lookout for:
RC01 Project based on an unsound premise or an unrealistic business case
RC02 Buyer failure to define clear project objectives, anticipated benefits and success criteria
RC04 Lack of Buyer Board-level ownership/commitment or competence

> **RC05** Buyer's funding and/or timescale expectations unrealistically low
> **RC06** Buyer failure to break a complex project into phases or smaller projects
> **RC09** Failure to achieve an open, robust and equitable Buyer–Vendor relationship
> **RC11** Buyer lack of sufficient involvement of eventual end-users
> **RC14** Failure to actively manage risks and maintain robust contingency plans
> **RC15** Poor project planning, management and execution (by the Buyer)
> **RC16** Failure to clearly define roles and responsibilities in the contract/ subcontracts
> **RC34** Buyer failure to manage the change implicit in the project (people, processes, technology)
> **RC35** Inadequate user/systems training

The key questions you must answer

> The most common question to ask the Buyer is 'How satisfied are you with the Vendor's performance on this project?' But the large size of the Root Causes panel above highlights other crucial issues. Is there Board-level visibility of the project and is an accurate picture of the project being portrayed to the Buyer's Board? How committed is the Board to the project? How competent is the Buyer's team? Are they meeting their contractual responsibilities? Is there a good relationship between the Buyer project manager and the Vendor project manager, enabling them to deal effectively with project issues? Is the Buyer approaching implementation with due regard to the need to manage culture change and user training?

To answer these questions, speak with a Buyer representative – normally the Buyer's project manager. You cannot ask many of the questions directly. For example, it would be impertinent to question the Buyer's competence or the commitment of the Board. However, you can form an opinion on these matters from an in-depth discussion. The conversation with the Buyer can also confirm that several other root causes of troubled projects might be 'waiting in the wings', including:

> **RC36** Catastrophic failure of the system, with no effective contingency arrangement
> **RC38** Buyer failure to measure actual delivered benefit and take corrective action
> **RC39** Buyer failure to maintain/enhance system post-implementation

Obtain the approval of the Vendor project manager to meet or telephone the Buyer's project manager or another suitable representative, such as the chairman of the project board or steering committee. Speak with the production manager, client manager and business manager to build up a mental picture of the individual you will meet or speak with. The Vendor project manager should not be present during your conversation with the Buyer representative as this enables the Buyer to be more open.

Establish the Buyer representative's role and how long they have been associated with the project. Then ask predominantly open questions such as:

- 'what are your measures of success for the project?'
- 'how have your objectives changed since work began?'
- 'from where you stand today, do you feel that the business case remains valid?'
- 'to what extent do you feel that Buyer and Vendor share the same understanding of the business drivers and user expectations of the system?'
- 'what is your level of satisfaction with the Vendor organisation?'
- 'how well are the relationships between Buyer and Vendor working?'
- 'how visible is the project to your senior management/Board?'
- 'how is senior management/the Board briefed about project issues?'
- 'how much time per week would you estimate that the project sponsor devotes to the project?'
- 'what would you say we (the Vendor) are doing well?'
- 'what do you think we could do better?'
- 'what do you see as the key issues and risks during development and testing?'
- 'what do you see as the key issues and risks during implementation?'
- 'what contingency plans are in place in the event of a serious system failure in the early weeks of operation?'
- 'how are you managing the change faced by users of the system?'
- 'how did you assess the training needs of users?'
- 'how will you measure the actual business benefit delivered by the system?'
- 'how will the system be supported and maintained, post implementation?'
- 'with hindsight, what changes would you have made with regard to how the project has been structured and approached?'
- 'what other projects or initiatives in your organisation might impact this project?'
- 'what other matters would you like to raise?'

If you are undertaking a trouble-shooting review of a project in difficulty and you have the permission of the Vendor project manager, ask how willing the Buyer representative would be to participate in a joint workshop session to prepare a turnaround strategy and plan.

Issue management

Root Causes
Be on the lookout for:
RC15   Poor project planning, management and execution

The key questions you must answer

Is there a means by which individual team members or team leaders can raise issues for discussion and resolution, and is there evidence that issues are addressed effectively?

Good issue management is fundamental to good project management. Ask each team member you interview for their view of the key issues and risks faced by the project.

Things to look out for include:

- is there an issues log? If not, how are issues captured and recorded?
- do team members feel free to raise issues with team leaders and the project manager?
- do team members feel that issues raised are taken seriously and addressed?
- does the project manager hold weekly meetings with team leaders at which issues are reviewed?
- are these meetings minuted?
- are issues reported effectively and openly in internal and external progress reports?
- are issues being removed from the issue log or list before they have been fully resolved?
- are any issues caused by the Buyer being addressed effectively?

Risk management

Root Causes
Be on the lookout for:
RC14 Failure to actively manage risks and maintain robust contingency
        plans

The key questions you must answer

> Does the project manager and the team know what the key risks to the project are? Are the risks documented in a risk log or risk register? Are the risks being managed?

Ask each team member you interview for their view of the key risks faced by the project.

Things to look out for include:

- is there a risk log or risk register?
- does each risk have an estimated probability and a quantitative impact so that the project can focus on the 'big hitters'?
- does each risk have documented risk-reduction actions?
- are risk-reduction actions being progressed?
- are contingency plans defined and costed, at least for the high-impact risks?
- is the cost impact of the residual risk (defined in Chapter 10) known?
- is there a residual risk contingency which covers a percentage of the cost of residual risk?
- is the risk log reviewed regularly by the project manager and team leaders – are risk-reduction actions reviewed, new risks added, old risks removed etc. In other words, are the risks being managed?

> Unmanaged risks can become issues. Unmanaged issues lead to a troubled project.

Review the risk log and determine how many of the risks you have identified in the review are actually in the risk log. If appropriate, recommend a risk workshop to update the risk log.

Quality of monthly reporting

> **Root Causes**
> *Be on the lookout for:*
> **RC24** Poor Vendor standards deployment (design, coding, testing, configuration management etc)

The key questions you must answer

> Is the project manager producing informative internal and external progress reports to enable both Vendor and Buyer management to support the project?

> Do the reports reflect the true position with regard to progress, cost and quality?

You can probably answer the second part of this question better towards the end of the review. The project manager should have a file of all internal and external progress reports.

Summary

Project planning

Is the project undertaking effective planning using both 'top-down' and 'bottom-up' approaches? Are plans being baselined and all versions maintained to provide an audit trail? Does the planning horizon extend to the whole project timescale, with a moderate degree of detail in the planning or activities?

Project resourcing

If team members more junior than planned are deployed, are team leaders providing appropriate supervision and support? Are resourcing and HR functions providing an effective service to the project manager? If staff turnover is high, what are the underlying reasons? Have key team members committed to remain on the project for defined periods?

Project information management

Project information must be securely filed in a paper-based or computer-based filing system. A wide range of information must be held, including bid information such as early estimates and estimating assumptions. E-mails and other correspondence with the Buyer, subcontractors and third parties must be retained; this is vital to support project delivery reviews and any dispute which might arise.

Progress monitoring and control

Active control is needed, not *passive monitoring*. This requires regular comparison of actual and planned progress, the identification of non-performing teams or individuals, the clarification and investigation of issues, and swift action to address the issues. Plans and estimates should only be varied when this is necessary in order to ensure that time-line and resource plans remain realistic.

Financial monitoring and control

Revenue and cost forecasts must be maintained to support financial management. Forecast cost must be based on a realistic assessment of the effort required to complete the project. Falling GP must trigger the development of a profit improvement plan. Billing for completed work must be initiated in a timely manner. Late payment of invoices might indicate a Buyer satisfaction issue.

Contract management

'Frozen' requirements and design baselines must be in place to support change control. Every change requiring additional work must result in increased funding and movement to the right of all affected milestones. As a general principle, all non-essential changes should be postponed to a later software release to minimise the impact on work in progress.

Subcontracts and documents of understanding with Vendor-internal 'subcontractors' must be signed at the same time as the master contract between Vendor and Buyer. Subcontracts must 'flow down' the Terms and Conditions of the master contract, specify how product/service quality will be controlled, and define the metrics to be used to report progress. A subcontractor management system must be in place. Actions to be taken in the event of subcontractor failure to deliver to the subcontract must be defined.

Buyer relationship management

An interview with a Buyer representative can indicate whether success criteria have been defined for the project and whether the original business case has been compromised in any way. The interview can identify relationships which are not working and highlight the issues and risks which are uppermost in the Buyer's mind. The level of sponsorship and commitment within the Buyer organisation can often be established, as can the level of readiness of the organisation for live system operation.

Issue management

Good issue management is fundamental to good project management. Ask each team member for their view of the key issues. It should be possible for any team member to raise issues. There should be a formal issues log or list which is regularly reviewed and updated. Issues should be reported in internal and external progress reports.

Risk management

Ask each team member for their view of the key risks. There should be a risk log or risk register. The probability and impact of each risk should be defined, together with risk-reduction actions and contingency plans. Check that risk reduction actions are being progressed and that the risk log is regularly reviewed. Compare the predicted cost of residual risk with the risk contingency available.

Quality of monthly reporting

Is the project manager producing informative internal and external progress reports to enable both Vendor and Buyer management to support the project? Do the reports reflect the true position with regard to progress, cost and quality?

Postscript to Part 3

Congratulations if you have read the whole of Part 3. Checklists are heavy going. In my defence, I have proved that the focus areas covered in Part 3 *are* effective at getting to the root of a project's troubles. Try running project health check reviews and trouble-shooting reviews using these focus areas and see if you agree.

Part 4

PROJECT TURNAROUND AND ORGANISATIONAL LEARNING

Chapter 20

TURNING AROUND A TROUBLED PROJECT

Introduction to Part 4

Part 1 of this book presents 40 root causes of troubled IT projects, based on published studies and personal experience. Part 2 provides guidance on how to avoid the majority of these root causes during the planning or bid stage of a project.

I will be delighted if the principles set out in Part 2 reduce the occurrence of troubled IT projects. However, I am not under the illusion that troubled IT projects will be in short supply. For this reason, Part 3 sets out an approach to reviewing projects in delivery and identifying troubled project root causes. This approach covers routine project health check reviews for currently 'untroubled' projects. It also covers in-depth, trouble-shooting reviews for projects known to be in difficulty.

In Part 4, we are at the stage where we know that we have a project in trouble and we know what the root causes are. We have the report from a recent trouble-shooting review. We are no longer looking for problems. The adrenalin is pumping and we are looking for solutions.

This chapter sets out an approach to defining a turnaround strategy and plan for such a project. To set expectations appropriately, I have never come across a turnaround strategy which resulted in the project being delivered to its original budget, timescale and functional scope. That would be a miracle for a project which has already veered substantially off track. What we are looking for in a turnaround strategy and plan is not a miracle but rather:

- collaboration between Buyer and Vendor to avoid an otherwise inevitable project failure;
- the confronting of root causes by both parties;
- the definition of initiatives to address the root causes;
- improvements in the delivery efficiency of the team;
- the reshaping of the project to deliver tangible business benefit to the Buyer in an acceptable timescale and at an acceptable cost, which *will* mean revision of the original business case;
- the regaining and maintenance of control over the project.

We can see that a turnaround strategy is likely to be a combination of initiatives. Some initiatives will be directed at addressing the root causes of the project's problems. Some will be directed at improving the software development and project management processes to make the project team a more efficient delivery vehicle. Some will be directed at changing the shape of the project to deliver tangible business benefit earlier than would otherwise be the case.

The joint nature of a turnaround strategy is important. Vendors with a troubled project due in large part to Vendor-induced root causes will often attempt to formulate a unilateral turnaround strategy. This is usually done without the knowledge of the Buyer, with the primary purpose of improving profitability. Renegotiation of the contract is often high on the list of initiatives arising from such a strategy. This is very hard to achieve. Why should the Buyer provide additional funding to compensate the Vendor for the financial impact of poor Vendor performance?

A successful turnaround strategy will result in the project 'turning the corner'. However, we must recognise that it is not possible to define a turnaround strategy for every project. In some cases, the turnaround strategy exercise *must* result in the termination of the project. This requires great clarity of thought and high-quality decision-making on the part of senior management in the Buyer and Vendor organisations. It is in the interests of neither party for a turnaround strategy and plan to be formulated and for the plan to subsequently fail.

When leading a network strategy study for the Royal Navy section of what is now the Defence Logistics Organisation, I studied the performance of existing networks. A 'batch network' was used to transmit requisitions from Naval bases to the mainframe computer sites controlling the stock. It was also used to transmit forms and reports from the mainframes to the bases for local printing. The batch network comprised a number of mid-range servers connected by dedicated leased lines. Data was read from magnetic tapes and transmitted in batches across the network.

Two problems were apparent. The rate at which data could be transmitted was low and printing at the Naval bases was ineffective. I had some success investigating the data rate problem. I noticed that, during transmission, the disc drive was vibrating like the spin dryer my mother used to have and that the tape drive was also juddering in an alarming manner. The source code confirmed my suspicion that tape reads and writes were being performed a record at a time. Inserting a few lines of code to implement a double buffer approach increased the data rate by an order of magnitude and enabled the organisation to reduce the hours of operator cover at the Naval bases.

The printing problem was more elusive. The operator could direct a print job to Printer A or Printer B. Either printer would print at full speed provided the other printer was not in use. If both printers were in use, the sound was reminiscent of a box of fireworks exploding, as both printers slowed to half their normal print rate. It was clear that the printer driver was not handling concurrency correctly.

I studied the program, which ran to about 20 pages of source code. The programmer who had written the program was no longer with the organisation. I desk-checked the code with one print job and with two print jobs. The program used a large number of 'flags' to maintain control over character

> buffers, printer status and print job status. After a couple of days it was clear that I was unable to follow the structure and logic of the program. I would never be able to debug it. A rewrite was necessary. We later rewrote the program, very elegantly, recursively and re-entrantly. The source code was about three pages long and both printers operated at rated speed.

The above example is presented to make the point that it is sometimes necessary to abandon a software work product, a project phase, or even a project, and to start again from scratch.

Published troubled project remedies

The survey on 'runaway projects' conducted by KPMG Management Consulting in 1994[1] asked respondents which of a range of remedies they had applied to runaway projects. The results are shown in Figure 20.1, reproduced by permission of A P Publications Limited.

Three of the four most popular remedies involve applying additional resources to the project without changing its shape or project processes in any way. Two of the remedies involve the Buyer applying extra pressure on the Vendor by with-

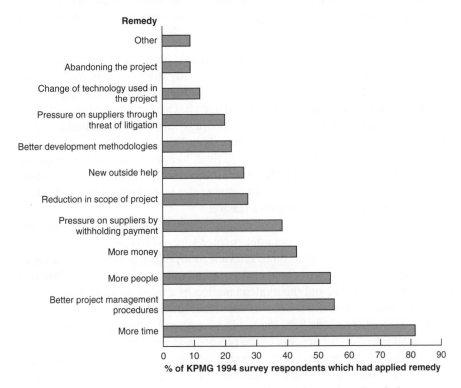

Figure 20.1   *Runaway Project Remedies from the 1994 KPMG Survey*

holding payment or threatening litigation. Once again, neither of these remedies reshape the project or improve its processes.

Only 4 per cent of respondents had carried out their threat and resorted to the Courts. Of course, litigation is not actually a remedy for an ailing project. However, it could represent an element of an exit strategy from a troubled project and it certainly could be a financial recovery strategy, depending on the merits of the plaintiff's case. Similarly, abandonment of the project is not really a remedy, but it is certainly a step which needs to be taken, and taken quickly, if no turnaround strategy can be found.

Remedies in the KPMG survey which do reshape the project or improve project processes include:

- better project management procedures;
- reduction in the scope of the project;
- employing new outside help;
- better development methodologies;
- change of technology used in the project.

The focus of the report *Improving the Delivery of Government IT Projects*[2] is on providing advice to government organisations on how troubled IT projects can be avoided. The report does not set out specific remedies for troubled IT projects. However, it does contain some nuggets relevant to a turnaround strategy, as follows:

- It concludes that 'end users must be identified before the project commences so that their needs are taken into account fully during design and development.' I believe that the involvement of end-users in the development of a project turnaround strategy is particularly vital as they are best placed to advise on what level of functional de-scoping is feasible for an initial release.
- It notes that 'Government Departments should consider whether their overriding priority is to deliver the project to time, to cost, or to a particular quality specification.' This is good advice for all Buyers. During the development of a turnaround strategy, Buyer clarity on priorities is essential as this will inform which re-shaping approaches are feasible.
- It recommends that 'Departments should draw up contingency plans to cover the risk that the system is not implemented successfully on time and as specified.' This advice is even more relevant to a project implementing a turnaround plan because a troubled project has a higher probability of failure than an untroubled one, and the implementation of a turnaround plan does imply additional funding and the risk of additional financial loss.
- It notes that 'relations between the Department and the supplier will have a crucial effect on the success of the project, and that Departments should ensure that all parties have a clear understanding of their respective roles and responsibilities, and a shared understanding of key terms and deadlines.' During the development of a turnaround strategy, cards must be laid on the table

and both parties must step up to their responsibilities, including financial responsibility for past mistakes.

Parliamentary copyright is reproduced with the permission of the Controller of Her Majesty's Stationery Office on behalf of Parliament.

Another UK Government paper, *Successful IT: Modernising Government in Action*,[3] was published by the Cabinet Office in 2000. The focus of this paper is on improving IT delivery performance in Government and on avoiding the mistakes of the past. Once again, advice is presented which is particularly relevant to the development of a turnaround strategy and plan:

- 'Business cases must reflect all of the business change to be delivered.' This recommendation recognises that successful IT projects do not focus solely upon IT delivery but also embrace the design and delivery of business process change and change management initiatives. The relevance of this to the development of a project turnaround strategy is that the work includes, probably on more than one occasion, examination and adjustment of the business case underpinning the project. It is essential to include all relevant costs in the business case, even if these were excluded from the original business case.
- 'All IT-supported change projects or programmes must have a single, named Senior Responsible Owner (SRO). This individual is responsible for ensuring that the project or programme meets its overall objectives and delivers its projected benefits.' This recommendation recognises the need for leadership, responsibility and ownership within the Buyer organisation. Its relevance to the development of a turnaround strategy is that such a strategy will generate initiatives to be implemented by both parties, not just the Vendor.
- 'Departments and agencies must adopt a modular and/or incremental approach to projects, unless there are very strong reasons for not doing so.' This recommendation recognises that IT projects which attempt to provide support to an organisation's entire range of business processes are likely to fail; it is better to address the requirements of one functional area at a time. The recommendation also recognises the wisdom of initially providing an 'entry level' of IT support for a functional area and expanding the richness of IT support by means of subsequent releases of the application. These modular and incremental strategies are of immense value when defining turnaround strategies.
- 'Departments and agencies must ensure that they put in place processes that will actively encourage co-operation and an open dialogue between supplier and client.' This recommendation recognises that a mature relationship between Buyer and Vendor can have a substantial positive impact on project success. This is the underlying premise of Part 2 and Part 4 of this book. The parties must be open with each other during the development of a turnaround strategy and plan.

Crown copyright is reproduced with the permission of the Controller of Her Majesty's Stationery Office.

In his book *Crunch Mode*,[4] John Boddie notes that when a 'crunch mode' project is slipping, there are only three options – the functional requirements can be de-scoped, the delivery date can be slipped, or the project can be cancelled. By definition, the team on such a project is already operating at full capacity. He notes that the remedies often suggested by senior management – adding more staff to the team, and motivating the team to keep to the original schedule – are seldom successful. When a team is working at full stretch, they cannot sustain the burden of inducting new team members without falling even further behind schedule. And when a team is working at full capacity they cannot be further motivated; any attempt to do so will be seen by the team as somewhat of an insult.

Tucked away towards the back of Robert Glass's book, *Software Runaways*,[5] are some excellent 'principles to minimise the damage in IS development failure', some of which are reproduced below, with the permission of Pearson Education Inc:

- 'When outlining the project schedule, be realistic and include an adequate 'slack' time. Technical and other problems may occur.' This is of crucial importance when developing a project turnaround strategy. Team morale will have suffered badly as the project became troubled. To recover good team morale, the turnaround plan must be realistic, enabling each milestone date to be met.
- 'Executives should not make any 'calming' statements about the project status before they learn the facts. Making uncorroborated statements is not only unethical to the client, it may also send wrong signals to employees.' The relevance of this advice to the development of a turnaround strategy is that the work must start with a full analysis of the current situation.
- 'Most important: being dishonest may hurt your client, but it may also hurt you and your company. The financial impact of lost business because of a failure due to lies may prove much greater than the lost income from a single mishap. If it is not the monetary gain that drives your judgement but the reluctance to admit professional weakness, think again. Failure to disclose the real status of the project to the client may exacerbate the damage. Unfortunately, honesty is not always in one's economic self-interest. Often, there is economic incentive to lying (e.g. when the transaction is a one-shot deal and if information of the incident does not spread). But in this age of fast communication, especially in the IS industry, the news will travel fast. And your own employees may follow the bad example: they will lie to their superiors.' When developing a project turnaround strategy, honesty and straight dealing are essential. By definition, a troubled project has a higher probability than an untroubled one of ending up in Court. Any evidence that a Vendor or Buyer has attempted to cover up, mislead or lie will be immensely damaging.

A composite list of generic project reshaping options

Table 20.1 contains a selection of potential project reshaping options, one or more of which, when coupled with a set of initiatives aimed at implementing the recommendations of the most recent trouble-shooting review and addressing the root causes of the project's problems, may yield a viable turnaround strategy. The options in Table 20.1 should only be considered when Buyer and Vendor are agreed on the overriding priority for the project – time, cost or functional quality.

Inputs to the development of a turnaround strategy

A key input to the development of a troubled project turnaround strategy is the report prepared by a trouble-shooting review team. Such a review will thoroughly investigate the state of health of the project, review project risks and containment plans, highlight the root causes of the project's problems, and make recommendations to address all issues found. It should also scope and plan an exercise to develop a turnaround strategy.

The nature of this exercise will depend on the size of the project and the seriousness of the issues. For a small project with a few problems, a one-day workshop might be sufficient to bottom-out the issues and determine the initiatives the Buyer and Vendor teams must take to correct matters and refocus the project. For a large project, Vendor and Buyer management might establish a task force or commission a team of external consultants to recommend how the project problems should be tackled. My belief is that a project turnaround strategy is best undertaken as a series of one-day workshops, each addressing a step in the process. The process typically extends over several weeks, as Buyer and Vendor project teams will need to consult with their senior management and this consultation takes time.

The turnaround strategy process

The turnaround strategy process is shown in Figure 20.2.

There are four steps in the process. Step 1 seeks to establish the facts of the current project situation, in order to provide an answer to the question 'Where are we now?' – the basic starting position for any strategy. The Vendor is best placed to lead this step as the Vendor organisation is closer to the design, development, integration and testing issues and will have access to the findings of all delivery reviews undertaken on the project. The parties review the issues and root causes impacting the project. The project plan is reviewed and adjusted, if necessary, to derive realistic dates for milestones and project completion. Vendor and Buyer cost projections are adjusted to take into account the impact of any slippage. Step

Table 20.1   *Generic Project Reshaping Options*

General

- Strengthen/replace/refocus/reorganise management and skills in both Buyer and Vendor teams where this is needed.
- Implement improvements in the development and test environments if lack of server/PC power or other bottlenecks are delaying development.
- Consider redistributing project work to new, specialist Commercial Off-The-Shelf (COTS)/services Vendors.

Requirements

- Put all Buyer-generated change requests through a Buyer-led review panel before releasing any 'must have for initial release' change requests to the Vendor.
- Review functional scope and totally remove support for any business function where the business case is weak, or robust alternative IT support already exists, or suitable IT support can be made available using COTS packages.
- Prioritise business functions and determine which functions must be supported in the initial release and which can be supported by later releases.
- Review any package customisation being undertaken and determine whether the Buyer could use vanilla functionality through modest business process change.
- Prioritise functional requirements in each functional area of the business into 'must haves for first release', 'must haves for subsequent releases', and 'non-essentials'. Remove all the non-essentials.

Design, Development and Integration

- Evaluate the solution and determine whether there is a case for changing the underpinning technology, including more use of COTS application software.
- If time is the overriding priority, implement more streams of development by partitioning the development project into sub-projects, each with clear functional scope. These teams can operate in parallel but their outputs must be mapped onto defined software builds and releases. (This approach will require additional funding.)
- Adopt an early integration approach to solve as many integration and infrastructure issues as possible and demonstrate that non-functional requirements can be met before the application development is complete.
- Consider whether interfaces to external or legacy systems can be simplified (even to the extent of making them batch interfaces in the first instance) or whether advantage can be taken of middleware such as IBM MQ Series.

Testing and Implementation

- Mobilise end users to work with the Vendor's testing teams well ahead of user acceptance testing.
- Consider the concept of a functional pilot, with roll-out to other groups of end users delayed until Release #2.

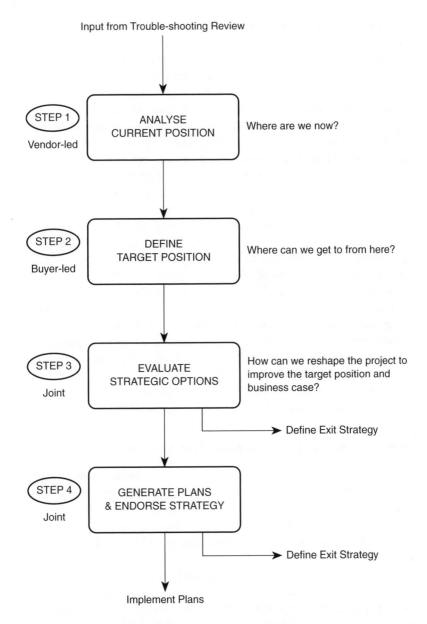

Figure 20.2 *The Basic Turnaround Strategy Process*

1 is a fact-finding step which leads directly to Step 2, any delay being that necessary to prepare for Step 2.

Step 2 seeks to define a feasible target position for the project, answering the question 'Where can we get to from here?' The Buyer is best placed to lead this step as the Buyer organisation owns the business case. Issues and root causes are confronted and a package of costed initiatives is drawn up designed to bring the project, more or less in the same shape as originally defined, back onto an even keel. It is inevitable that the feasible target position is not the same as the original target position. The Buyer's business case is adjusted to take account of slippage and the costed initiatives. If the Buyer's adjusted business case is tenable, Step 2 could lead directly to Step 4. However, Step 3 is still worth undertaking as it has the potential to improve the target position and business case.

Step 3 evaluates strategic options, in order to provide an answer to the question 'How can we reshape the project to improve the target position and the business case?' This is a joint activity which attempts to define alternative packages of initiatives and project reshaping options, evaluate them and propose a 'strawman' turnaround strategy. This strategy is defined and costed, and the business case is once again adjusted. If the adjusted business case is still not tenable, an escape route is provided. This escape route allows the Buyer and the Vendor to define an exit strategy. Hopefully, this will be a bilateral exit strategy, not involving litigation. If the adjusted business case now 'works' for the Buyer, Step 3 leads directly to Step 4, any delay being that necessary to prepare for Step 4.

Step 4 seeks to prepare detailed cost estimates and plans as if the project was a new one, which it is. A revised project charter and business case are prepared, and Buyer and Vendor senior management meet to commit to proceeding with the turnaround strategy and plan. In the event that this commitment is not obtained, an exit strategy is defined. If commitment is obtained, plans are laid to relaunch the project.

Each of these steps is described in more detail later in this chapter, following some advice on the groundwork necessary to prepare for the workshops.

Preparing an environment for success

Select a neutral location for the workshops. A nice quiet hotel in the country with conference facilities and a very good restaurant is best. There are going to be some sizeable egos in the room, so make sure that you select a large room, with ample whiteboard space and several flip chart stands. You will also need some syndicate rooms so that Vendor and Buyer teams can break out of the workshop for private discussions.

Employ the services of an experienced facilitator. They have the skill to ensure that the agenda is acceptable to all participants, that outcomes are placed on the table, that emotion is kept to a minimum, that no one person hogs the airtime or imposes their views on the meeting, that peripheral issues or those requiring substantial debate are put 'on ice' for later, and that the workshop makes reasonable progress against the agreed agenda.

Agree some ground rules, up front. These will vary with the project and contractual situation, but they might include several of the following:

- Our overriding objective is to discover a way of turning the project around.
- Both parties will work together to achieve this objective.

- Both parties are prepared to compromise and give ground in a fair and reasonable manner.
- The contract will not be used as the ultimate arbiter on every issue.
- We are going to keep emotion out of the workshop as much as we can.
- We are going to be honest and as open as commercial confidentiality permits.
- We are going to lay our cards on the table with regard to our ability to sustain further financial pain.
- For each project issue we will agree how responsibility (not blame) rests with the parties.
- We are going to step up to our responsibilities.
- Our overriding objective is to discover a way of turning the project around.

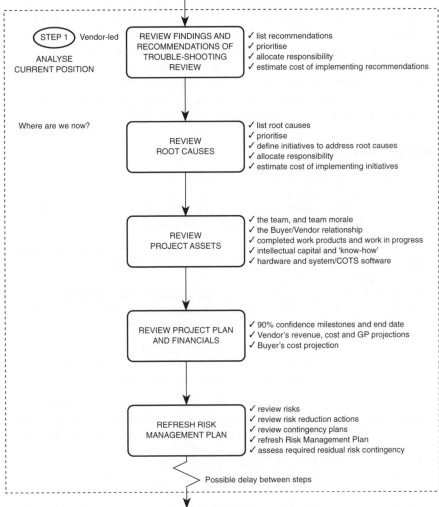

Figure 20.3   *Activity Outline for Step 1*

Step 1 – analyse current position

The activities required to undertake this step are shown in Figure 20.3. Each activity is described briefly below.

Review findings and recommendations of trouble-shooting review

List the findings and recommendations of the most recent project review. For each finding which highlights an issue or a process improvement opportunity, ensure that there is a corresponding recommendation; if there isn't, create one.

Prioritise the finding/recommendation pairs in a column down the left hand side of a whiteboard, with the finding/recommendation with the largest potential positive impact on the project at the top. Add five further columns to the whiteboard. In column 2, allocate responsibility for the original issue (Buyer, Vendor or Joint). In column 3, allocate ownership of the recommended action (Buyer or Vendor – actions need a single owner). In column 4, estimate the cost of implementing the recommended action. In column 5, estimate the cost to the project of *not* taking action. In column 6, estimate the future saving which will accrue after the recommended action is taken. Remove every finding/recommendation for which there is no compelling reason to implement.

Review root causes

I'm not going to pretend that this activity is easy. As Vendor staff will, most likely, have constructed the list of root causes in the first place, this will be the first time that the Buyer team is confronted with the analysis. The Buyer team is likely to roundly disagree with some root causes placed at their door, such as:

RC01	Project based on an unsound premise or an unrealistic business case
RC04	Lack of Buyer Board-level ownership/commitment or competence
RC05	Buyer's funding and/or timescale expectations unrealistically low

If one or more of these root causes are present, careful crafting is required to remove any pejorative wording, while clearly expressing the underlying issue.

Several other Buyer-induced root causes may have been at work, such as:

RC06	Buyer failure to break a complex project into phases or smaller projects
RC08	Buyer failure to define and document requirements (functional and non-functional)
RC11	Buyer lack of sufficient involvement of eventual end-users
RC17	Full-scope, fixed-price contracting (requirements, design and development)

These are less likely to cause an emotive response as there is substantial evidence in the literature that these are common causes of troubled IT projects.

There will be pain for the Vendor team also when root causes such as the following are disclosed:

RC07	Vendor setting unrealistic expectations on cost, timescale or Vendor capability
RC10	Vendor failure to invest enough resources to scope the project prior to contract
RC12	Vendor underestimation of resources (predominantly person-effort) required
RC13	Vendor failure to define project tasks, deliverables and acceptance process
RC15	Poor project planning, management and execution
RC19	Poor choice of technical platform and/or architecture
RC24	Poor Vendor standards deployment (design, coding, testing, configuration management etc)

So, expect some blood on the floor during this activity as the Buyer and Vendor teams seek to agree which root causes *have* been present on the project. It is not necessary to resolve all disagreement during this activity, as Step 2 contains an activity to confront the root causes and reach agreement on initiatives to address them. A delay between Step 1 and Step 2 provides a cooling-off period.

List on a second whiteboard the troubled project root causes set out in the report of the most recent project review. Prioritise the root causes in a column down the left hand side of the whiteboard, with the 'biggest hitters' at the top. Add five further columns to the whiteboard. In column 2, define an initiative or action to address each root cause. In cases where nothing can be done, just leave an exclamation mark at present. In column 3, allocate ownership of the action (Buyer or Vendor). In column 4, estimate the cost of implementing the action. In column 5, estimate the cost to the project of *not* taking action. In column 6, estimate the future saving which will accrue after the action is taken. Remove every root cause for which there is no compelling reason to implement an action.

Compare the two whiteboards and remove any duplication between findings/recommendations and actions to address root causes.

Review project assets

This activity prepares and reviews a schedule of project assets, covering both tangible and intangible assets.

Start by summarising the Buyer and Vendor teams deployed on the project – the size of the teams, their strengths and weaknesses, the degree of motivation which is evident on both sides, and the level of morale on both sides.

Assess how well the teams are working together at the various levels of interaction. Assess the quality of the Buyer/Vendor relationship overall.

Next, review a schedule of completed work products and work in progress (prepared prior to the workshop). Show a qualitative assessment of the quality of each completed work product, indicating whether the item is of wholly acceptable quality, needs some rework, needs substantial rework, or should be discarded. For work products in progress, indicate the '% complete'. This is a metric with a poor reputation in the IT services industry, but if it was easy to find a better one, we would have done so.

Next, summarise the intellectual capital and 'know-how' which exists on the team and which will be the springboard for any turnaround strategy and plan.

Finally, list the hardware platforms, system software and COTS software which has been purchased for the project and which is being used for development or is set aside for production.

Review project plan and financials

Review the project plan. In most troubled projects, slippage of milestones and pressure on the end-date are evident. Sketch the current high-level plan on the whiteboard and adjust it to show revised dates which the Vendor feels are achievable with 90 per cent confidence. For the purpose of this exercise, assume no change in the overall shape of the project and ignore for the moment the budgetary and business impact of the revised plan on both parties. The important thing is to understand the degree of pressure on the current plan and the amount of movement to the right which would have to be introduced to generate a high-level plan representative of reality.

Review the Vendor's revenue, cost and GP projections. It is normal for Vendors not to disclose their actual-to-date and projected-at-completion costs and this exercise can be conducted by the Vendor team in a breakout room. However, the Vendor team should consider opening the kimono and sharing the numbers as it is valuable for each party to be aware of the degree of pain being suffered by the other party. Projected Vendor cost to complete the project should be increased to take into account the slippage introduced during the previous activity (i.e. assuming the Vendor will fund all the slippage).

Review the budget committed by the Buyer for the total project, including all Buyer activities and contracts placed with other Vendors. Capture actual-to-date and projected-at-completion costs, the latter increased to take into account the slippage introduced during the plan review activity (i.e. assuming the Buyer will fund all the slippage).

At this stage worst-case financial out-turns are defined for both parties. Discuss the appropriate funding split and reach an interim agreement. Both Buyer and Vendor emerge from Step 1 with defined first-cut financial out-turns.

Refresh risk management plan

Review the risks, risk reduction actions and contingency plans in the project risk register. Update the risk register with any new risks arising from the workshop so far, and assess the level of residual risk contingency required. Compare this with risk provisions currently held by Buyer and Vendor.

Step 2 – define target position

The activities required to undertake this step are shown in Figure 20.4. Each activity is described briefly below.

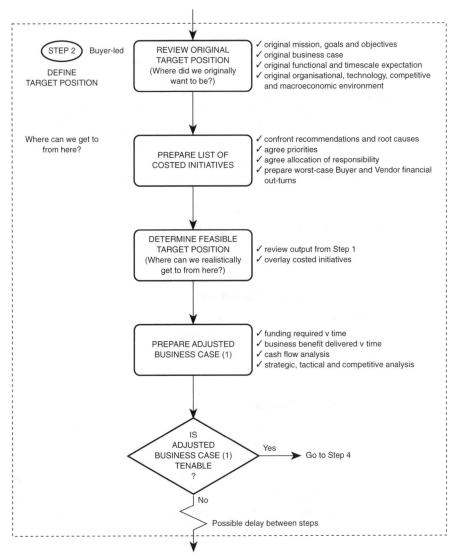

Figure 20.4   *Activity Outline for Step 2*

Review original target position

Summarise the original mission, goals and objectives of the project, defined at project start. Also summarise the original business case – the funding profile, the benefits delivery profile and the anticipated strategic positioning benefits – based on the original functional and timescale expectations.

Review the organisational, technology, competitive and macroeconomic environments at the start of the project and note how they have changed from project start to the current time.

Prepare list of costed initiatives

In Step 1, prioritised lists of project review recommendations and initiatives to address root causes were prepared. The issues and root causes must now be confronted and agreed upon. Review root causes for which no initiative can be defined and determine whether these, collectively, represent a showstopper for the project. Prepare a consolidated list of high-priority, costed actions, each with an owner. For each action, agree whether the Buyer or the Vendor should fund all the work, or what funding split is appropriate. Add the appropriate share of these costs to the Buyer's and Vendor's first-cut financial out-turns, developed during Step 1.

At this point, there is a substantial degree of clarity over the current position of the project. Both Buyer and Vendor have a clearer view of the financial out-turn if the project is allowed to continue in more or less its current shape but with initiatives in place to improve the project processes and to address root causes.

Determine feasible target position

Review the output from Step 1, particularly the adjusted high-level plan showing the milestones and project completion date which the team believed were feasible. Overlay the costed initiatives and determine the impact on the milestones and project end-date.

Prepare adjusted business case (1)

Adjust the original business case to reflect the revised timescales and costs. Set out the Buyer's funding profile, including the cost of all associated tasks (such as culture change management, training, infrastructure, relocation etc). Also define the likely profile of business benefit delivery. A full cash flow analysis might be a little premature at this stage, but the Buyer should assess the likely impact on their business of the funding and benefit delivery profiles. Summarise the strategic, tactical and competitive consequences of reaching the feasible target position.

Is adjusted business case (1) tenable?

The Buyer now assesses whether the adjusted business case is tenable, i.e. whether there is a net return on the investment needed to complete the project, more or less as originally scoped but with initiatives in place to address issues and root causes. When making this assessment, consider the cost and business impact of cancelling the project and taking whatever steps might be needed to address the original business need in an alternative manner.

The Vendor also assesses whether the revised cost profile, generated by taking responsibility for funding certain recovery actions, is sustainable by the business.

If the adjusted financial positions are acceptable to both parties, Step 3 could be bypassed completely. However, Step 3 may provide the opportunity to improve the target position and business case, so it should not be abandoned lightly.

Step 3 – Evaluate Strategic Options

The activities required to undertake this step are shown in Figure 20.5. Each activity is described briefly below.

Review list of costed initiatives from step 2

Retrieve the list of costed initiatives developed during Step 2 and summarise them on the whiteboard.

Brainstorm potential project reshaping options

Review the generic project reshaping options in Table 20.1. Determine which of these could possibly be deployed and summarise them on the whiteboard, with the option with the highest potential at the top.

Taking into account the specific issues and environment of the project, brainstorm further reshaping options and add them to the prioritised list. You must exit this activity with one or more reshaping options, so be creative.

Prepare 2–3 candidate turnaround strategies

The objective of this activity is to prepare 2–3 alternative 'packages' of costed initiatives and project reshaping options for evaluation. Each package is a candidate turnaround strategy. You can include the same set of costed initiatives in each package if it makes sense to do so, but there may be circumstances in which it doesn't make sense. For example, if one of the costed initiatives relates to the partial redesign of the online requisitioning function, and one of the reshaping options is to remove this function totally and continue to deploy legacy functionality for a period, then these two measures would not sit well together.

Consider tackling this activity in two breakout groups, each containing Buyer and Vendor representation. Aim to develop a minimum of two potential turna-

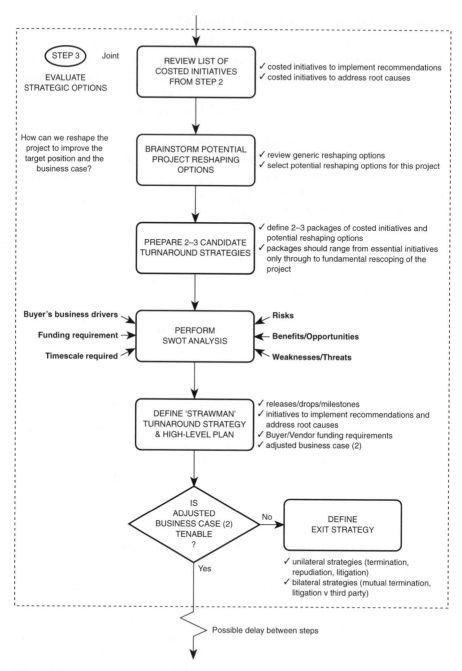

Figure 20.5   *Activity Outline for Step 3*

round strategies. One way to approach this is for one candidate strategy to embody essential initiatives and reshaping options only, and for the other to contain a wider range of initiatives and more fundamental reshaping options.

Perform SWOT analysis

For each candidate turnaround strategy, list on the whiteboard:

- the degree of support offered to key Buyer business drivers;
- the additional or reduced funding requirement (Buyer and Vendor);
- the impact on project timescale;
- the risks;
- the additional or reduced benefits delivered;
- the weaknesses or threats.

Define 'strawman' turnaround strategy and high-level plan

Define the package of costed initiatives and reshaping options which appears to deliver the best 'benefit per buck'. This might be one of the candidate strategies evaluated in the previous activity or a composite turnaround strategy containing parts of two or more candidate strategies.

Sketch a high-level plan for the reshaped project on the whiteboard, showing the major milestones and software drops/releases.

Adjust the projected Vendor cost to complete the project to take into account the reshaped project and the initiatives which are to be taken forward which are wholly or partly funded by the Vendor.

Adjust the Buyer's budget to take into account the reshaped project and the initiatives which are to be taken forward which are wholly or partly funded by the Buyer.

Note that both Buyer and Vendor emerge from this activity with second-cut financial out-turns defined.

Is adjusted business case (2) tenable?

If the Buyer's business case is tenable and the Vendor's financial exposure is sustainable, then the parties have the basis of a viable turnaround strategy and can proceed to Step 4. When making this assessment, the Buyer must consider the cost and business impact of cancelling the project and taking whatever steps might be needed to address the original business need in some less ambitious manner.

Define exit strategy

If no way forward is found, the parties must define an exit strategy. Ideally, this will be a bilateral strategy for terminating the contract, probably with some financial settlement.

Step 4 – generate plans and endorse strategy

The activities required to undertake this step are shown in Figure 20.6. It is not essential to conduct these activities at an off-site location. Each activity is described briefly below.

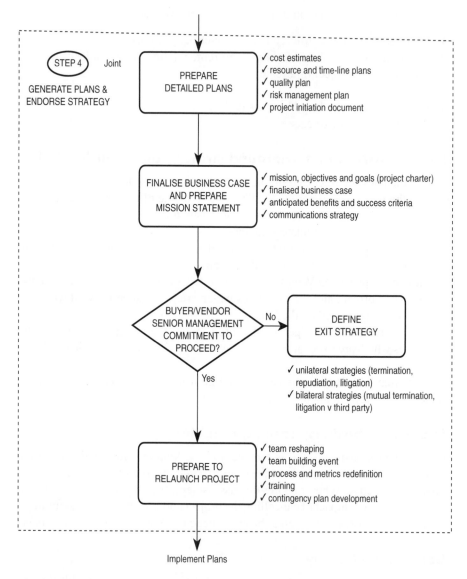

Figure 20.6   *Activity Outline for Step 4*

Prepare detailed plans

The work involved in this activity is virtually identical to that required when planning a new project, as described in Part 2 of this book. The difference is that the various types of plan should already exist and will simply require modification to suit the reshaped project. Clearly, the more the shape has been changed, the greater the degree of modification required.

Start by preparing a revised work breakdown structure to provide the foundation for detailed, activity-based cost estimates. Next prepare resource and timeline (Gantt) plans, driven by the cost estimates.

Modify the Quality Plan to detail any changes to the software development processes, the revised schedule of work products and any changes to the Verification and Validation (V&V) techniques to be used for each work product type.

Update the Risk Management Plan with the risks identified during the SWOT analysis undertaken in Step 3. Calculate the residual risk contingency required.

Generate a succinct and crisp Project Initiation Document (PID). Populate the section on Project Mission, Goals and Objectives, once the team has produced the output from the next activity.

Finalise business case and prepare mission statement

Buyer and Vendor representatives should generate a project charter, setting out the mission, objectives and goals of the revised project.

The Buyer team should then complete the detailed work on the business case. This will highlight the anticipated business benefits of the reshaped project and enable project success criteria to be defined.

Meanwhile, the Vendor team should complete the detailed work on setting out Vendor target financials for the project.

The two teams should then assemble to consider how best to communicate the new project charter and plans to Buyer and Vendor project teams, end-users and third parties.

Buyer/Vendor senior management commitment to proceed?

Hold a formal meeting at which Buyer and Vendor senior management commit to proceeding with the relaunch of the project. If either Buyer or Vendor senior management are unwilling to commit, or unable to secure the necessary approval for additional funding, an exit strategy must be developed as outlined in Step 3.

Prepare to relaunch project

The final activity is to prepare to implement the turnaround strategy and plan.

Make any necessary personnel changes or changes to the structure of the project teams. Hold an off-site event to communicate the project charter and initiate the team-building process.

It is likely that some of the costed initiatives will be to improve software development or project management processes. Train the project teams in their use.

The relaunched project cannot be allowed to fail. This requires the implementation of regular, formal progress reviews. To allow these reviews to make objective assessments of progress against the revised plans, define the metrics which will be gathered and reviewed. These will include financial metrics and progress metrics (such as actual number of test cases completed each week against a defined target). Define the metrics to reflect the nature of the project and the stage reached in the development life cycle.

Finally, define the contingency plan which will be followed if the relaunched project veers off course.

Maximising the chance of a successful turnaround strategy

It is not possible to turn around every troubled IT project, but if you follow the four-step process set out above you should generate one of three outcomes:

1. The project is reshaped, process improvements are implemented, root causes are addressed, and the delivery of the (redefined) project is achieved in the face of what would otherwise have been failure.
2. Project delivery is improved and the project completes earlier than would have been the case without the turnaround strategy intervention.
3. The parties decide to pull the plug on the project to save further money from being wasted.

All of these outcomes are positive and can only be achieved through dialogue between Buyer and Vendor. The earlier in the life of a troubled project that a turnaround is attempted, the higher the chance of success as:

- the Vendor/Buyer relationship will not have deteriorated as much and the parties are more likely to be open with each other;
- the damage will be less severe and easier to correct;
- a smaller percentage of the project budget will have been spent, allowing more project reshaping options to be explored.

To turn around a troubled project, root causes must be confronted and hard decisions must be taken. There may be a need for senior people on either or both teams to be replaced. This would not be done simply because heads must be seen to roll; it would be necessary if one of the key players was felt to lack the ability, commitment, self-belief or leadership skills necessary to deliver the reshaped project. It is important in this situation to test the views of the project teams. A team can refuse to commit to a project relaunch unless the project manager is changed. A team can also refuse to work for a new project manager.

Summary

The most popular troubled project remedies in the literature are 'more time', 'more people', and 'more money'. Another remedy in widespread use is the motivation of the team to work harder and even longer hours of (generally unpaid) overtime. I do not believe that these remedies are particularly effective.

Recent UK Government reports, focusing on the reasons why projects become troubled, correctly stress the value of modular and incremental approaches to development and the importance of a co-operative and open relationship between Buyer and Vendor. These considerations point the way to an approach to the development of a successful turnaround strategy – it requires Buyer and Vendor teams to engage, in an open, honest and collaborative manner to consider how the project can be reshaped. This often means delivering less functionality, but delivering it earlier.

A composite list of generic project reshaping options is presented in this chapter which, when taken into consideration with project improvement initiatives arising from recent project reviews and the confronting of the root causes of the project's problems, may enable a project turnaround strategy to be formulated.

A four-step process is set out which, if followed, will lead to a positive outcome. Either the project will become deliverable, albeit in a somewhat reshaped form, or its delivery performance will improve. The third possibility, which is also a positive outcome, is that the Buyer and Vendor will decide to cancel the project before any further money is wasted.

The earlier in the project's life that a turnaround exercise is undertaken, the higher the chances of success.

Exercise

1. Try it!

References

1. Andy Cole, KPMG, *Runaway Projects – Causes and Effects*, Software World Vol. 26, No.3, 1995.
2. House of Commons, Session 1999–2000, Committee of Public Accounts, *First Report – Improving the Delivery of Government IT Projects*, HCP 65 99/00 The UK Stationery Office.
3. The Cabinet Office, *Successful IT: Modernising Government in Action*, 2000.
4. John Boddie, *Crunch Mode*, Yourdon Press, 1987.
5. Robert Glass, *Software Runaways – lessons learned from massive software project failures*, Prentice Hall, 1998.

Chapter 21

INDIVIDUAL AND ORGANISATIONAL LEARNING

Individual learning

While at university on a sandwich degree, I was sponsored by the Raytheon company. I enjoyed the industrial experience immensely. Periods in a drawing office and an engineering workshop developed skills which I enjoy to this day. Many printed circuit boards for hi-fi amplifiers were designed, manufactured and populated with components in those days.

There were some wonderful characters also. One such was Arthur Le Boutellier, a builder of improbable machines for the manufacture of certain components of radar systems, instrument landing systems and oscilloscopes. These machines were constructed, without drawings, using hand tools of the more violent variety and a treasure chest of surplus electronic components and relays. A much-abused lathe was used to turn down pieces of scrap steel using impossibly large cuts. Most of his inventions featured cams and the door of his shed bore the proud inscription, 'Boots the Camist'.

Boots was also famous as the inventor of 'electrolytic keying'. Under each key of his home-made electronic organ were five vertical wires. When a key was depressed, the wires dipped into tiny pockets of anti-freeze and connected the master oscillator outputs through to the voicing circuits. This unlikely arrangement led to a perfect church organ sound. Boots was the final port of call when an engineer had an intractable problem. He would generally find a solution. He showed me the value of an independent 'trouble-shooter' and lateral thinker.

An unsuccessful learning experience

Another memorable character was a lecturer at the local technical college. He looked like a Gary Larson rocket scientist and wore a pair of glasses held together with sticking plaster. The college had been asked to provide a three-month day-release course to introduce the student apprentices into the world of electronics and production engineering. Several lecturers participated in the course. Mostly, they taught us sensible things like how to solder a component onto a printed circuit board and which way round a hacksaw blade should be inserted. The 'rocket scientist' gave us a postgraduate course in quantum mechanics.

In the first week he covered Newtonian mechanics, Bohr, and Planck's hypothesis. Next week he moved on to De Broglie, the Schrödinger equation,

Heisenberg's uncertainty principle and Einstein's special theory of relativity. By the end of the course, we were cantering through Fermi levels, state functions, eigenvalues and Hamiltonians. Several of us had 'A' levels, others had ONCs. Most of us could solve problems involving locomotives hauling trains up slopes, but we were not equipped to handle this. I developed a personal coping strategy. I copied down every formula and proof he put on the board and dumped it to memory as a meaningless string of sequential characters. Before the examination at the end of the course, I checked that I could accurately restore the information from memory onto paper.

In the examination I achieved a perfect score and the rocket scientist beamed at me in a crazed manner. Unfortunately, I had learned absolutely nothing. More importantly, when I studied quantum mechanics in my degree course, I found it very hard to understand and developed a deep loathing for both particles and waves.

A successful learning experience

I had another, more rewarding, learning experience at Raytheon a few years later. As a systems engineer, I spent a great deal of time writing the technical sections of proposals. All the text for these proposals was passed to 'old Ted' in the technical publications department. Old Ted was a mild-mannered, quietly spoken fellow who had been an editor at a publishing house for many years.

I was surprised to note just how many corrections he made to my manuscripts. I discovered that he would only tolerate the words 'therefore' and 'however' if they started a sentence and were followed by a comma. I found that he always replaced the word 'significant', which he deemed to be meaningless. I learned the difference between 'principle' and 'principal', 'dependent' and 'dependant', 'complement' and 'compliment'. He would split long sentences in two or rearrange them to move the end of the sentence to the front. I was not allowed to start or finish a sentence with a preposition (although I often break this rule now, to make text more conversational).

I started to change my writing technique. Short sentences were in. Split infinitives were out. Over a period of 2–3 years, the amount of blue pencil on my manuscripts reduced, until more than half the pages required no corrections. I had learned to write clearly. This has been both a valuable skill and a pleasure throughout my career. I found that the skill could be used not just for technical writing but also for the key 'selling sections' of proposals.

I had learned by making mistakes. As Aristotle said, 'What we learn to do, we learn by doing.'

Know who you are and what baggage you have

Of course, the way *I* learn is going to differ from the way *you* learn. All individuals are different – even identical twins. The differences are embodied in our mental 'maps', our psychometric profiles and our learning and thinking preferences.

To advance one's career in business today, it is essential to know in broad terms who you are and what baggage you have. When risk assessing bids or trouble-shooting projects in delivery it is essential to be dispassionate and totally objective. This means that we have to be aware of any tendency we have to form instant judgements or any preference to match or mismatch what we are told. This helps us to correct any in-built distortions – like correcting the Hubble telescope – so that we can see clearly.

Our mental maps define how we see the world and embody our value system and beliefs. They are a function of our upbringing, education and experiences and are used to inform the way we react to everyday events at home and at work. To us, our map is reality and we use it to judge other peoples' behaviour and performance. However, just as medieval maps may have obvious distortions and omissions when compared with modern maps calibrated using global positioning system information, our mental maps may also contains errors. The map is not the territory. Our maps can also be distorted by incorrect empowering beliefs or unhelpful limiting beliefs which cause us to either be over-confident in our ability or to fail to meet our full potential. The good news is that our maps can be changed.

Forward-thinking companies know that the provision of training in 'soft skills' can offer huge potential for staff development – arguably higher than that offered by traditional competency-based training. There is still a long way to go; most project management training still focuses more on methods and tools for the planning, control and management of projects than on how to obtain peak performance from the individuals and groups within the project team.

Group learning

The work group is a vital concept in Japanese management science and it differs from the Western model. In Japan, group well-being, values and morale are as important as group performance. Group leaders must earn the respect of the group and group members have an obligation to other group members. Continuous improvement of both individual and group performance is expected. This extends to working smarter as well as harder – making changes to business processes in order to improve quality or reduce cost. It has been found that groups larger than 15–20 are less effective per capita than smaller groups. When a group becomes too large it is split into two groups. This concept of small teams being more effective than large ones certainly matches my own experience on projects.

Group learning is a very powerful concept and cannot be better demonstrated than on an IT project, where individuals are brought together to form a project team. The group will contain developers, testers, team leaders and a project manager. There may be some business analysts or domain experts. There may be a project office manager, a secretary, a configuration manager and a project librarian. Increasingly, the team may be part permanent staff, part contract staff. The group will go through the Forming, Storming, Norming and Performing stages, defined by Barry Tuckman, as it gels into a team. An enormous amount will be learned about the business requirements, about the product or system under development, about the development environment and tools, and about software development processes. Most of all, much will be learned about the individuals on the team – their strengths, weaknesses and ability to be 'team players'.

At the end of the project, the team disperses. Individuals join existing projects or new projects and the process starts again. It is often the case that much of what has been learned is apparent only to team members and not visible to colleagues outside the project team. When the team is disbanded, this knowledge can be lost.

Of course there are other groups to which members of a project team will belong. For example, it is likely that there will be a professional development structure within the company, designed to provide a career structure and fraternity for application developers, technical architects and project managers. These communities provide a valuable means for projects to promulgate learning into the wider organisation and they need active encouragement to do so. It is human nature *not* to want to spend much time raking through the ashes of a failed project to find out what went wrong and *not* to want to broadcast these failures to one's peers. Executive sponsorship and a 'no blame' culture is needed to ensure that these learning opportunities are seized.

Organisational learning

Intuitively, one could define a learning organisation as one which instinctively and routinely avoids repeating previous mistakes. But organisations cannot *really* learn as they are not organisms. They cannot *really* have a mission, values, goals and objectives. Nor can they actually *care* for their customers. These are concepts defined by individuals and groups within the organisation and passed down the line to employees for the purpose of setting organisational, business unit, group and individual goals and objectives.

However, the organisation does have a 'map'. It is embodied in its business plans, its processes, its policies and procedures, its standards, its marketing material and its sales proposals. As with our own maps, organisational maps may have distortions.

As an example, most IT services organisations have methods and standards for project management and application development, whether they operate at Level 1 or at Level 3 of the Capability Maturity Model (see Chapter 9). Sales proposals often draw the clients' attention to the excellence of these standards and to the fact that they are deployed on every project. For companies operating at CMM Level 1, we know that this is not the case. This problem may not be visible to business managers or salespeople in the business, who assume that the corporate standards are being deployed. There is an organisational map mismatch.

We can also define a learning organisation as one which senses map mismatch and endeavours to correct it, either by ensuring that groups within the organisation do match the corporate map, or by modifying the corporate map itself to reflect a lesson learned by a group within the organisation. This feedback mechanism is central to organisational learning. The process can be summarised as:

- **Step #1** – Detect map mismatch (failure by the project team to 'walk the talk') as early in the project as possible. Don't leave it until the project completion report.
- **Step #2** – Assess whether the project needs to change its approach or the organisation needs to change its map (processes, standards etc).
- **Step #3** – Change the project map or the organisational map, or both.
- **Step #4** – Promulgate these 'learning opportunities' to all relevant groups in the organisation and ensure that they become 'lessons learned'.

We have mentioned above the communities which can pass on learning opportunities – the project manager community, the architect community etc. It is also important to encourage interchange between the communities so that they do not become isolated 'towers'. There are many ways to achieve this, both formal and informal. One such is *action learning*, which involves bringing together individuals from a variety of functional areas or disciplines across the business to explore and expand their own learning using the support and coaching of group members.

Summary

In this chapter we have briefly considered how complex we are as individuals and how this complexity can affect the way we learn as individuals. We have noted how important it is to develop 'soft skills' in addition to the normal competencies associated with our work.

We have discussed how groups can learn and how the learning of a transitory group like a project team can be lost at the end of the project. Other, more permanent groups or communities provide a means of promulgating learning opportunities.

We have looked at how organisations can learn and proposed a definition based on the detection of map mismatch. To learn, an organisation must be prepared to bring projects into line with its map. It must also be prepared to change its organisational map when this is indicated.

Exercises

1. Think back to situations where you learned a lot in a short time. What do these tell you about your preferred learning style? What factors made the learning enjoyable and successful?
2. Talk to your HR professional about 'soft skills' training, such as influencing skills and accelerated learning.
3. Look up Myers Briggs, Belbin and Learning Styles on the Internet and get yourself profiled. What new insights have you gained? How will you use this information?

4. How does your organisation capture learning points from projects? How are learning points passed to appropriate communities? How can the process be improved? Consider the use of *action learning*.

5. What mismatches can you see between the way your company says it works and what actually happens? What mismatches can you see between the way projects should be run and what actually happens? What will you do about it?

6. How would you rate your company as a learning organisation? What are you going to do today to raise the visibility of organisational learning in your company?

7. If you feel that this book has helped you to improve your project management, selling or 'trouble-shooting' skills, please recommend that a copy be given to your company's project management, sales, delivery and QA professionals!

APPENDIX

'Key Lessons' extracted from the UK House of Commons Committee of Public Accounts First Report – *Improving the Delivery of Government IT Projects* – published on 24 November 1999.

'Key lessons' regarding the inception and design of IT projects

'Departments should ensure that they analyse and understand fully the implications of the introduction of new IT systems for their business and customers. In particular, it is important that:

- the introduction of new systems is seen to be based on a clear business need;
- departments have considered fully the implications of any other changes that may coincide with the introduction of a new IT system; and
- departments should base their project plans on ensuring that the identified business benefits are delivered by a high quality team with clearly defined roles and responsibilities.'

'Departments must consider carefully the scale and complexity of projects to assess whether they are achievable. In particular, departments should consider whether:

- the proposed timetable for a project is realistic;
- IT initiatives should be broken down into manageable projects, with each successive one being considered in the light of the outcome of the earlier ones;
- an incremental, as opposed to 'big bang', approach to IT projects should be adopted, with regular milestones, each delivering an auditable business benefit. If there is no feasible alternative to the 'big bang' approach, then they should ensure that the timetable for implementation is realistic;
- their overriding priority is to deliver the project to time, to cost, or to a particular quality specification;
- enough high-level review points have been built in to the project to ensure that it is not allowed to continue if changing circumstances mean that the business benefit is no longer going to be achieved cost effectively; and

- senior management are sufficiently aware of the importance of halting a project that has been overtaken by events, rather than continuing to spend money.'

'Delays in implementing projects place them at risk of being overtaken by technological change. In particular:

- it is vital that project plans are sufficiently flexible to allow for the insertion of technological advances where relevant; and
- there are considerable benefits in introducing systems in phases.'

'The project specification must take into account the business needs of the organisation and the requirements of users. In particular:

- business cases must be based on an analysis of requirements and priorities that have taken account of the reasonable needs and preferences of system users;
- desirable, but not essential, features should be kept out of the specifications, which must be focused on delivering the core business benefits; and
- the benefits of using the new system must be sold to staff.'

'Key lessons' regarding the management of projects

'Senior management in all public bodies have a crucial role to play in championing the successful development of IT systems. In particular, it is essential that senior staff:

- recognise the opportunities that information technology can give them to improve their administration and provide other business benefits;
- create an environment within their organisation in which project management can succeed, for example, by supporting the development of high-quality project management skills and experience;
- ensure that there is clarity about the aims and objectives of major projects, and there are clear criteria against which the success of a project can be judged;
- insist on having regular feedback on the progress of projects and do not have information on progress filtered out;
- use trusted sources of advice on the benefits that technology can bring;
- where they are not IT specialists, are provided with appropriate training so that they have sufficient awareness of risk management and evaluation; and
- are accountable for ensuring that specific anticipated benefits from IT projects are achieved.'

'The development of high-quality project management skills within Government is essential. In particular:

- the Committee consider that the professional status and standing of project management within Government as a whole needs to be developed and enhanced. This could be done by establishing project management as a distinct profession within Government, along similar lines to the position of the new Government Procurement Service;
- work should be undertaken to ensure that the principles of good project management are understood and followed throughout Government;
- Government must find ways of rewarding project managers for their part in delivering IT projects successfully, and so retaining them to provide continuity and experience for future projects; and
- project managers must be encouraged to draw risks to the attention of senior management in order to alert them to problems. They must be encouraged to undertake active management of changes to project contracts, costs, benefits, risks, timescales, technology and organisation, and not simply adhere to original project plans or project management methodologies.'

'It is vital that Departments pay attention to the management of risks and have contingency plans in case projects are not implemented as planned. In particular:

- decisions on projects, both prior to inception and during development, should be soundly based on a rigorous assessment of costs and benefits, and a realistic assessment of risks;
- major IT projects call for competent risk managers, who quantify and prioritise risks on an ongoing basis throughout the life of the project, and raise issues at an appropriate level;
- there should be a risk management framework for projects, within which people are empowered to make decisions as the costs, benefits and risks change during the project's life; and
- risk assessments should be carried out throughout the project, in particular, to assess whether the business case continues to be viable in the light of actual costs incurred and changing business requirements.'

'Key lessons' regarding relationships with suppliers

'Relations between the Department and the supplier will have a crucial effect on the success of the project. In particular:

- Departments should maintain a close relationship with suppliers, but avoid undue reliance on them, and maintain overall ownership of progress to achieving the intended benefits;
- Departments should ensure that all parties have a clear understanding of their roles and responsibilities, and a shared understanding of key terms and deadlines; and

- where suppliers sub-contract work arising from PFI contracts, departments should satisfy themselves that the prime supplier's arrangements for managing the sub-contracts are consistent with the requirement of the main contract.'

'Contracts between departments and suppliers must be set out clearly. In particular:

- it is essential that the roles and responsibilities of all parties are fully defined;
- there should be an ongoing process of contract management during the life of the project to allow for the almost inevitable change to requirements. The aim should be to manage, rather than police, project contracts;
- departments should ensure that the business implications of late delivery are reflected in contractual incentives; and
- in highly complex deals, it may well be unavoidable that some matters cannot be settled in detail at the time that the contract is signed, but it is undesirable for contracts to leave key issues to be decided later.'

'Key lessons' regarding post-implementation issues

'Departments should seek to review the success of projects as soon as possible so that lessons can be fed back into consideration of later projects. In particular:

- reviews should seek to understand the reasons for cost overruns and slippage in the delivery timetable, as well as the way in which changes to requirements were considered and authorised;
- they should monitor the achievement of the anticipated benefits, which were part of the basis on which the project was originally approved. Where these have not been achieved, the reasons should be fully investigated; and
- reviews should be undertaken in a constructive and open manner with the aim of improving future project performance.'

'Sufficient time and resources should be spent on ensuring that staff know how to use the IT system. And proper consideration should be given to the possible effect the new system may have on productivity in the period following implementation. In particular:

- a realistic assessment of the impact of the introduction of the new IT system on the productivity and effectiveness of staff should be made and taken into account when planning;
- implementation of new IT systems must be accompanied by the provision of training appropriate to the required organisational change to deliver the business benefit; and
- departments must recognise that training may take time and staff may respond to different types of instruction.'

'It is essential that departments learn from past mistakes and consider how they can co-ordinate better their considerable resources to ensure better value for money in the future from IT projects. In particular:

- there may be a need for increased central co-ordination and monitoring of the way in which Departments implement IT projects, and the promulgation of more explicit standards against which departmental performance can be measured and benchmarked;
- Government as a whole may wish to co-ordinate better the way in which it takes forward major IT projects, making better use of its purchasing power, and prioritising the projects it would like to see implemented, to avoid contributing to an overheating of the market where relatively limited skills are available;
- there may be scope for encouragement of the development of greater professionalism in project management across Government; and
- where projects cross departmental and other organisational boundaries, and, possibly, costs lie in one body and benefits in another, an appropriate senior level "board" should be formed for the project to champion it and drive it through.'

INDEX